"*Abusing Donor Intent* tells the story, which
incredulity in its portrayal of how top brass
callously disregarded the wishes of Charles a
immense gift of $35 million (in 1961) being deployed to promote the education
of young Princetonians for government service in foreign lands."

—*Jim Watson, Chancellor Emeritus, Cold Spring Harbor Laboratory
Recipient of the 1962 Nobel Prize for the discovery of the DNA double helix*

"Doug White's careful and fair study of the seminal Robertson Foundation
endowment litigation against Princeton University should be read by all donors
and donees. As a former head of the New York State Law Department's Charities
Bureau, I know donors have to have both courage and resources to enforce their
rights, especially against iconic donees. Fortunately, the Robertsons had both."

—*Bill Josephson, Former head of the Charities Bureau,
New York State Attorney General's office*

"*Robertson v. Princeton,* the mother of all donor intent cases, is must-know
material for everybody involved in the giving or receiving of large charitable
contributions. Happily for his readers, Doug White has turned what could have
been a dry legal text into an engaging human story. The lessons to be learned,
which are both heuristic and institution-shaking, go down easily in his smooth
narrative."

—*Neal B. Freeman, Chairman, Foundation Management Institute*

"Who cares about donor intent? Donors do. And therefore they need to heed
Ronald Reagan's dictum: "Trust but Verify." As Doug White outlines in his
engaging new study, replete with fascinating family history, arrogant administrators, and trusting donors, there are far too many illustrations of institutions
simply disregarding donor intent and turning aside questions from donors who
are wondering if their wishes are being followed. The infamous Robertson case
against Princeton University—in which Princeton ultimately paid tens of millions of dollars to the Robertson family—is a clarion call to donors everywhere
to demand clarity of expectations, clear communication of results, and strict
regard for donor intent."

—*Anne D. Neal, President, American Council of Trustees and Alumni,
Co-author,* The Intelligent Donor's Guide to College Giving

"As a philanthropist I am very interested in how charities use their money. As the nonprofit sector grows increasingly important and vibrant around the world, society needs to better understand the relationship between those who support good causes and the organizations that put donated money to use. Doug White's narrative is at once engaging and exacting. And while he even-handedly examines the legal arguments in *Robertson v. Princeton,* he also describes a family's humanity—a dimension of the philanthropic process that is far too often overlooked. *Abusing Donor Intent* will undoubtedly be the authoritative chronicle of this epic lawsuit, as well as an indispensable guide for all charities and future philanthropists."

—*Dame Stephanie Shirley, Philanthropist*
The British Government's Founding Ambassador for Philanthropy, 2009-2010
Author, Let It Go

"Can the phrase, 'The Arc of Embezzlement,' play a credible role in a book about finances at an Ivy League university? Read on. Doug White's meticulous, patient research documents a story about a massive moral ill in our nation today: the unregulated billions of untaxed dollars in the endowments of the nation's wealthiest colleges and universities. The trustees and university officers managing these endowments are accountable to no one and can operate with reckless disregard for the purpose of the charitable dollars in their control. Doug White's story would strain belief as fiction—but this story is true."

—*Wick Sloane, Author of "The Devil's Workshop,"* Inside Higher Ed
Former Visiting Fellow, Higher Education, Federal Reserve Bank of Chicago

"Doug White has certainly captured the depth of Bill Robertson's tenacious and resolute dedication to his parents' intent when they made their magnificent gift to Princeton University. *Abusing Donor Intent* fairly and judiciously explains Princeton's morally inexcusable actions, both in the manner that the university committed its misdeeds and in the way it resorted to feeble legal arguments to excuse its actions."

—*James W. Schubauer*
Former Chairman of the Board, Bucknell University

Abusing Donor Intent

Abusing Donor Intent

The Robertson Family's Epic Lawsuit Against Princeton University

Doug White

PARAGON HOUSE

First Edition 2014

Published in the United States by

Paragon House
1925 Oakcrest Ave, Suite 7
St. Paul, MN 55113
www.ParagonHouse.com

Library of Congress Cataloging-in-Publication Data

White, Douglas E., 1952- author.
 Abusing donor intent : the Robertson family's epic lawsuit against Princeton University /
Doug White.
   pages cm
 Summary: "Details the lawsuit that the children of one of Princeton's largest donors brought
against the university, including the family history of the donors, the 40-year build-up to the
lawsuit, essential legal arguments of both sides, and a discussion of what charities and donors
should take into account when a targeted gift is made"--Provided by publisher.
 ISBN 978-1-55778-909-9 (pbk.)
 1. Robertson family--Trials, litigation, etc. 2. Robertson Foundation for Government--
Trials, litigation, etc. 3. Princeton University--Trials, litigation, etc. 4. Woodrow Wilson
School of Public and International Affairs--Finance--Law and legislation. 5. Charitable
uses, trusts, and foundations--United States. 6. Princeton University--Benefactors--Legal
status, laws, etc.--United States. I. Title.
 KF228.R635W45 2014
 346.749'0642--dc23
                                        2013042465

The paper used in this publication meets the minimum requirements of American National
Standard for Information Sciences— Permanence of Paper for Printed Library Materials,
ANSIZ39.48-1984.

Manufactured in the United States of America
10 9 8 7 6 5 4 3 2 1

For current information about all releases from Paragon House, visit the website at
http://www.ParagonHouse.com

This book is dedicated to
Jessie Lee Washington,
who risked her reputation to help correct an injustice
at an organization she loves.

With Appreciation:
The attorneys who represented Princeton
The attorneys who represented the Robertson Family

Individual Thanks:
Roberta d'Eustachio
Harvey Dale
Bill Josephson
Dick McPherson
Carl Schafer
Rick Schubart
Marcia Stepanek
Eric Swerdlin
Ginny Tranchik

Special Gratitude:
Brooks Hornsby
Mari-Anne Pisarri

And . . . With Warmth
Barbara L. Merk
"A woman of daring and courage"

Contents

Introduction

"Look at what this project could accomplish for the country."[1]

The words were whispered, although not intentionally, as Bill Robertson's emotions emerged. The weight of some years—more likely, some decades, as he thought of it—was being lifted, as he would finally be able to tell his immensely personal story that just happened to be about the largest lawsuit in the history of philanthropy.

During a period of six and a half years, beginning in the summer of 2002, the actions of this man, whom most everyone would assume by his outward demeanor of gentleness and accommodation could do no harm, at first surprised, then irritated, then upset, then offended, then riled, and then, finally, exploded the sensitivities of those who work in the patrician atmosphere that permeates the charitable organization that is Princeton University.

From his perspective, his goal wasn't to inflict damage. But he did think it was high time Princeton stopped inflicting its damage.

He wanted the voices of his parents to be heard. They had spoken through their enormous charitable gift forty years earlier, and their altruism was intended to accomplish something. Charles and Marie Robertson actually wrote it all down on a piece of paper, a carefully drawn, legally binding document hovered over by several attorneys—the family's as well as the university's—before it was declared satisfactory.

To the casual observer of Princeton's world-renowned Woodrow Wilson School, things seemed to be going swimmingly. What at such a place couldn't? But by 2002, Robertson, who sat on the board of the foundation his parents created, had put up with enough. "The whole idea had gotten so off course," he says, "it was time to pull the plug."

He wanted nothing less than to remove the original money and all of its earnings from Princeton's control and go elsewhere with it, not to benefit himself or any other individual, but to use it at another, more deserving university, one that would adhere more faithfully to his parents' wishes.[2] So, with his brother and two sisters, he went to court. The genteel environment of the boardroom would be replaced by the much more daunting rough and tumble venue of the legal system.

The arguments, the animosity and the money were about a basic idea: assuring that the dream of two people would become a reality. Like tens of millions of other donors—some wealthier, many far less wealthy—they wanted to do good things for the world, and they committed a sizable portion of their fortune and intellectual capital to make that happen.

This is a story about their children, led by Bill Robertson, who were determined to ensure, at whatever cost, that their parents' intentions would live in perpetuity. The good people at Princeton say they were ensuring the Robertson legacy, but they may never have suspected, when disagreement on that point arose, that the children would be as resolute as they were.

It was the largest one-time amount—$35 million—anyone had ever donated to benefit a university.[3] Charles and Marie Robertson were specific about the way the money was to be used. It was intended to help Princeton's Woodrow Wilson School for Public Policy and International Affairs focus on sending its graduates into those areas of the federal government concerned with international relations. "But the university," the son says, "was ignoring my parents' intentions." Furthermore, he maintains, Princeton's administrators were "harming the country as well."

That's not, as you might imagine, the way Princeton saw it—or sees it today. The people there say they not only assiduously honor the concept of donor intent for all its supporters, but that in this case they were particularly faithful to the donors' intentions. "Princeton," a top administrator once said, "has always used the funds given by Marie Robertson solely for the purpose for which she made her $35 million gift in 1961."[4] The university contends that the Woodrow Wilson School has been and continues to be one of the best in the country for public administration and policy with an international orientation, and that it was unfairly disparaged.

By 2002, the corpus of the gift, even after annual expenditures were accounted for, had grown to almost $700 million, a sizable portion of Princeton's endowment. By the spring of 2008, the fund had grown to $850 million. In part because of the sheer amount of money and in part because of Princeton's prominence in American academia, the lawsuit, the longest and most debilitating litigation ever in the history of American philanthropy, was destined to draw scrutiny. Among nonprofit executives, board members, donors and students of philanthropy, it is the most discussed legal case relating to donor intent. As the lawsuit wended its way through the court, it was covered extensively in the media, not only in outlets that specialize in nonprofit news, but in the general-circulation media as well.

In addition to the sum of money at stake and the audacious, public challenge to a pillar of the most academically revered group of universities in the country, another, more important reason the world took note—and why all donors and all nonprofit organizations should never forget what happened—is that this dispute, at its heart, sharply raised the awareness of the need for trust and honor in the sector of our society that most demands and depends upon those qualities.

Princeton officials claim they fulfilled their obligations. The Robertson family claims Princeton made a mockery of them. No matter what the defendants might say, Robertson insists he wasn't the bad guy; he was just trying to protect the family's honor.

When the lawsuit was filed, I was more than twenty years into my career advising nonprofits, many of which are among the most successful, both in their fundraising and their effectiveness, in the United States, as well as many individual donors, some of whom are well known. Based on what I had read of the case until that time, I assumed, as did many others in the nonprofit fraternity, that Princeton could not possibly have been in the wrong, that such an esteemed university could not have committed the sins Robertson accused it of committing.

I had just begun my second book, *Charity on Trial,* and was still trying to make sense of the anger that was directed at the American Red Cross after many of its donors' wishes were ignored in the wake of 9/11. *Charity on Trial* was originally intended to celebrate the good works of charities,[5] but I concluded from my research that many ignore the solemn promises they make to their donors and to society. When a charity accepts donated money so it can do the work it promises to do, and then doesn't spend the money as agreed upon, it is violating the deal—with its donors, as well as with the public in general. Still, in an interview after that book was published, which was while the lawsuit was in progress, I said that I thought Princeton had a strong case.[6]

My next book, *The Nonprofit Challenge* was a plea for nonprofit boards to better employ intelligent, ethical decision-making procedures when they go about their business. By then, the lawsuit at Princeton had been settled. Although that book didn't concentrate on the Princeton case, as part of my research I interviewed Bill Robertson for the first time and I began to question the weight of Princeton's arguments. I had gone from a mindset that Princeton had a strong case to something more nuanced: "The search for clarity," I wrote, "demands that everyone connected to the nonprofit world pause and think about donors' rights, financial accounting in accordance with the terms of an agreement, and just how strong a dead hand continues to be."[7]

Then I decided that this story, wherever it took me, needed to be told.

The book would ideally encompass the spirit, as well as the essential facts, of the lawsuit. It was also important that the legal drama be informed by the family's private journey. "This is an exceedingly personal story to me," Robertson said, his words at once gentle and determined. We were talking casually, over lunch in the conference room that housed the offices of the Banbury Fund and the Robertson Foundation for Government— the *new* Robertson Foundation—both of which he and his family ran at the time of our first interviews in Juno Beach, Florida.[8]

The topic on the table was his parents' gift. The agreement, the one that had been so carefully written in 1961, had, by 2008, when the law-suit came to a close, been parsed, pummeled, and ravaged, and the foundation it created had been completely and permanently dissolved.

By looking at Robertson you wouldn't suspect that he would be capable of such an assault on a place like Princeton. He stands at a modest 5'9", is bespectacled, has unkempt, naturally blond hair, looks youthful, even though his 60th birthday is behind him, and sports a goatee. He shows up for work more often than not in a golf shirt, baggy shorts, and flip-flops. He is disarmingly polite. Bill Robertson is, by all accounts, a nice guy.

But people can be unwavering as well as nice, and he was determined to ensure that his parents' wishes, as he so clearly understood those wishes, would be honored. By 2002 his parents were long dead and unable to speak for themselves, and Robertson undertook the task, as he saw it, to make certain their voices would be heard—now and forever, just as they wanted and for which, yes, they *contracted* with Princeton. "A deal's a deal," he says, "and Princeton had no right to now claim otherwise," a sentiment that could well reflect a growing cynicism that far too many of our nation's charitable organizations are dishonest—or worse.

One of the fundamental ethical issues a nonprofit must face, although it is almost never discussed at board meetings, is that of honoring its donors' wishes. As a result of a stunning indifference to the topic at far too many of our nation's nonprofits, I believe that donors have reason to be skeptical before they commit large sums of money to a charitable cause. As things stand now, donors pretty much have no way of knowing if a charity actually cares about how it spends the fruits of their philanthropy, regardless of how it is intended.

But the donor-intent issue isn't only about honoring a donor's intentions; it's also about making sure everyone knows what those intentions were. Given that, the first task is to determine whether the charity and the donor are on the same page from the outset. Not doing that is where the problems generally begin. Once that is established, the goal then becomes ensuring that, going forth, the charity acts honestly and competently. The question that pervaded my research for this book was this: In an increasingly scrutinized world, by the regulators and the public, was Princeton, in its dealings with the Robertson Foundation, part of a growing problem?

Some people, including many state and national legislators, may pause: What is a charity? Is it a renowned university with the largest endowment per student of any in the country?[9] Is it a behemoth like the American Red Cross? Or is it more like the neighborhood soup kitchen, the homeless shelter, or the HIV medical recycling program? The answer to all these questions is: Yes.

In the American nonprofit world, a million public charities and foundations, with countless and often competing missions, are compiled under the umbrella of what is commonly referred to as *501(c)(3)* organizations. Regardless of size or purpose, the rules for all public charities are the same. Some people feel that should change, that there should be different categories and different tax benefits for different kinds and sizes of charity, but right now, that's the way it is.[10] Although a large, well-endowed university has essentially nothing in common with a local homeless shelter, those organizations, along with a million others, are, through the lens of Congress and the IRS, identical.

The reason it's important to point that out is that this account is relevant not only to Princeton and the offspring of one of its donors. It could be the story of any charity and those who support it. This is simultaneously a case study of one failed donation and an examination of one of the most profound challenges in the world of philanthropy. Its repercussions can be felt well past Princeton; they can easily affect almost any of those one million charities that depend on the public's support to survive and thrive.

What follows is not a courthouse post-mortem. Instead, it is a human drama that at once encompasses and surpasses the legal issues. Alone, a cold attention to the law lacks the compassion that a true understanding of what takes place between donors and charities requires. The Robertson narrative is filled with history, complexity, and humanity. As philanthropy speaks primarily through the voice of the human heart, adhering only to the legal documents in telling the story would inflict a severe injustice on the vision that inspired the gift.

Besides, because the case was settled out of court, we don't have closure on the merits. At this point, we are left only to surmise the legal parameters of a donor's rights and a charity's obligations when it comes to the issue of donor intent.

Although I primarily make my observations through the perspective of Bill Robertson, I realize that the lifeblood of any honest telling is fairness. On the one hand, it would be easy to criticize Robertson. The son whose energy and passion were responsible for the lawsuit could be characterized as simply the antics of a bored rich heir with too much time on his hands. While personal financial greed was not a component in this drama, he has had his share of detractors—and not only from Princeton. But, as you will see, Robertson's drive was born of a reasoned sense of injustice.

On the other hand, it would be easy to criticize Princeton and conclude that its administrators practiced reckless disregard. But, while you will read the words of those who find fault with Princeton, I separate that criticism from the respect I have for those who run that world-class educational institution. Besides, as some of the evidence—part of it from Charles Robertson's own hand—suggests, Princeton's position was not devoid of merit.

Bill Robertson provided full access to available documents[11] and individuals related to the case. In all I perused more than 5,000 pages, many of which were produced during the proceedings (such as depositions); others were original, typewritten and hand-written notes, the earliest dating from the 1930s and 1940s. Some are extremely personal; several, particularly letters written by Charles Robertson, are breathtaking in their richness and compassion. In addition, Princeton maintains a website devoted to the case. It contains links to dozens of documents of fact and rationale available to the public. [12]

The best source of information for this book, however, came from the participants themselves. Although almost everyone associated with the gift in 1961 is now deceased, a few survived into the time of the lawsuit, so we do have some testimony that preserves contemporary voices for us to hear today. Of those who are now living and were involved in the case or were connected to the Robertsons' story, I interviewed as many as I could. Every person quoted had the opportunity to review his or her comments. I had no interest in tricking anyone or repeating a provocative comment if it wasn't relevant to the story or didn't fit into the context of what the person was saying. I sensed that there would be enough to write about—the two sides slugged it out in front of a judge and in the media for the better part of a decade, after all—without inventing false or unfair controversy.

As Bill Robertson undertook the messy task of ensuring that his parents' voices would be heard, the bright light of public scrutiny pricked the provinces of discretion and courteousness that typically characterize the nonprofit world. And it raised questions, honest explorations of which tend to make those who run nonprofits uncomfortable: What oversight should a charity maintain to ensure that the wishes of its donors are honored? How do we know, after they have died, what donors really meant? How long should a dead hand exert its authority? By making significant philanthropic gifts, what right do donors have to impose their priorities on future generations? While Bill Robertson speaks nostalgically of his parents' gift and what it "could accomplish for the country," does he own, and thus define, their sentiment? Or did Princeton come to own that perspective, free to tweak it as its leadership, immersed in the day-to-day tumble of actualizing the gift's directives, determined changing circumstances dictated?

Charles and Marie Robertson knew they couldn't save the world with their gift, but they hoped to make it better. "Our situation," their son says today, "is a very good example of encompassing a vision that had not been known before. No wealthy family had ever done this kind of thing. It was more or less unheard of. Who would have thought that in this way the tax-exempt sector would come to the rescue of the country—of the government?" A nonpartisan way, at that.

But did Princeton really reject that heady thought?

In a donor-be-damned way that should put every charity on alert, this question might well be asked: Did the Robertsons entrust their treasure to a charitable organization that simply took the money to do what it wanted?

The Robertson story contains this epic cycle: a birth, a death, and a rebirth. The birth took place in 1961, when the Robertson Foundation was created. The death took place in late 2008, when the foundation was dissolved. The rebirth took place when a new foundation, guided by Charles and Marie's sentiments, was created in the wake of the legal proceedings.

Chapter 1

The Gift

"How many of you who are going to be doctors, are willing to spend your days in Ghana?

"Technicians or engineers: How many of you are willing to work in the Foreign Service and spend your lives traveling around the world?

"On your willingness to do that—not merely to serve one year or two years in the service, but on your willingness to contribute part of your life to this country—I think will depend the answer whether a free society can compete."[1]

An Era of Optimism

The speech wasn't planned. It was 2:00 a.m. on October 14, 1960 when Massachusetts Senator John Kennedy arrived at the University of Michigan in Ann Arbor. No time of the day or night, it seems, is off limits in presidential campaigns that are coming down to the wire. Just a few weeks remained before the election, and Michigan was both important and hanging in the balance. When Kennedy arrived on campus, he unexpectedly found himself thronged by 10,000 students, and so mustered up his impromptu remarks—the thought, if not his syntax, had been forming for some time—in what he said was "the longest short speech I've ever made."[2]

Within weeks, well over one thousand students signed a petition and pledged to volunteer, supporting the objective that young people would serve their country by helping others around the world. The idea of helping people in other countries to make the world a better place wasn't original to Kennedy. For centuries, religious missionaries everywhere

1

have been acting on a philosophy of helping others. In the United States, shortly after World War II some members of Congress, with a secular approach, began calling for volunteers to work in developing countries. Indeed, as a young representative in 1951, Kennedy himself had suggested, "young college graduates would find a full life in bringing technical advice and assistance to the underprivileged and backward Middle East. In that calling, these men would follow the constructive work done by the religious missionaries in these countries over the past 100 years."[3]

But Kennedy's plea in 1960 was the first to be made by a candidate for President of the United States.

There was at that point nothing to actually volunteer for, however, and so, bolstered by the growing enthusiasm his remarks generated, shortly after taking office Kennedy asked his brother-in-law Sargent Shriver to put the idea into action. Defying most people's perceptions of the way the federal government works, it took Shriver and his task team only 21 days to complete the job.[4] On March 1, 1961, less than five months after extemporaneously stirring the souls of thousands of students, Kennedy signed the offspring of his comments. Executive Order 10924 formally established the Peace Corps—a good idea whose time had come, undoubtedly buoyed by one of the more enduring rhetorical flourishes in presidential inauguration history: "Ask not what your country can do for you—ask what you can do for your country."

One of the Americans infected with the optimism of Kennedy's inaugural—and an important participant in the Robertson cause—was Bill Josephson. Now in semi-retirement and serving as of-counsel to Fried Frank, a law firm based in New York, Josephson has had a long career in public service and served as an expert witness for the Robertson family in the lawsuit. "The Robertsons were extremely motivated by President Kennedy's Inaugural Address," he said. "One of the reasons that I agreed to be an expert witness is that I was present at that address. At the time I was a relatively mid-level State Department person and very shortly thereafter, by a series of strokes of luck, became the founding counsel to the Peace Corps, which I served from 1961 to 1966. So their purpose particularly resonated with me."[5]

Another person similarly inspired by government service—and another important voice before and during the lawsuit—was Robert Halligan, a Robertson family relation by marriage and a future trustee of the Robertson Foundation. He vividly remembers the Kennedy aura at the time. Halligan worked at the Agency for International Development then and recalls, "Kennedy was President, and government employees would be let out of work when a foreign dignitary came to Washington. We would be let out of work so we could stand on the sidewalks. We would be let out of work for two hours. We'd walk over to Pennsylvania Avenue from the State Department, and we'd see Kennedy in the limousine—with the top down—and then we'd go back to work. I saw Kennedy and Jackie and the King of Jordan once. Once, my wife and I went to the White House and we remember the band playing Hail to the Chief. Then we'd walk into Blair House. It was a very different time. It was a wonderful time. And it was exciting. We all felt the excitement of the international stuff . . . the inaugural . . . and I was entranced by that. We had lots of pride in that work."[6]

Taking into account the skepticism and even cynicism that pervades our public discourse on the role of government in the lives of Americans today, it is difficult to comprehend the innocent awe people felt when President Kennedy said, in another memorable phrase from his inaugural, "Let the word go forth from this time and place, to friend and foe alike, that the torch has been passed to a new generation of Americans."[7] The sense of possibility was vibrant. And it was real.

Yet, even though many people might look back on the late 1950s and early 1960s with nostalgia, the world was a mess. The twenty-year interregnum between World War II and the beginnings of the serious military buildup in Vietnam was bursting with angst.

The Cold War Environment

- Although the House Un-American Activities Committee (HUAC) was in decline by 1961, its residue of fear and suspicion was still strong. Begun in 1938, the committee investigated allegations of the communist activity that had been festering in the United States since the Great Depression. Many well-known writers, movie executives, and others were hauled before Congress to be grilled about their political beliefs. Many who refused to testify were blacklisted by their employers.

HUAC's crowning achievement—also a moment of great controversy—was the testimony of Whittaker Chambers, a former Communist Party member, which ultimately resulted in the conviction of Alger Hiss, a former high-ranking state department employee, for spying on behalf of the Soviet Union.[8] But by the end of the 1950s, the tide had turned against the committee's tactics. Although he was not involved with HUAC, Senator Joseph McCarthy from Wisconsin[9] added to its eventual demise with his ultra-hysterical accusations that just may have inspired people to think of other ways to advance America's cause on the international stage.

- Yuri Gagarin orbited the earth on April 12, 1961, and the Soviet Union declared that it "had won the space race." For Americans, however, the race was only beginning. In May of that year, the United States sent Alan Shepard and Gus Grissom into suborbital space, but had to wait until early the following year, longer than it hoped, to send John Glenn orbiting around the world three times.[10]

- A week after Gagarin's historic journey, Kennedy wrote a memo to Vice President Lyndon Johnson to look into whether the United States could get to the moon.[11] He publicly upped the ante the following month when, on May 25, he spoke before a Special Joint Session of Congress. "I believe that this nation should commit itself to achieving the goal before this decade is out," he said, "of landing a man on the moon and returning him safely to the earth. No single space project in this period will be more impressive to mankind, or more important for the long-range exploration of space; and none will be so difficult or expensive to accomplish . . . But in a very real sense, it will not be one man going to the moon—if we make this judgment affirmatively, it will be an entire nation. For all of us must work to put him there."[12]

Then, in a September 1962 speech at Rice University, Kennedy described how he saw the space challenge as the pursuit of a worthy goal that would bring out the best in America. "We choose to go to the moon in this decade and do the other things, not because they are easy, but because they are hard, because that goal will serve to organize and measure the best of our energies and skills, because that challenge is one that we are willing to accept, one we are unwilling to postpone, and one which we intend to win, and the others, too."[13] Announcing America's intention to reach the moon—a seemingly impossible task to be accomplished in a very short time—was, if nothing else, a call for the United States to play a dominant role in world affairs.

- Dag Hammarskjöld, the second secretary general of the United Nations, was killed in a plane crash in 1961. He was on his way to negotiate a cease-fire in the African country of Katanga. This was a blow to international stability at a time when things seemed to be going crazy, particularly in Africa. United Press International reported, "The United Nations was deeply affected by the loss, and for a time its very existence as an effective force for peace seemed to be at stake."[14]

- 1961 also brought the disastrous Bay of Pigs invasion in Cuba; the execution of Adolf Eichmann, the Nazi leader who, acting on behalf of Adolf Hitler, was charged and convicted of slaughtering millions of Jews during World War II; and the construction of the Berlin Wall, which for 30 years served as a symbol of East-West tensions in the Cold War.

Even though the United States emerged as an undisputed world power after World War II, by the late 1950s it was struggling with the increasingly belligerent Soviet Union and trying its best to form relations with less powerful but influential countries, many of which, it seemed, were faced with the stark choice between democracy and communism. Strife and hope spanned the distance from Washington, DC to Katanga, and beyond to the moon. The United Nations was thought to be in danger of crumbling. New missile technology, and growing secret intelligence communities made the world far more complicated and dangerous than most people in the general population could have anticipated in the wake of winning World War II. American school children learned to hide under their desks. Their parents, driven by a unique mix of Cold War angst, naiveté, and fear, were contemplating building underground bunkers in their backyards to prepare for a nuclear attack.

It was in this environment—an optimism severely tempered by the world's realities—that the Robertsons would, in their aspirational founding document, call for an educational program "to strengthen the government of the United States and increase its ability and determination to defend and extend freedom throughout the world."[15] America needed men and women with high ideals and equally high intellect to administer the country's foreign affairs.

The project at Princeton would be a bold, long step forward, its vision spanning generations into the distant future.

The Woodrow Wilson School

The Woodrow Wilson School started out in 1930 as the School of Public and International Affairs within Princeton's undergraduate liberal arts college. John Hibben, Princeton's president at the time, set the stage by quoting his immediate predecessor, Woodrow Wilson: "We dare not keep aloof and closet ourselves while a nation grows to maturity."[16] The prose in the school's first catalogue laid out the program's promise: "Throughout its history the sons of Princeton have been prominent in the service of the nation—statesmen, soldiers, judges, diplomats, men of science and men of letters, leaders of religious thought at home and abroad. It was this background which prompted Woodrow Wilson in 1896"—when Wilson was teaching at Princeton and before anything was named in his honor—"to define the University's destiny as: 'Princeton in the Nation's Service.'" The idea then, as it is today, was to prepare its students "for the new movement in national and world affairs."[17]

The university describes Wilson as an idealist. "President Wilson was motivated by the desire to end aggression forever and to free mankind from the terror and suffering of war. The causes he championed have not yet been achieved, but his ideals are the guides that help keep America great."[18]

The graduate program was added in 1948, and the school was also renamed to honor Wilson, who, in addition to serving as Princeton's president from 1902 to 1910, had graduated from the university in 1879. He served as governor of New Jersey from 1911 to 1913, and then as President of the United States from 1913 to 1921. Although his plan, after what was then called the "Great War," to establish the League of Nations, the precursor to the United Nations, couldn't survive a vote in the United States Senate, his legacy is closely connected to his attempts to establish a lasting peace in the world. For those efforts, in 1919 he was awarded the Nobel Peace Prize. Wilson coined Princeton's motto, "Princeton in the Nation's Service"—later expanded slightly by president Harold Shapiro to "Princeton in the Nation's Service, and in the Service of All Nations"— and is a "concept that Princeton and the Woodrow Wilson School regard as an essential component in their educational mission."[19]

It was the graduate program at the Wilson School that Charles and Marie Robertson had their eye on. Applicants would undoubtedly be inspired by the noble traditions of public service in this country. Students would earn a free and uniquely intense graduate-level education in public administration at one of the nation's leading universities, and would look forward to serving America's foreign policy objectives by helping to strengthen the government of the United States. Alumni would undertake careers in government service, with particular emphasis on . . . international relations and affairs."[20] Political leanings would be irrelevant. The learning in the classroom would not promote any dogma.

That was the broad plan. As the gift's tree bore fruit into the indefinite future, the opportunity would forever be available, as undoubtedly the need for qualified and motivated students would be always present and pressing.

Preparing to Make the Gift

Although the Robertsons were undoubtedly swept up in Kennedy's oratorical enthusiasm and buoyed by the creation of the Peace Corps, they had been planning their historic gift for a while before then. Serious talks with friends and advisors actually began two years earlier.

In late 1959, inside an office at the Carnegie Corporation in New York, Robertson met with John Gardner, Carnegie's president, as well as a future cabinet member in the Johnson Administration and the future founder of Common Cause and Independent Sector; and Eugene Goodwillie, one of Robertson's attorneys, as well as his best friend, to discuss international relations and what would be needed to ensure America's ability to address world problems. That same year Robertson and Gardner also visited with General A. J. Goodpaster, President Eisenhower's top military aid, at his office, which was adjacent to the President's in the White House.[21]

The oldest document relating to the gift that remains today is in the form of a note, written in Charles Robertson's hand. Dated March 8, 1960, it said, "Consider a small committee to undertake a study of the need for a training school for government employees—1 to 2 year course—no frills . . . " ("No frills" was underlined twice.)[22] Less than two weeks later, another of Robertson's hand-written notes, with the heading "Project X" at the top, said, "Consider a fully endowed small government training school at graduate level—part of Woodrow Wilson School—for candidates for gov't. departments—State, Commerce, Labor, Interior, Budget, Welfare, etc., etc."[23]

Later that spring, after a round of golf with Robert Goheen, Princeton's president, Robertson invited him to his home in Huntington, New York, for a discussion about a possible gift. Marie Robertson was also present. Goheen was well aware of their interest in world affairs. Earlier that year, through the Banbury Fund, the Robertson family foundation, the two had made a $500,000 gift to Princeton that was intended "to prepare young men for careers in international fields of endeavor and to improve understanding of foreign nations and peoples."[24]

It was at that meeting, as Goheen would later recall, that "Charlie first indicated to me that Marie and he wanted to consider some further and much more substantial way of advancing their interest in education for the public service, especially in its international dimensions. Perhaps," Goheen said, responding to what he inferred as mild criticism, "to put me on my mettle, Charlie indicated that some of his Harvard friends thought that the Littauer School would be a fine place to do that sort of thing." Littauer, at Harvard, was renamed in 1966 the John F. Kennedy School of Government. "At the same time," Goheen said, Robertson "invited us to consider areas of the Woodrow Wilson School's Graduate Program that it might be . . . desirable to enlarge or revise, provided the financial support could be provided."[25]

By the late fall of 1960 Robertson began discussions in earnest with Princeton. In the last week of November, he met with Goheen in New York. The following week Goheen wrote to tell him that individual appointments had been arranged with three influential people in Washington, DC, so that he could lay out his plans for the gift. Those people, who, along with Robertson himself, could fairly be considered the original brain trust for what would become the Robertson Foundation, were Livingston Merchant, A. J. Goodpaster and Allen Dulles.

- Livingston Merchant was a United States official and diplomat, two-time ambassador to Canada and, at the time of his meeting with Robertson, was Undersecretary for Political Affairs at the State Department. He was later an attorney and a partner at Scudder Stevens and Clark, an investment-counseling firm. Merchant graduated from Princeton in 1926.

- Andrew Jackson Goodpaster was a Brigadier General, and, when he met with Robertson, was serving as Staff Secretary and Defense Liaison Officer to President Eisenhower. (This was at least Robertson's second meeting with Goodpaster.) He would later be an advisor to Presidents Johnson, Nixon, and Carter, and serve as the Supreme Allied Commander of NATO Forces. In 1975, after he retired, for the first time, he was named a senior fellow at the

Woodrow Wilson School. Goodpaster was the salutatorian in his
class at West Point in 1939, and earned degrees in civil engineering
and politics at Princeton in the 1940s.[26]

- Allen Dulles was the Director of Central Intelligence. Among
  other achievements, as an employee of the Office of Strategic
  Services, the predecessor of the CIA, he negotiated an early sur-
  render of German forces in Italy during World War II. He is also
  credited with discovering, in the early 1920s, the source of the
  documentation proving that the controversial document "The
  Protocols of the Elders of Zion" was fraudulent—a landmark discovery in its time. Dulles graduated from Princeton in 1908.

"Each of these men," Goheen wrote, "is pledged to the strictest
secrecy about your interest in the matters we discussed in New York last
week. Each of them has expressed to me a very great interest in talking to
you about these matters from the standpoint of their experience in government." He then added, "Here in Princeton, Gardner Patterson"—the
director of the Woodrow Wilson School at the time—"and I are engaged
in rethinking and reshaping our proposed program in the light of the
larger scale of development and the more immediate schedule which you
put before me. I would hope to be ready to present our ideas to you early
next week."[27]

The meetings went well. Goodpaster, whose participation was essential to the success of the project, as well as to the foundation once it was
under way, followed up by writing, "You may be sure that I will continue
to have an interest in the project."[28] Two months later, he again wrote to
Robertson explaining that he would be glad to serve on the board once
his boss, General George Decker, chief of staff of the United States Army,
examined the issue: "I assure you that I was delighted to be able to help in
any way on a constructive project like the one you and Mr. Goodwillie"—
Charles Robertson's attorney—"discussed with me."[29]

Even in private correspondence, Goodpaster remained secretive
about Robertson's plans. After the meeting with his boss, he reported
that General Decker thought it would be "entirely appropriate for me to

go forward with preparatory discussions *such as we have had*," and " . . . he does not anticipate any problem with *the project* . . .." [30] Nowhere in that letter, or in any other contemporary correspondence, is "the project" identified.

In addition to being secretive, Robertson, a businessman, expressed some frustration as he went about converting his idea into action. When Goheen wrote that he and the dean of the Wilson School were "rethinking and reshaping our proposed program in the light of the larger scale of development and the more immediate schedule you put before me," he was responding to a sense of urgency to which many academics are generally not accustomed. Upon being presented with the idea, Princeton had apparently taken it up with the slow deliberations characteristic of the scholarly class. No doubt, that is why Goheen concluded his letter: "I hope to be ready to present our ideas to you early next week."[31]

Even though both Robertson and Princeton mutually envisioned a need, they were not in complete harmony.

Challenges at the Wilson School

In 1960 Robertson didn't think much of the graduate program at the Woodrow Wilson School. After his meetings in Washington, and after talking again with Goheen, as well as others, he thought it time to let his critique of the status quo be known.

- About the head of the program: "Although liked, the present director of the School is not considered qualified for the job." He was speaking of Gardner Patterson, whose career included various roles on government economic missions in Tunisia and Turkey, and as a consultant to the State Department.[32]
- About the school itself: "The W.W. School does not enjoy a particularly favorable reputation with a majority of the men with whom we talked. As men in public service, they did not seem to be aware of any substantial contribution by the School to the Federal public service."

- About the school's advisory council: "We did not gain the impression that the Council exercised any particular influence in formulating school policy."

- And about the school's objectives at the time: "The men interviewed were public servants, anxious to improve the quality of that service by adding dedicated men with good minds to government service. The need is great, is ever present, is not organized."

These comments are important. Without Princeton's commitment to making changes, there would be no gift.

As far as Robertson was concerned, the current director needed to be replaced. A new director, he said, "must be a really top-flight man with a really good mind, well liked, well known and trusted in Washington. He should be able to move easily in the top echelons of Washington." He will know 'whom to recommend to whom.'" And, "His graduates will not be lost in Washington's 'grinding mill.' His graduates will be placed in jobs with the expectation that if they possess what it takes, promotion into areas of policy-making will follow." The director, Robertson wrote, should also attract "top flight, interested public servants to participate in the Princeton seminars."

Robertson was realistic about how long it would take to ramp up the program to his expectations. "It may take time to attract to the school the really fine minds it seeks. The school's reputation, based on the excellence of its faculty, size of its fellowships, quality of seminars and its success in job placement in exempt positions under top-flight men in Washington will all have a direct bearing on the recruitment program."

Robertson also outlined some of his thoughts relating to a newly structured curriculum. He wanted a "period of training limited to two years" and expected that graduates would receive "a recognized graduate degree." Graduates should "possess a competence in at least one foreign language" while the program would also "stress the importance of international economics." Nevertheless—an important matter, Princeton's fidelity to which would be debated decades later—the curriculum should "not be limited to areas pertinent only to foreign service." He anticipated a need "for understanding the problems and aims of labor," as well as a need for "a thorough knowledge of the history, political institutions, economy, etc. of the United States."[33]

Robertson hoped his recommendations would help the school attain a better status among potential students as well as with the federal government.

Princeton was in the middle of a $53 million capital campaign, at the time second in size only to Harvard's $94 million—quaint numbers compared to the several multi-billion campaigns at universities and other charities that are taking place today. The Robertson gift would clearly be a huge boost toward meeting that goal, but Robert Goheen wanted to be sure that the needs identified for the campaign, which did not include major cash influxes at the Woodrow Wilson School, were still going to be met. "It was very clear that the needs of the campaign were very real needs," he said. "We needed that $53 million-plus in addition to what-ever might come in this way, so we were trying to make that very clear to our workers out there and all our possible donors."[34]

One point of clarification: There was only one donor, not two. Marie Robertson was the granddaughter of George Huntington Hartford, the founder of the A&P supermarket company, and had inherited approxi-mately $85 million. While her husband Charles was a successful stock-broker, he did not have anywhere near the wealth of his wife. The reason news stories about the gift, at the time it was made and during the lawsuit, often refer to "the donors" is that Charles provided much of the motiva-tion for the gift to be made and its direction afterward.

The Structure: Tax Considerations and Oversight

The Robertson gift was not a gift to the university. Instead, it established a foundation. That was yet another source of controversy in the lawsuit. Victoria Bjorklund, a retired partner at Simpson Thacher & Bartlett, one of the law firms that provided counsel to Princeton during the law-suit, says, "This was a negotiated agreement to establish a *supporting*

organization, even though it was not called that at the time." Bjorklund
is a leading national expert on nonprofit law, and her concern is helping
donors and charities achieve their goals while complying with federal and
state law. She is, by the way, a member of Princeton's class of 1973, the
first class that included women, and the university's first female basket-
ball player.

Even though it was only five pages long, the Certificate of
Incorporation was constructed with care. As the evidence shows, the
agreement and the decision to execute such a gift did not come quickly
or easily. In a manner never done before, or since, the written agreement
established the Robertson Foundation so that it was, in effect, the gift.

To emphasize that a lot of time and effort went into putting together
the agreement, Bjorklund says, "Both parties were represented by counsel." Furthermore, she points out, "This was a very unusual gift in the way
it was made. This was not a gift by a deed of gift *to* a charity. This was
somewhat different in that it was an organization that was going to be set
up for the benefit of the Woodrow Wilson School with the participation
of the Robertson family members. And there was a lot of back-and-forth."

And the back-and-forth wasn't about just the mission or the purpose of the gift. According to Bjorklund, the Robertsons had three
tax-related issues to take into account. "We have the federal income tax
matter. Clearly, Marie Robertson wanted to claim an income tax charitable deduction for her contribution." At that time, the federal income
tax rate on those who filed jointly, as Charles and Marie Robertson did,
was 91 percent on incomes of over $400,000, an earnings threshold the
Robertsons exceeded. "Also," Bjorklund then explained, "at the time, the
deduction was not available for a newly formed entity unless the entity
was controlled by a public charity." Enter Princeton as that controlling
charity. Although tax law permitted then, as it does today, a greater
deduction for gifts made directly to a charitable entity, the Robertsons
gave up that benefit and intentionally designed their philanthropy to permit future family input.

The second concern was the gift tax deduction. To be entitled to that,
the same rule applied.

The third issue was that, to be certain of getting the deduction, donors who made charitable gifts could apply for and receive a Letter Ruling from the IRS. "That's exactly what happened," Bjorklund said, "and that process was conducted by Jack Myers, Robertson's attorney."

A fundamental part of the equation to satisfy the IRS was that Princeton needed to control things. But the university had other motives to ensure its influence. "Princeton, for reasons of academic freedom and academic stewardship, could not permit anything less than to exercise the right to maintain full control," says Bjorklund, "and could not take on important obligations, such as appointing tenured professors and undertaking other long-term commitments, unless they had the assurance that they would be in control."[35]

This thought would become important when Princeton defended itself in the lawsuit.

Another consideration was oversight, which was every bit as important as a potential tax deduction. Even though a restricted gift to Princeton would have been easier and more traditional, as Seth Lapidow, who would serve as the family's New Jersey attorney during the lawsuit, says, "Using the corporate form, even in the minority, the Robertsons had rights that Princeton could not trample. Minority directors cannot simply be steamrollered by the majority. Robertson and Goodwillie were aware that about that time Harvard was having a dispute with a donor who was unable to do anything about the use of his gift. I think Charles chose the corporate form because he wanted to preserve the rights of his family to act as directors. He acknowledged that Princeton would have control, but he did not want them to have *unfettered* control"[36]

While there is no reason to think that either the Robertsons or Princeton anticipated future problems at the time the gift was made, the document, as any good legal document should, was written to clarify the roles of the foundation and Princeton, and to minimize potential conflicts. The language in the portion where the goals are outlined was clear: The foundation's "objective is to strengthen the government of the United States and increase its ability and determination to defend and extend freedom throughout the world by improving the facilities for the training and education of men and women for government service."

It was not clear enough, it would turn out.

Signing the Certificate of Incorporation

They gathered on the morning of March 16, 1961 at the Robertson home in Huntington, New York, a posh Long Island suburb a little over an hour's drive from New York City. The day had a not-yet-Spring feel, cool and blustery, about 45 degrees, with a dusting of snow the night before that had melted by 11:00 a.m.[37] In addition to the handful of lawyers representing the Robertsons and Princeton were those who would affix their names to what would be known as "The Composite Certificate of Incorporation of the Robertson Foundation." The incorporators were Charles Robertson, Marie Robertson, and Eugene Goodwillie.

No doubt, the assembled were warmed by the wood burning in the fireplace, its gentle heat and familiar crackling, along with the home's elegant furnishings and decorations, conveying tradition and wealth. A mighty sense of purpose loomed. The physical centerpiece in the Robertsons' foyer also provided an iconic and philosophical focus to the moment: Lurking conspicuously was a large original canvas of Dwight D. Eisenhower. No guest to the Robertson home could miss the radiant smile of the five-star general and former President of the United States or, as all guests to the Robertson home would have a deep interest in world affairs, its owner's impact on the international stage. Charles and Marie Robertson revered Eisenhower, whose legacy they wanted to honor, in addition to their earlier $500,000 gift to Princeton, with this new, much larger gift, a supreme and transforming act of philanthropy.

The expectation for this historic gift was that the donors' stunning and self-imposed sense of obligation to generosity would shape America's future, the expectation being that the document to be signed that day would provide an avenue for America's most capable young men and women to pave the way for the country's ongoing greatness among the nations of the world. Every day, but on that day in particular, under Eisenhower's watchful eye, Robertson's Huntington home was alive with

Jack Kennedy's optimism. As the rarified air electrified the dreams of everyone present, the donors affixed their signatures to the piece of paper that would, once the IRS gave its approval, create a new foundation to further the goals of one of Princeton University's most important graduate programs.

After the IRS finished its deliberations and gave the go-ahead for the tax deductions—although it took more than a year for the IRS to send its formal letter[38]—on May 29, 1961, Marie Robertson transferred 700,000 shares of her A&P stock to the Robertson Foundation. The total value, with a per-share mean of just under $49.60, was $34,715,625. The stock funded the largest single gift ever made to that time to Princeton, and the largest single gift to benefit any university in the history of American philanthropy.[39] The gift added substantially to Princeton's endowment, which in the early 1960s was approximately $400 million.

Charitable giving has grown since then, to be sure, even after taking inflation into account. In early 2013, for example, Michael Bloomberg, New York City's former mayor and software and media entrepreneur, made a gift of $350 million to his alma mater, Johns Hopkins; his total giving to that university to that time was $1.1 billion, the largest amount to any university from a single donor in the history of American philanthropy.[40] According to *Giving USA*, which conducts annual surveys of giving, education receives about 13 percent of all philanthropic gifts, the second highest group—religion is first, with about 32 percent—among eleven broad charitable categories of recipients.[41]

The Robertsons were the Bloombergs—as well as the Gateses, and the Buffetts—of their time.

A Father's Letter: A Vision and A Warning

On July 3, 1962, the eve of America's 186th birthday celebration, during the in-between of the high hopes that accompany ideals and the grittiness of actually putting a plan into action, Charles Robertson wrote a letter to his 12-year-old son Bill. Following are the important portions relevant to the father's thoughts about the gift:

"Your Mother and I decided last year that the time had come for us to acknowledge the tremendous debt we both owed to this country. Possessed of a large fortune ... we for years had searched for a cause, a project, an idea that might serve to strengthen the government of the United States and, in so doing, to assist people everywhere who sought freedom with justice. In due course and after a diligent search we, solely on our own initiative, decided to finance through a foundation a school in which outstanding college graduates truly dedicated to the service of the public would be educated to assume the responsibilities of the important positions in those areas of the Federal Government concerned with international affairs.

The Robertson Foundation was created in 1961 as a vehicle for underwriting the initial costs of establishing and operating, through the Trustees of Princeton University, the new Woodrow Wilson School of Public and International Affairs, a graduate school at Princeton. Mother made a magnificent gift to the Foundation more than adequate to achieve our purpose. In characteristic fashion she insisted upon and secured complete anonymity. We are determined to make this new School the pre-eminent graduate school of its kind in the world.

You will note that provision has been made for the active participation by members of our family in its affairs.

Mother and I know that you will maintain a sincere and deep interest in the School and in the Foundation. Some two hundred years ago Rousseau said, "As soon as public service ceases to be the chief business of its citizens, and they would rather serve with their money and not with their persons, the state is not far from its fall."

Although the school will be an integral part of Princeton University its administrators, faculty, lecturers and student body will be recruited from the entire country as well as from abroad. The Foundation serves a two-fold purpose. It permits members of our family or their chosen advisors to take an active part in the planning for and growth of the School, and it affords the members of its carefully selected advisory committee, composed of men of excellence and accomplishment in fields related to public service, an opportunity to bring to bear on the School's policy and curriculum the experience and judgment acquired in the course of their varied and highly successful careers.

We are all prone to take for granted the gifts of freedom and justice as we Americans enjoy forgetting that these great privileges simply do not just happen and flourish—bestowed on us by a benign and generous Providence. Men by the millions have fought for freedom and men by the uncounted thousands have died that you and Mother and I, along with our fellow countrymen, might live secure and happily in this free country. Recently the President of the United States said, "Ask not what your country can do for you—ask what you can do for your country"—and the late distinguished and extraordinarily capable Secretary of the United Nations, Dag Hammarskjold, who gave his life in its service, wrote, "I inherited a belief that no life was more satisfactory than one of selfless service to your country—or humanity."

It may well be that your life and the lives of those who follow you will be enriched by reason of your and of their identity with this project, which was conceived with the express and clearly defined purpose of strengthening our government and our country. As many times as you travel abroad you, like Mother and I, will return with the firm and lasting conviction that "this is my own, my native land"—by all and every means cherish and protect it.

Our love and deep devotion to you—always.
Dad [42]

In many other letters, Charles Robertson would sign letters to his children with *Old Grumble*.

To ensure that its profound meaning and purpose—so vibrant in the father's heart that they demanded to be written down early on—would be understood from the perspective of an adult's mindset, Charles Robertson waited six years, until the son was 18 years old, before presenting him with the letter. Then, from the day he read it, Bill Robertson committed himself to passionately defending his parents' wishes. Connecting those wishes with Eisenhower's accomplishments and Kennedy's words, and making them real, would become a lifelong labor of love.

Chapter 2

The Family

Marie Hartford Hoffman Robertson's fortune was the product of a most unlikely relationship. She was the granddaughter of George Huntington Hartford, "raised as a God-fearing farm boy" in Augusta, Maine. In 1859 Hartford met George Francis Gilman in New York City. Gilman, another Augusta, Maine native, whose ancestors could be traced to the *Mayflower*, was flamboyant and ran his life on the principle, "Modest success in life is worse than failure."

The Early A&P Years

By the time he and Hartford got together, Gilman had begun two businesses, one selling leather and the other selling tea. In 1860 New York City's Business Directory listed Gilman as a "Hide and Leather Dealer," and Gilman & Company as "Importers of Tea." "Gilman had the vision and flair to promote their new tea enterprise in grand fashion," while Hartford had the "intensity and persistence to conceive, develop and operate the business."

Even though their personalities were entirely different, they did well together. "Hartford taught Gilman how to operate a successful business, and Gilman taught Hartford how to dream bigger dreams."[1] Nevertheless, even though the two men have been described as partners, during the early years Hartford was only an employee. Gilman did not initially give or sell him part of the business.

In 1859, the first store-warehouse of the company was located at 31 Vesey Street, in lower Manhattan.[2] That address is located inside an area known today as Ground Zero, where the twin towers of the World Trade Center were located before the 9/11 attacks brought them down.

At the time, tea was considered a necessary luxury; coffee wasn't yet commercially available and it certainly wasn't the dominant aid for Americans waking up in the morning. An expensive commodity from the Orient, tea arrived with a vast mark-up as several people took their cut on its journey to the United States. Hartford, early on, wanted to make tea less expensive by removing as many of the middlemen as possible. He and Gilman did just that.

In 1861, as the company grew prosperous, the two men came up with the name "The Great American Tea Company." By the end of the decade, inspired in part by the completion of the transcontinental railroad, Gilman, in an effort to give the impression of an operation without territorial boundaries, renamed the enterprise "The Great Atlantic & Pacific Tea Company." Later generations would come to know the behemoth grocery chain simply as "The A&P."[3] Although George H. Hartford would secretly become a partner in 1878, it wouldn't be until 32 years later, the day after Gilman's death, that the company would actually be incorporated.[4]

Although nobody knew about it at the time, Hartford had effectively taken control of the business outright. More than two decades before he died, Gilman had wanted out of the day-to-day operations.[5] His flair and flamboyance led Gilman to make a mess of his life and personal finances. But he also wanted to maintain the image that he was in control, and so he kept his name on the A&P bank account. When he died on March 3, 1901, Gilman left no will. His heirs—he had no children but did have many nephews and nieces, as well as two surviving half brothers—wanted in on an inheritance that was thought to be worth $40 million. In addition, other people who had been befriended by Gilman wanted money, one of whom sued the estate.

Then, in the midst of what was turning into a probate circus, another lawsuit was filed—this one by George Hartford.

Hartford explained to the court that back in 1878 he and Gilman made a secret pact. The A&P, it turned out, wasn't just Gilman's company, and, since well before Gilman's death, Hartford was no mere employee. Hartford persuasively argued that the agreement, which was not written down, gave him control of the company, as well as all its assets, with both men sharing the profits equally.

After the accountants finished plowing through the books while the estate was being administered, two things became clear: Gilman's estate was worth nowhere near $40 million, and, as it slowly dawned on all the hopeful beneficiaries that Hartford was the business brains behind the company's success, the heirs needed him at the helm if they were to get anything at all.[6] For that reason, even though no one had any absolute knowledge of Gilman's intentions, the family conceded control and ownership of the enterprise to Hartford.

A year later, Hartford became president and sole owner of the A&P. Even then, valued at just over $2 million, it was already among the largest grocery retailers in America.[7] In 1951 A&P was the largest retailer in the country.[8] The company's assets would grow to something just shy of $1 billion by the time Hartford's granddaughter Marie Robertson—nee Marie Hartford Hoffman—and her sister and cousins would take outright ownership of the stock in 1957. Along the way, the company would be the target of an antitrust lawsuit and several political attacks, all of which failed. Because of its price-setting tendencies, and because it was very popular, the company would later be thought of as the Walmart of its day.

Marie Hoffman's First Marriage

Charles Robertson was not Marie Hoffman's first husband. And in looking back on her first marriage, it seems a minor miracle that she even survived to marry him. In 1931, when she was 19, having decided not to go to college, Marie Hoffman married Louis Reed, Jr., a handsome, but shallow, society playboy.

After being together only one and a half years, during which time a girl was born, they separated. "He abused her," recalls Bill Robertson, interpreting the whispers through the decades that permeated the upper-class code of silence on all things unpleasant. Reed's behavior, as described by Robertson, practically killed her. "He was a violent man. He once pushed her down the stairs and she was injured, so much so that she thought she'd never have another child. These were the days when men could get away with such things. Still, my mother divorced him."

The divorce didn't come easily. Reed initially wanted one million dollars, but after two years of bickering Marie agreed to pay alimony of $1,650 per month for the rest of his life.[9] She would have custody of the child.

They decided on Reno, Nevada, where the divorce would be quick, and valid in any state, but when Reed got there he demanded $500,000 and equal custody of their daughter. Marie refused and returned home without a divorce decree.[10]

Years later she said, "I was compelled by the violence, drunkenness, and general misconduct of my then husband to separate from him and return to the home of my father. During the time we lived together, he failed to support me. On the contrary, he incurred debts, which I paid. After our separation Reed demanded $1 million. When I refused, he began suit in Supreme Court in January 1934, for custody of our child, Marie Louise."

Although Reed eventually agreed to the alimony, the $1,650 was less than the $2,250 per month that he wanted. That victory might sound like small potatoes for a wealthy heiress, but she was trying as best she could to cling to her dignity. He did, however, manage to claw out from her about a quarter-million dollars outright before the divorce.[11]

"It was really blackmail," said Robertson. "She didn't want the scandal of her being so mistreated to get out."

Eleven years later, in March 1946, by which time she had married Charles Robertson, Marie Hoffman Robertson stopped her payments. "Charlie went ballistic," Bill Robertson says of his father. "My dad found out Reed was blackmailing her"—she had kept the alimony agreement secret from the public, her family and her husband—"and that she was paying him money under the table." She said in court that she felt the alimony agreement was "invalid, illegal, and of no force and effect in that it is unconscionable, was obtained by fraud and violates the law and public policy."[12] So, as Charles took control of the situation when he discovered what was going on, Marie just stopped paying.

This, of course, displeased the easily angered and emotionally unstable Reed. He felt entitled to the money. His annual income before he was married was about $6,000; hers, he estimated, was about $1 million. A year and a half after the payments stopped, he filed a complaint with a Manhattan court demanding the back payments and their continuation going forward. Not only did her debt to him "add up to $28,050," he lamented, "but it also adds up to a breach of contract and considerable discomfort."[13] He took the moment to whimper that he had come to rely on the monthly checks too much to give them up. His legal papers contended, "In reliance upon fulfillment" of the agreement stipulating the alimony payments, "plaintiff"—Reed—"has entered into certain financial commitments so that if the breach of said contract continues, plaintiff's own source of income will be endangered or wiped out even though said contract will be ultimately enforced."[14] Marie's perspective, with Charles's backing, was that, even though she was wealthy, she had no obligations to a man who had regularly beaten her up.

That move set off a public discussion about whether wives should pay alimony, a highly unusual concept in 1948. At the time, nine states permitted alimony for husbands and the idea was just beginning to pick up traction. Charles Rothenberg, a New York attorney who wrote books about marriage and divorce laws, said of the contract between Reed and Hoffman, "Public policy in this country definitely favors the preservation of the bonds of matrimony. An agreement such as this, signed while the marriage was in force, could therefore be considered contrary to public policy."[15]

The first judge to hear the complaint agreed with Reed. He said the alimony contract was valid. As that decision came several months after the complaint was filed, the back payments by that time totaled almost $45,000. It probably didn't help that the daughter—Marie Louise, nicknamed Mimi—publicly supported her father in his efforts to extract money from her mother. "She testified for her father at the trial, against my mother" Bill Robertson says, "and my father never forgave her for that."

But the appeals court in New York disagreed with the lower court, and ruled that she could stop the alimony payments. The court echoed Rothenberg's legal logic: The agreement was in violation of "domestic relations laws and public policy."[16] As of February 1, 1950, 19 years after she married him, 18 years after they were separated, 17 years after her divorce, and 15 years after she remarried, Marie Hartford Hoffman Reed Robertson was free of Louis Reed.

Reed really was a piece of work. In the summer of 1935, while Hoffman was writing her very first check to him, the freshly divorced Reed married Marion Snowden, an heiress of the Standard Oil fortune. That marriage didn't even last through the honeymoon, however, and it was back to Reno for Reed. Apparently, extortion didn't impress Snowden and there is no record of her paying Reed money. He would have to learn to live on his $6,000 annual income, as well as the payments from his first ex-wife of more than three times that amount.

In 1948, shortly after the alimony payments stopped, and a month after Reed cooked up his scheme to sue Marie for their continuation, the police arrived at his home, by now in Bennington, Vermont, after receiving a distress call. He was "conked with a beer bottle by a blond factory worker," according to the local paper. "I think I've killed Reed," the woman said in her call to the police. He wasn't dead, however, and, when the police arrived, Reed, perhaps still groggy so soon after he regained consciousness, said of the blond, "She's out of her head. She came to supper six weeks ago and hasn't gone home yet."[17]

Just another episode in the life of a playboy who, when he wasn't otherwise getting into mischief, thought he could feed off rich heiresses.

One of the reasons Charles Robertson would be unforgiving toward Mimi for what he considered her traitorous behavior toward her mother was his understanding that Reed's violence upon Marie resulted in her not being able to bear more children. As this naturally also weighed heavily on Marie, she may have found some solace when an opportunity later arose during the Second World War. A non-governmental organization in Britain, the Children's Overseas Reception Board, arranged for thousands of children to be evacuated from London so that they would be safe during Hitler's blitzkrieg attacks. When he read that many of the children would be evacuated to the United States, Robertson called his wife to ask if she would be interested in temporarily sheltering any and, if so, how many. "Without a moment's hesitation," she responded, "the entire shipload."[18] They took in two children.

Nuala Pell

The oldest living direct descendant of George Huntington Hartford is Nuala O'Donnell Pell. Although she is at the same generational level as Bill Robertson and his siblings—a great-grandchild—she is more than 20 years older than Robertson. Her grandfather, Edward Hartford, the third son of the A&P co-founder, was the only child to make a successful business life for himself outside of the grocery chain. Although he served as A&P's corporate secretary, took part in strategic decisions, and, of course, derived income and wealth from the success of the company, he was less drawn to the world of grocery stores than that of automobiles. He invented what has become one of a car's most basic components: the shock absorber. He also invented brakes, jacks, and other auto components, all of which were produced at the Hartford Suspension Company in New Jersey, next door to A&P's headquarters.[19]

As was true of all of Hartford's grandchildren, Nuala Pell's mother—Edward's daughter, who was at the same generational level as Marie Robertson—was one of several income beneficiaries of a trust that had been established in 1917. Pell's mother's name was Marie Josephine Hartford, although she was known as "Jo." "Mother was talented," Pell remembers. "She was very good at the piano, a concert pianist." Also, "she spent time in Paris, and every house she had was perfect in design and comfort." She was also a well-known breeder of racehorses.

Altogether, Jo had four husbands and lived the high-society life. "One husband was the son of a famous Russian admiral and another (the fourth), Ivar Bryce, was a close friend of Ian Fleming, whom Jo met while vacationing in the Bahamas," the locale of some of the early James Bond novels. "I met Ian Fleming at my mother's house in Bennington," Pell says, "and when the movies started coming out, I saw Sean Connery often."

Life was good. Yet to hear Pell tell it, even though her mother was receiving about $1 million a year from the trust, Jo "was always broke. Rich as she was, she spent more than she had. Since she got a great deal, I could never understand it," Pell recalls today. "Jo was constantly on the financial verge, waiting for that next trust distribution."

One of Jo's advisors in those years remembers her as an eccentric. "A lawyer in her employ," says the advisor, "once called to inform her that her husband Bryce, who had recommended investments in oil and gas, a business in which he had an interest, was secretly overcharging her and cooking the family's books. Her response? 'If he's taking me for a ride, I'm really enjoying it.' She then called the most senior partner at the law firm where the lawyer who reported the overcharging worked, and told him that if the firm didn't fire the lawyer—in her view nothing more than behaving as an unwanted tattle-tale—she would fire the firm. So, simply because of Jo's eccentric whim, they fired the guy, even though he was doing his job and trying to protect her interests."[20]

Pell grew up unaware that her family had a lot of money. "I didn't know anything about the A&P," she says. "I didn't think we had any money. We had detectives around all the time, but I didn't know why. Nothing was ever said."

In the 1930s the Hartford family was one of the wealthiest in the United States and, despite her lifestyle, Jo carried a concern about publicity that her cousin Marie shared. "I think it was because of the Lindbergh baby," Pell says, recalling the kidnapping of Charles and Anne Lindbergh's 20-month-old son in 1932. Around the country and the world, but particularly in New Jersey, the kidnapping was a sensational story and people everywhere were mesmerized by it. Most of the Hartford family lived in Orange, New Jersey and the Lindberghs lived in Amwell, 50 miles south. But that information, when Nuala Pell was growing up, was not connected in her mind to her own family's prominence. "The first I learned of my family's history wasn't until I got married."

Miss Nuala O'Donnell became Mrs. Nuala Pell when she married Claiborne Pell in 1944. Pell followed what might be described as an ideal career path, although he didn't attend the school, for a Woodrow Wilson School graduate: After graduating from Princeton and serving in the Coast Guard from 1941 to 1945, he was a foreign service officer for seven years, worked in government positions for several years, and then, in 1960, was elected in Rhode Island to the United States Senate, where he served until 1997. Despite his own family history—five ancestors, from his father back to a great-great-great-grand-uncle, served in Congress—Pell was known for his lack of pretension. To the degree his name is recognized today, especially by those associated with higher education, it is because in 1973 he was the primary sponsor of the "Basic Educational Opportunity Grants," better known as Pell Grants, which provide financial aid to college students.

"My mother disapproved of Clay," Pell recalls. "She didn't think he would amount to much. But he didn't approve of my mother either; 'she was married too often,' Clay said. It all worked out, though. Afterwards, she would refer to her son-in-law as 'the Senator.'"

Another memory takes Nuala Pell back to the time she and her husband were newlyweds and living in Princeton while he was teaching military affairs and government. "We had a little house in front of Albert Einstein's home. He was so nice, and I was terrible at math. When he wasn't too busy, he would come over to my house to balance my checkbook for me. He was a sweet old man."[21]

Wealth and a Second Chance in the Great Depression

In 1935 the nation was deep in the Great Depression, the unemployment rate had *fallen* to 20.1 percent, and, even though the broad consensus was that the economy was recovering, the average annual income was $1,500. That was the year that, at the age of 23, the wealthy Marie Hoffman remarried.

She would be considered a good catch for obvious reasons, but Charles Robertson was a good catch, too. He was born and grew up in

New York City, and graduated *magna cum laude* from Princeton in 1926 with a degree in English. He started out in real estate, the family business; once the Depression began, there wasn't much else to do, even for an honors graduate of Princeton.

One day, in the early 1930s, when he was at his desk at the Sammis Real Estate Agency in Huntington, Long Island—Sammis was his grandparents' name—an attractive young woman walked in. She had just been through a grueling divorce and wanted out of New Jersey, so went looking around for a place to live on Long Island, one of the glamorous residential areas in the eastern United States at the time. Money was no object. Robertson sold her sixty acres of land that sloped down to the eastern shore of Cold Spring Harbor.

He then sold her on himself and they were married shortly thereafter. Afterward, during World War II, he was an intelligence officer in the Navy and was stationed off the eastern coast of Long Island to watch for German submarines. He was also an explosives expert. After the war, he became a limited partner at the investment firm, Smith Barney.[22]

In 1957, when the last of the five children of George Huntington Hartford died, the trust established upon his death in 1917 dissolved. The terms called for his grandchildren to receive the A&P stock outright; now they could live off of more than just the income. The grandchildren split up their parents' one-fifth distribution depending on how many brothers and sisters they had. That meant Marie Robertson would evenly split her mother's 20 percent share with her sister. Ten percent of the A&P fortune was valued at about $85 million in 1957.

Financially astute, Charles Robertson took on the responsibilities of what might be described in later decades as wealth management—hers, which became theirs—with intensity, astuteness, and a sense of altruism. With the stark juxtaposition of his marriage into unbelievable wealth with the depths of the Great Depression as motivation, Robertson felt a moral obligation to use, with his wife's enthusiastic support, a good portion of their fortune for charitable causes.

By then, after two decades of marriage to Charles, Marie Robertson's life was at least steady, if not fully stable. "All along, she was a sweetheart,"

Nuala Pell says of Marie. "Unlike what she had to endure with Louis Reed, she and Charles shared a solid value system and a good life together."[23]

Bill Robertson's Childhood

Bill Robertson was not born into the Robertson family. He was adopted. So were two of his siblings, Anne and John. Bill was the youngest of the three. "I found out from Anne when I was around six years old, and she found out from our next door neighbor," Bill recalls. "She said, 'I found out we're adopted.' And I said, 'What's that?'"

And there was to be a fourth. Marie eventually did get pregnant. "Katherine came along unexpectedly. She was the only child my parents conceived," says Robertson. Katherine was Marie's second, and last, natural child.

Despite the happiness of finally having conceived, Charles and Marie, according to Bill Robertson, showed no favoritism when the four were growing up. "I think any intelligent person would realize that there is some difference," Robertson says. "I've always had it on my mind; you know, some sort of extra feeling on the part of my parents? My father's only genetic child? He must have had a preference. But there was never any attitude about it. We were all treated equally."[24]

The following language is usually boilerplate in trust documents that provide for future generations, but it was with special relevance that Charles and Marie added to the Robertson Foundation's Certificate of Incorporation, the document that established the gift to benefit Princeton, "The term 'descendants' . . . shall include adopted children."

Although he will never know to whom he was genetically bonded, Bill Robertson describes his childhood in idyllic terms. "We spent winters in Florida when I was little. I remember waking up in the morning and then building castles in the sand. Altogether, we had three homes—the one in Huntington, New York, the one in Del Ray Beach, where a pool house adjoined the main building, and the apartment in the City. We also had a governess, Maria Min, who took care of me most of the time. She was fabulous. Life was filled with a lot of fun. I have happy memories of going back and forth to Florida on the train in the 1950s. I never heard my parents argue and I never saw either one of them unhappy. To me it was all harmony and happiness." One of Bill's singular memories was when his parents "gave my brother and me a motor boat. I was around ten at the time. This was in Long Island, and every day I'd drive the boat to the Cold Spring Harbor Beach Club."

Bill remembers his father as "a pretty cool guy. He was quite liberal with us. He let us go as we pleased. He was tolerant. He would even buy us beer to drink when we were on vacations—not when we were really young," he quickly clarifies, "but later. When I brought my high school friends by the house, he would keep a cooler filled. He asked his driver to keep it filled. He was fun, a regular guy, and we were all very fond of him. He was a good dad, and I give him high marks."

In New York, the Robertsons' lifestyle was "modest," as Bill remembers it; this, even though his parents owned three homes. His parents, with the same philosophy that Nuala Pell's parents employed, kept him in the dark about the family's fortune. "They didn't tell me anything," says Robertson. "When I was ten, I played on a Little League baseball team in Huntington. Every team was identified by who sponsored them. Ours was 'The A&P' team, and I didn't know what that meant. My parents didn't talk about the A&P. There was never any discussion about money, and there was never any talk of religion or politics either, not at the dinner table."

Robertson was a teenager when he suspected for the first time that his family was wealthy. He remembers the cars. "My mother drove a little black Thunderbird and my father had a Chrysler Imperial. It had those big fins." To confirm his suspicions of the deeper meaning of the big fins, he asked Jim Snedeker, a friend of his. "He said, 'Don't you know? You're loaded.'" Snedeker knew this because his mother, a friend of Bill's mother, had told him so. It's quite possible that the only dinner table in Huntington around which a discussion of the Robertsons' wealth never took place was the one in Charles and Marie Robertson's home.

Marie built the Huntington house—a small mansion, really—with her own money, shortly before she and Charles were married. "People took note of how beautiful it was, and they raised their eyebrows," Bill recalls. "I later realized how unusual it was that my mother was able to afford that kind of house—when she was in her early 20s. That's a tender age to be so fabulously well-off." Today the estate, including the home in which she and her husband lived until her death in 1972, is owned by Cold Spring Harbor Laboratory.[25]

Bill Robertson's father worked hard and went in early to the office, about an hour's drive into New York City. "I remember that he had breakfast with us, and then his driver, George Taylor, a great guy, would take him to New York."

"I know it sounds strange," Bill says—and he reiterates this often—"but I don't remember any discord." In his particular case—Bill can't speak for Anne, from whom he is today estranged, or John, who died tragically in a boating accident in 2003—he admits to feeling "lucky." He says he was chosen. "I have a powerful loyalty to my parents. They adopted me. I would certainly have loyalty to natural parents, but I have an extra sense of loyalty *because* I was adopted. They came and they chose me . . . and they *saved* me. Who knew what my fate would be? They gave me an incredible childhood, not to mention an inheritance and an education. I feel like I'm a blessed man."

No life, however, is completely idyllic. No memories, if honestly conjured, tell such a one-sided story, not even if they include bonding father-son beer moments. Extreme wealth can bring on strange behavior and feelings. When pressed, Bill does remember things that weren't always so happy. Charles Robertson would leave for the City on only those mornings he was in Huntington the prior evening, which wasn't all the time. "I didn't see a lot of my parents. My father was always working," Bill remembers, "and he often stayed in the City. He stayed in the East Side apartment a lot."

And Marie struggled. "My mother was probably unable to be a great mother because her own mother died at 51 when she was only 13. She grew up in East Orange, New Jersey with servants running around."

Privilege may have left Marie fragile and uncertain, with a lack of self-confidence that led her to the charming but disastrous Louis Reed. Even strong support from Charles Robertson, an emotionally level-headed man, could only do so much to stabilize her internal struggles. When Bill was in high school and then at college, his mother never wrote. "She didn't call either," the son says. "Dad was the communicative one. He would call me every Sunday morning when I was at Lawrenceville." Although he was later expelled, Robertson had been enrolled in the exclusive Lawrenceville School near Princeton, New Jersey. "Dad wrote lots of letters, too, two or three every week, and most of them were hand-written." While the family always kept up its decorum and while there existed an on-and-off again intimacy, Bill says reflectively of his father, "We never celebrated his birthday."

Bill Robertson Grows Up

Officials at Princeton today would have no difficulty believing that, among the four Robertson children, Bill and his brother John were the troublemakers.

"My brother John taught me how much fun drinking beer was," Robertson remembers. "Johnnie got people to buy us beer, and then, after we were 18, we'd buy it ourselves. We'd sneak out of the house." He wonders if his parents might have been too liberal. "One summer we got into trouble. We were too young to have jobs, if you can be too young for that, and took a bunch of paraphernalia—life preservers, paddles, a hodge-podge of things—off of yachts moored at the fashionable Seawanhaka Corinthian Yacht Club in Oyster Bay, and put them in dinghies, which we also stole, and then towed it all out and tied everything to a navigation bell just outside of the harbor. It was all out there for three days before anyone figured out what happened. I was stupid enough to tell some-one—I thought he was a friend—that I had done this. And then he told his father, who then told my father, who laid it on me. When he found out, my father yelled, 'I hope you're proud. You've embarrassed me in front of the entire community!'" Bill Robertson reflects on this memory for a moment, and then says of the tattletale, "He was a nasty kid."

Some 40 years later, Robertson heard from one of his long-ago neighbors, Ann Brower, who, upon remembering the incident, told him that Oyster Bay's town fathers actually thought the stunt was a "riot. We stirred up a hornet's nest at that fancy club." To this day, Robertson does not take full credit for the caper. "Tommy Dubosque—he goes by *Hutch*—really came up with the idea, and I would be remiss in not permitting him to share in the glory of that riot."

A few years after that incident, when Bill was 16 and had just obtained his junior driver's license, he got into another minor mess. "A friend, Flipper Powers, and I were driving out to go surfing. It was raining. I went for the brakes, but I wound up on the accelerator, and, when I finally found the brakes, I fishtailed. We went through a fence between a tree and right into the Roosevelt estate on Oyster Bay. Teddy's family. Right through his picket fence. We were so smart. We didn't want anyone to find out, so we pulled out the fence pieces and then took off. We fled the scene of the crime. But of course we got found out." Home that night, presumably, wasn't a cozy place.

His parents weren't very happy about his expulsion from Lawrenceville either. "I didn't graduate," Robertson says self-effacingly. "The problem was both behavioral and academic." Charles Robertson was worried that, even with the gift he and Marie made several years earlier, his son would not be able to get into Princeton. So, after being kicked out of Lawrenceville, Bill Robertson says, "I was shipped off to Upper Canada College in Toronto."

Upper Canada College is a high school where, according to its web site, "endless opportunities await boys." Bill played hockey well enough—"I wasn't that great, but I was good enough to make the first team"—and studied hard enough that, combined with his parents' pull, he received an acceptance letter from the admissions office at Princeton. "Upper Canada was my father's way of getting me through the back door at Princeton," Robertson admits. "Although my father had influence, Upper Canada was a very nice added feature to make me look legitimate." His application wasn't all that dreary, actually. He says his SAT scores were "more than acceptable." Then, introspectively: "I wasn't a complete legacy."

His mother, even though often distant and never communicative, supported Bill in the limited ways she could. And he found solace in her efforts. After Lawrenceville, he says, she was kind. "Even though she was disappointed that I did so poorly at school, my mom was great. I'd always go to my mom when I got in trouble."

At Princeton, Robertson made the freshman hockey team. But then, he says, "I blew out my knee. If I'd been healthy," he wonders as he seems to be recalling an unfulfilled dream, "and had my stuff together . . . I don't know." Then, reality: "Keep in mind that I was a married man with a child at the time"—he had gotten married in college—"and so I had a lot of other things on my mind. And, frankly, I didn't like the travel. Here you were in the dead of winter on some beaten up old school bus riding around in the sleet and snow at night going to a flea-bag motel in, uh, places like . . . Ithaca and Buffalo."

College, marriage, and fatherhood seemed finally to have knocked a sense of adulthood into Robertson. He got his first job after college at Merrill Lynch and, as his father did, has spent his professional life in the world of investments.

Something happened early in his career that helped develop his professional acumen and played a part in his decision to later sue Princeton. In the early 1980s, as a director of his family's trust, he invested in a company whose owner, Robertson says, "was disregarding the investors. One day I confronted him. I told him the company wasn't growing and that I and several other people had put in considerable funds. When I asked what he planned to do about it, he told me, in effect, 'Well, kid, you put your money in and since I didn't sign a formal shareholders' agreement, you're out of luck.' He then told me, 'To remedy this, you're going to have to prove fraud.' So I filed suit against him for securities fraud and common law fraud, and a jury found him guilty on all counts."

That success, in part, gave Robertson the confidence to sue Princeton when he felt similarly ignored. "I had been through the process and saw how the court system could work to redress a wrong."

Bill made enough of an impression as a fiduciary on his father that, just a few years after he graduated from Princeton in 1972, Charles asked him, alone of the four children, to serve as a trustee of the Robertson Foundation at Princeton.

This would open up a new and profound set of responsibilities for him.

Keep in mind that, when Bill was younger, there was never any discussion about his parents' gift to Princeton. "I didn't know until I was 18. Right after they made the gift, Dad wrote a letter to me explaining it all, but he didn't show it to me. It went into a great big case with an album about the gift and into a safe deposit box, and so I didn't actually see the letter for a long time. He didn't want us to know early on, but he wanted a record of the correspondence. They wanted to shelter us from knowledge of the money."[26]

That letter, beautifully written, omitted one important detail. Bill Robertson discovered only as he was to enter college that the X Foundation, as it was known for over a decade after it was established, was actually the Robertson Foundation. As was the case with Nuala Pell's mother, her first cousin Marie was intensely protective. Although the gift to Princeton was made almost thirty years after the Lindbergh baby was kidnapped, Marie Robertson, one of the wealthiest people in the country, and extremely publicity-shy at that, was concerned for her and her family's safety. In addition, she was still, as she always would be, humiliated about the publicity her alimony trial with Louis Reed had generated. It was best, she thought, to stay out of the newspapers.

The End of an Era

The Hartford era at the A&P began in 1878, when George Gilman quietly handed operational decisions to George Huntington Hartford. At his death in 1917, the company's management was transferred to two of his sons, George and John, who were of one mind and ruled the company with a singular determination. Nuala Pell says that the two "were a perfect combination. John would spread the word. George would take care of the books; he was a real businessman."[27] It was under their leadership that the A&P grew into one of the most successful companies in the history of American business.

By the late 1940s, the two aging Hartfords began planning the succession of the company's leadership. In 1949 they appointed David Bofinger, a long-time employee and executive, as the company's president. That put him in a public role for the first time, however, and he panicked when, in December of that year, the Senate Agriculture Committee asked him to testify on the price of coffee. The company was the target of much wrath in the 1930s and 1940s, when much of the public, including many people in Congress, thought A&P was just a bit too monopolistic. When Bofinger delayed his response, the Committee threatened to subpoena him. Shortly after that threat, he died of a heart attack.

Next up was Ralph Burger. Described as "an A&P lifer" and "a backstairs operator," he would have to balance running the company and dealing with ending the company's longstanding feud with the government. Although it was eventually settled, in 1949 an antitrust suit threatened to break up the A&P. Burger's job was to run the company, but, after John Hartford died, Burger had to do it without Hartford's legendary vision and marketing savvy.[28]

John, who lived until he was 79, died on September 20, 1951. George, who lived until he was 91, died on September 24, 1957.[29] After 79 years, the Harford era at the Great Atlantic & Pacific Tea Company had ended.

Both brothers, neither of whom had children, bequeathed all their shares, which amounted to 40 percent of the company, to the John A. Hartford Foundation. Established in 1929, it today has assets of approximately $550 million and annual charitable distributions of just under $25 million.[30] According to its executive director, Corinne Rieder, "for the past 30 years the foundation's goal has been to improve the health care of older people." Its board of trustees has, by tradition, included one of the Hartford heirs.[31] Toby Pell, one of Nuala Pell's children, and therefore a direct descendant of the founder of the A&P, sits on the governing board.

When the A&P trust, which was established in 1917, came to an end, the stock was no longer in the hands of the directors, but in those of the heirs. Burger's goal was to maintain control, and he could do that only by pressuring the family members to pool their voting power. Burger had also been named the president of the Hartford Foundation. Because the foundation owned 40 percent of the company, Burger needed only another 10 percent to keep control under one roof. And he got it, from Josephine Bryce—Edward Hartford's daughter and Nuala Pell's mother—as she was on the foundation's board and was friendly with Burger.[32]

Charles Robertson had been anticipating the day when A&P's golden era would be over. By the late 1940s, he too was worried about what would happen to the company's stock when the trust dissolved after the Hartford brothers died. His investment instincts told him that things would not go well, a lack of confidence that, combined with his personal dislike for the Hartfords, led to animosity between him and the Hartford brothers, who were, remember, Marie's uncles.

A meeting that Charles and Marie had with the brothers in 1946 to discuss the succession issue did not go well. They and their advisors wanted Robertson not to persuade Marie to sell her stock after the trust dissolved. Their efforts, viewed as strong-arm tactics, upset her. "When she did not wish to discuss her financial affairs," Robertson later wrote, "she would go for a drive or her eyes would fill with tears and she would disappear into her bathroom until she was sure I was out of the mood to report to her."[33]

Marie Robertson might have been upset because her uncles didn't like her husband. But after what happened in her first marriage, anyone might have had reason to question her judgment. It wasn't her marital judgment, however, that was at play when the A&P elders took a disliking to Charles. Before he and Marie stormed out of that meeting, Robertson had explained that he was opening an office for the purpose of investing, a clear signal that he knew that the A&P stock would, soon after the trust terminated, become publicly traded and that he could be expected to immediately diversify his and Marie's asset base.

The Hartfords did not like this at all. According to Bill Robertson, "At that meeting John Hartford told my mother, 'Don't you know that Charlie could clean you out?'" To which, Marie responded, "Let's go, Charlie!"[34]

In a letter to his children, Charles Robertson wrote, "Your mother joined me as we departed from the meeting in some haste because I was about to blow my stack. As we emerged from the office of the president, we were stopped by Mr. Ralph Burger, secretary to both of the Hartford brothers, who pleaded with us not to go in such haste and in such a mood, but your mother replied gently but firmly, 'Please!' and Mr. Burger, later head of the A&P, stepped aside and we never saw either of the Hartford brothers in life but did attend both their funerals."[35]

There was no love lost between Burger and Robertson either. Burger, Robertson told his son, "was loath to release any of the stock to the beneficiaries while he attempted to wheedle your mother into voting with the Foundation to insure that he and Mother's cousin Josephine Bryce would control the tea company. He even offered to make a large donation from the Hartford Foundation to the Huntington Hospital of which I was a former president of the Board of Trustees."[36]

In 1958 the A&P announced that it would soon go public, which provided a ready market for family members who would then want to sell their stock. As soon as she could after the stock was released, which was still over a year after the trust was dissolved, Marie, at Charles's direction, sold 900,000 shares, about half her holdings. Because so much was being sold, however—others were also selling chunks of their ownership—the price dropped to $44.5, from over $70, which meant that, before capital gains taxes, she received just under $40 million by selling half her shares.[37]

The other half would be used to benefit Princeton. As it happens, even though the stock price was higher by the time the gift was made, the result of a booming economy, it was falling by the middle of 1961 and there wasn't much time. A&P was losing its luster. Charles Robertson's concerns were vindicated as he saw that the new management after the Hartford era wasn't keeping up with the times. "There may never have been a major company so ill suited to public share ownership," wrote Marc Levinson, the author of *The Great A&P.* "The A&P was still extraordinarily secretive, as it had been under George L. and John A. Hartford and under their father before them. Researchers from the Bureau of Labor

Statistics who checked on prices for the monthly consumer price index were turned away; the company refused to cooperate with the National Labor Relations Board as it tried to resolve workers' complaints; and the company also declined to provide sales data on items for A. C. Nielson, the market research service. It alone saw proprietary value in its internal information."

Things were going downhill fast. "The speed of A&P's decline was shocking," Levinson wrote, "At the start of 1961, it was still the largest retailer in the world," but "signs of rot were everywhere." A few years after the deaths of the founders, "the once-mighty A&P was a basket case, staggering from one failed strategy to another as better-run companies passed it by."[38]

Levinson describes the decline over the next two decades, and how, as the owner of so much of the company, the Hartford Foundation hurt its own charitable purposes. In early 1961, A&P's stock traded at $70.50 per share. At the end of May 1961, when the gift to the Robertson Foundation was executed, the stock was valued at $49.60. By mid-1964 it was trading at $34.50, less than half its high.

By 1978, "the [Hartford] foundation's trustees finally decided that the game was up. A buyer from Germany bought 42 percent of the stock, "an implied value of $190 million on a company that had been worth $1 billion 20 years earlier. After fending off decades of government efforts to destroy it, A&P had all but destroyed itself."[39]

In 2010, A&P filed for bankruptcy.

"My dad," Bill Robertson says, "was astute and he knew that once the family lost control of the stock, the company wouldn't do well. He didn't trust the new management—and he was right."[40]

The Family's Philanthropy

"My mother wanted to be charitable early on, and my parents set up the Banbury Fund in 1946," Bill Robertson recalls about the family's first foundation. And Charles had just the right temperament and ability to help her establish and fulfill their philanthropic goals.

Which was good, because Charles Robertson didn't think much of inherited wealth. He wrote to his children, "Mother's fortune was a burden to her. Large fortunes endowing young people did not appeal to us. When you were very young Huntington Hartford," because of his playboy lifestyle, "used to be in the newspapers daily. His sister"—Nuala Pell's mother, the one who had difficulty making ends meet on a $1 million annual income—"was divorced three times in a row. John"—one of the two sons who ran the A&P—"after forty years of married life, divorced his wife and married a bag. One in-law was shot and killed by his own son. Too much endowment would discourage individual initiative, we felt." Then, foreshadowing the philosophy about inheritance that Warren Buffet would reveal some years later,[41] Robertson said, "Heirs and heiresses were for the birds. We required normal children and that is what we have—not spoiled brats."[42]

While the Princeton gift was the largest the couple made, it was not their only gift. The list of their recipients includes the Community Service Society of New York City and its counterpart in Huntington, the Visiting Nurse Service, Columbia Presbyterian Hospital, the Boys Club of New York, the United Negro College Fund, the Red Cross, and several other charities.

A precursor to the Robertson Foundation also benefited Princeton. Charles Robertson explained to his children, "We decided, with a gift through the Banbury Fund, to honor one of mother's heroes, General and later President Dwight D. Eisenhower," an endowed fund set up to hire professors who would "prepare young men for careers in international fields of endeavor and to improve understanding of foreign nations and peoples."[43]

"The Banbury Fund," says Bill Robertson, who was a trustee of the fund, "was pure, unselfish philanthropy." But he wonders if "there might have been a small amount of personal consideration for a while when my dad made gifts from the Fund to Phillips Exeter Academy. It was a great program, providing scholarships for the boys who were accepted. I think my father was hoping I'd wind up at Exeter. But of course I didn't cut it."[44]

Exeter was an essential part of the Banbury Fund's early days. Katherine Ernst, Bill's sister, as well as a board member of the Banbury Fund and the president of the Robertson Foundation for Government, the foundation that resulted from the Princeton settlement, says, "My father knew Bill Saltonstall, the principal at Exeter in the 1940s, and my parents told him that if he encountered any boys—Exeter only took boys back then—who had tremendous potential but didn't have the money, then he should let my father know." The fund paid for many students. "They were called 'Banbury Boys,'" says Ernst, "and my parents' fund not only put them through Exeter, but college and graduate school as well."

The first boy to receive a scholarship under the program was Nicholas Yankopoulos, Exeter class of 1948. "His family escaped from Greece and came to Boston," says Ernst. "Mr. Saltonstall heard about this young man with fantastic potential but no money, and the Fund was able to help." Yankopoulos, who graduated from Harvard and then from the College of Physicians and Surgeons at Columbia, is today a cardiologist in California. In the small-world department, Ernst says, "While I was attending college in California, I became close to Nick and his family. He attended my wedding and he's my daughter's godfather."[45]

Today, at 84, Yankopoulos says, "I would have struggled to be educated if it weren't for Mr. Robertson and his wife. The Robertsons saved my life. The Banbury Fund paid for Exeter, through Harvard, and through Columbia Medical School. I think they would have paid more, but I was finally making $50 per month as an intern and so I told them I didn't need the financial help any more. They were very generous."

Yankopoulos remembers both of the Robertsons fondly. She was motherly, he says, as if invoking Marie's spirit when she took in British boys during World War II. Yankopoulos also remembers a moment when he was visiting Charles Robertson after Marie had died. "We were sitting in the living room talking," he recalls. "There was a framed picture of Mrs. Robertson on the piano. In the middle of the conversation, he got up to wipe off the dust from the picture's frame. I don't think there was any dust, though. I think he just wanted to touch it."[46]

In the early 1980s, a short while after his father died, Bill Robertson visited Dr. Richard Mayeux at the Columbia University Medical Center. Today, Mayeux is the chairman of the Center's Neurology Department. He also runs the Gertrude Sergievsky Center and co-directs the Taub Institute for Research on Alzheimer's Disease and the Aging Brain. Robertson was visiting Mayeux because the family was interested in supporting research for Alzheimer's, the disease that led to Charles's death. He was an assistant professor then and just getting his career started. At lunch with Mayeux and the then-chairman of the Neurology Department, Robertson mentioned that a gift would most likely be made to either Johns Hopkins or Albert Einstein College of Medicine, both of which had better-established programs in Alzheimer's research than Columbia did at the time. When it seemed that Columbia wasn't in the picture, Mayeux, says, "My chief lost interest in the discussion."

On the walk back to Robertson's car in the parking lot after the dispiriting lunch, Mayeux gave it another shot and asked how much money they were talking about. When he heard what it was, Mayeux said, "You know, if you give it to those guys it's not going to get them anywhere. I'm at the beginning. If you give it to me, it will help me build a program. I said that the money at either of the other two places might fund a postdoc or something like that, but here the money could launch a career for a bunch of us because we could use it as development money. And Bill looked at me, and he said, 'I like that. I like that idea.' I then told him that I had no other place to get grants." After a reflective pause, Mayeux says, "A few days later he called to tell me they were going to give me the money. And every year since then the Banbury Fund has supported my program."

Note to fundraisers and other nonprofit executives: Mayeux says, "I didn't take 'no' for an answer." He did that not by speaking ill of the other two deserving medical centers, but by explaining that the amount of money in question—which, by the way, was about $25,000—could do so much more at Columbia's nascent program than anywhere else. Of course, he had to convey to Robertson that the program had potential, but he had done that over lunch, describing his plans and establishing his medical authenticity and commitment to Alzheimer's research. "My chair said afterwards, 'You have a lot of chutzpa.' And I said back, 'Well, what's the worst he could say? No?'"

The potential has been realized. In 1992, Mayeux received the Leadership and Excellence in Alzheimer's Disease award from the National Institute of Aging. In 2004 he received a MERIT award for his work on the genetic epidemiology of familial Alzheimer's disease. Since 2002 he has led the National Institute on Aging—Late Onset Alzheimer's Disease family study.[47]

And that gift, repeated and increased every year since, "has meant everything," Mayeux says. "I've been able to develop new faculty with the money." In fact, "Half the faculty here got their initial grant from Bill. They don't know that, but the Robertsons do." Mayeux describes the process with pride for his faculty. "When a new faculty member has an idea and needs some money, I can give it to him or her. It's not much—maybe $20,000 or something like that—but that's what Bill did for me, and now I do it for my faculty whenever I can. I've never spent a penny of it on my own research—at my level you're supposed to get federal grants—but I have people who are now full professors who started off with a grant from the Robertsons."

From mouse genomics, where one of the faculty figured out how to give a mouse an MRI, to developing new cognitive tests, the Robertsons' philanthropy, in demonstrable ways that Mayeux is eager to explain to the family members every year, has helped society in a very real way. He is clear: "You can't push the edge without the right funding. It really is like venture capital. Without that money this would not have happened." After a discussion about the outlook for a cure for Alzheimer's, Mayeux, as a result of his work and the work of many others throughout the world, admits that he is optimistic. "There is no question that Bill got me started. It was that seminal start—that $25,000, negotiated in the parking lot— that got us off the ground."[48]

Today, given impetus by the initial Robertson gift, the Taub Institute at Columbia University is a national leader for Alzheimer's research.

Another recipient of the Robertsons' philanthropy is the Cold Spring Harbor Laboratory on Long Island. "The year after my mother died," Robertson says, "my dad gave $8 million to the Laboratory." At the time, Cold Spring had only a $20,000 endowment.

The laboratory's then-president, Dr. James Watson, is best known as one of the three people awarded the Nobel Prize in 1952 "for," as the Nobel Prize people put it, "their discoveries concerning the molecular structure of nucleic acids and its significance for information transfer in living material." That means they discovered the Double Helix, the molecular structure of DNA. The other two who shared the award were Francis Crick and Maurice Wilkins.

Watson describes the momentous accomplishment in this self-effacing way: "It was going to happen anyway. Somebody would have done it. It was a competitive race. Three horses. Two horses fell and so we walked over the finish line." One of the other two horses was Linus Pauling, one of the most influential chemists in history and the recipient of two other Nobel prizes, in Chemistry and Peace, who, as Watson says, "*should* have found it." The other horse in the race was a team from London, "a man and a woman who didn't talk to each other because they couldn't work together."[49]

At Cold Spring "we had begun researching neuroscience," Watson explains, "but we didn't have the money to do it. And Charlie comes along and gives us all this money to do it. This institution was about to fall apart—no endowment, no staff. Charlie's gift saved this place."

As with much about philanthropy, altruism and pragmatism blended. Watson explains in a book that he wrote, with its double-entendred title, *Avoid Boring People,* that Robertson's attorney recommended that he take up residence in Florida to save taxes, and that he dispose of the family home, preferably to a worthy charitable enterprise. He did both. Cold Spring Harbor Laboratory would be an appropriate charitable enterprise: the mission was agreeable and exciting, and it was nearby. But Watson wasn't comfortable taking just the property, as that didn't accomplish either his or Robertson's primary objective of executing real science at the lab. He needed money. "I had to confess, nervously, that dividing our research facilities into two sites was not realistic. Yes, I saw the best use of his land," Watson said to his would-be benefactor, "as a high-powered conference center, similar to the CIBA Foundation in London." But he felt compelled to be frank, even if it meant giving up a valuable gift. "Spending time to raise monies for conferences on Banbury Lane"—the estate's location and the inspiration for the family foundation's name—"would divert us from raising funds to expand our cancer research program."

The honesty paid off. "Charlie took less than a day to reach a decision that far exceeded our most optimistic hopes," Watson says. "Late the next morning, we learned that he had decided it made no sense to give his estate to an institution surviving hand to mouth. He would soon have his lawyer, Eugene Goodwillie, draw up documents establishing an *$8 million* endowment"—Watson then confesses that he doesn't have any idea why Robertson chose that number—"to support research on the lab grounds. That amount would become the Robertson Research Fund. In return, we would accept the gift of his estate, which he would separately endow with an additional $1.5 million." That amount was intended not only to pay the estate's operating expenses, but also to provide money to the village of Lloyd Harbor in lieu of real estate taxes.

Another note to fundraisers and other nonprofit executives: Accept gifts that work and don't accept those that don't. James Watson was schooled in science, not raising money, but he had the good sense to know what would work and what would not. The honesty did not chase the donor out the door. Instead, that Watson honestly and starkly laid out the scenario *inspired* Robertson to provide what was needed.

"We were in a daze," Watson explained. "We actually worried that becoming rich would destroy the Lab's unique way of doing science. But we soon returned to our senses."[50]

The Robertson Research Fund, according to Watson, was "set up in the same way Robertson's gift to Princeton was: as a separate corporation, with five members from the lab and four members from or representing the Robertson family." In contrast to what happened at Princeton, things are going well. "The family is very happy with us," Watson says, noting the obvious juxtaposition, "because we do everything his father wanted us to do. We just respected the donor. Charlie was a straightforward, honest man, and he wanted his children to be proud of what he and Marie had done, and he wanted their involvement in what they had done for the rest of their lives."[51]

Today, that $8 million gift, even taking into account annual payouts and the economic recession of 2008-2009, is worth well over $100 million, more than a third of the lab's $280 million endowment.[52]

The Robertsons were charitable people, they had big dreams, and they wanted their money to make an impact on society. With their most significant gifts—those to Cold Spring Harbor, Columbia, and Princeton—they wanted their children to be partners with the recipients as they stewarded those dreams. They did what they could during their lifetimes, knowing that the day would come when the torch would be passed.

Passing the Torch

Marie Robertson was a beautiful woman. Her face was innocent and sweet, with a small nose and eyes that would look deep, with the interest of someone eager to learn, hungry to know others. Although modest in its dimensions, her figure was the type that caught the eye of men. She kept her hair short, the style women preferred when she came into her womanhood in the 1920s. She was quiet and demure, the way women of means in her era were taught to behave.

And she had a steady income. It was large on the day she was born, and it grew larger every year. By the time she was 45, the trust her grandfather established when she was five years old provided her with about $20,000—per month, *after* taxes—more of an intake than most people, even today, could ever hope to enjoy.

Then, when the A&P trust dissolved in 1957, she came into real money.

While most people think that an enormous amount of money would solve most of their problems, it seems to have created most of Marie's. Sheltered as a young girl, she grew up unaware of the way the world works and her responsibilities in it. On some level she knew she was wealthy, but family tradition dictated that no one speak aloud of money, especially within earshot of the children. Like Nuala O'Donnell, the young Marie knew almost nothing about her link to the A&P fortune.

Some children can't act out their innocence. Their lives, say, in the inner city or with cruel or absent parents, demand an almost-instant growing up; they skip right past the carefree years of exploration and calm that we all know—we really do—is best for children to experience. Such a life anchors their growth into adulthood.

But Marie's problem was the opposite. She was provided everything, and yet, as a young adult, she was unable to deal effectively with some important challenges. Could the well-intentioned sheltering that her parents imposed upon her have had the same stunting effect that a too-difficult childhood might have had? Could the vastly different experiences, because of their absence of what we think of as normal childhood activities, create similar emotional responses in the adult? This is not a banal question: Can the rich kid's burden be just as severe as the financially or socially bereft child's?

Married at 19—possibly pregnant and unhappy on her wedding day—she separated from her husband less than two years later to begin a difficult and arduous ordeal of divorce, and then a dozen years of alimony payments, kept secret from her second husband and parents because she was being blackmailed. Her first husband married her for her money and treated her cruelly; so cruelly, he didn't care that he almost killed her when he threw her down the steps in the home she paid for. The mental confusion of trying to right that situation, all the while keeping it from the world, must have been unbearable, and to deal with it Marie would have been excused had she psychologically retreated into her own world.

With those conflicts dominating her mind, who knows what her internal outline of existence looked like?

Charles was a good man. He knew his wife was fragile. They may not have talked much about it, even between the two of them at their most intimate, but he knew. And she knew he knew. Their life together was one of a basic understanding that Charles would be fully engaged in her social and financial affairs.

Charles did not look upon Marie's fortune in the same gluttonous way that Louis Reed did. It was the opposite, actually. Charles harnessed her innocence—the innocence that drove her insecurities and allowed her to trust the wrong man, when she was far too young to trust any man with her future—to provide her with a purpose money can't buy. In his care, Marie's innocence was rewarded not by becoming the subject of abuse but by being able to follow her altruistic instincts; she took in two boys from England so she could provide *them* with emotional shelter from the war. When she thought her injuries, inflicted at the hands of her first husband, prevented her from having more children, she adopted three to care for. That, along with Charles's strength and goodness, permitted Marie Robertson a far more fulfilling life than was her destiny when she was suffering in Reed's matrimonial prison and parole.

But it wasn't fulfilling enough to fend off the lurking demons of her many insecurities. Charles dealt valiantly with all the issues that took their toll on her life. But while that must have had its effect on the marriage, he never confused her struggles with her essential goodness. He began a letter to his children once, "Your mother was a lady of infinite wisdom."[53] Through her fragility, her husband observed her insight, astuteness and, yes, strength.

It may have been a bout of feeling enormously sad—and why, if that was the case, we will never know—that led her to a fatal lack of self-awareness. She was alone in their apartment in the River House at 435 East 52nd Street in New York on the evening of April 19, 1972. Charles was in Florida. The children were away at their schools. The housekeeper had the night off. It was the middle of the week and no social commitments were on the calendar.

Afterward, the governess mentioned the absence of an expensive bracelet. Could there have been a burglary? But nothing else was missing. The police concluded that no one had broken in and that the bracelet had simply gone missing. Although no autopsy was conducted, the coroner determined that Marie had fallen and hit her head on an unforgiving and-iron in front of the fireplace. There was blood, although not a lot, and the impact didn't kill her, not immediately. She somehow made it to her bed, perhaps thinking that, even though she was a Red Cross-certified nurse, the injury wasn't so severe and that rest was all she needed. She made no phone call for help. She was dazed and confused and bloodied, but tomorrow would be another day. She just lay there, unaware that she was slowly dying.

Yet at some point she almost certainly became aware of what was happening to her, that tomorrow would never come.

Many people think there is a brief moment in the transition from this life to the next, especially when death comes slowly, when the person knows, even if for only the briefest moment before it's over. It is commonly understood that at the instant of crossing, a lifetime of memories flies through the dying person's consciousness.

If that's the case, one can only hope, as she appraised, one last time at the young age of 59, all her life's anguish and insecurities, that Marie Robertson could spend some of that fraction of a second knowing the wealth to which she was born would be used well, to improve society. If her most profound personal accomplishments were to make her family's fabric strong, the legacy of her marriage to Charles and being a mother to five children, three of whom were lovingly adopted, her most profound gift to humanity was her extraordinary philanthropy.

Charles Robertson's death almost a decade later was, although natural, equally as tragic. He remarried, but succumbed to Alzheimer's disease in May 1981. "Dad was 75 when he died," says his son. "He was diagnosed around 1977 or 1978, and it was rapid onset. But I strongly suspect he may have known in the early '70s," shortly after Marie died. "He was reading books on the brain obsessively. He went down fast after the diagnosis. I was with him when he died. He was living in Florida and had donated the Huntington house to Cold Spring Harbor Laboratory by then."

Although family life was far from perfect, Bill Robertson's loyalty to his parents was, and to this day remains, fierce. Senior administrators at Princeton might have benefitted if they had taken more notice of that.

Chapter 3

The Landscape of Good Intentions

Supporting a charity might seem like a pretty simple and benign process. Most people think that after a donor writes a check, or even donates something that doesn't come from a checkbook, such as stock or land or artwork or jewelry, the people at the charity use the gift in the best possible way. It's up to them, the people who work at the charity, to figure that out, of course, but who would know better how to use it best? Not the donor. While donors have a passion for the charity's cause, they have no idea how to actually spend the money in pursuit of that cause. They know how to make it in the commercial world, perhaps, but they don't know anything about running a nonprofit. The donor's job is to give the money; the charity's is to spend it. That's why charities employ professionals.

The mantra may seem this crude: Give us your money; now go away. Nothing could be simpler.

Or more arrogant.

The Dead Hand

At first blush it may seem odd, even morbid, but one of the terms swirling around conversations about a donor's intentions is *manus mortua*, "the dead hand." At once solemn and capricious, it suggests a person's intentions to control things after death. The body might be dead, but the spirit continues to rule from the grave. And some, as they ponder life after their death, assume their ideas should live forever.

And why not? The ideas of lots of good, smart people, now dead, are enshrined in our everyday life. Thomas Jefferson's list of self-evident truths; Abraham Lincoln's legacy of limiting and then ending slavery; Susan B. Anthony's pursuit of women's suffrage; even Branch Rickey's bold move to integrate major league baseball. No one today disputes the vision of these and many other people. And even though the ideas behind the breakthroughs weren't always original to the people who get the credit, they nevertheless did what was needed at the time to effect long-lasting change for the betterment of all.

But are these long-dead people, in the sense that the term is used in trust law or philanthropy, ruling from the grave? No—because their ideas have been embraced in society's fabric and are now priorities embedded within our legal system. The dead hand, on the other hand, is a source of controversy precisely because society, as reflected in our laws, has *not* embraced those intentions; not that people have rejected them, not that they are bad ideas, but because they are not sufficiently national or encompassing enough to rise to the level of priorities enshrined in our laws. The law says segregation is history, but no law, for example, insists that grown children be restricted to the income from a trust their parents have established. That kind of thing is permissible but it's not compulsory.

While some goals found in the nonprofit arena are public goals, and are funded partly by the government—such as public radio and television, the national parks and cancer research—most philanthropists give money to charities to endow their personal ideals, which, for better or worse, are not mandated by the government, no matter how good or desirable they might be. As the whole of society hasn't embraced those ideas, they are given life through private funds.

The well-meaning people who want their goals to be pursued in perpetuity can choose from over a million charitable organizations in the United States. Someone may want to give to a university an amount of money whose income, for example, will forever be used to provide scholarships for needy but academically capable students. Or someone might donate to a hospital to provide enough funds to build and maintain a medical research facility. Or donors might start their own foundation, with goals, as long as they are in accord with legally permitted charitable objectives, that they and their families can define.

These ideas, and thousands of others, don't have the weight of national sympathy, and so for the most part the government doesn't fund or enforce them. But they do, nonetheless, serve society. This is true even though many of the purposes conflict with one another.

While some objectives in the philanthropic realm live on and on, others don't—or shouldn't. A few that have outlived their usefulness:

- The will of one donor who died in the 1800s required that an orphan asylum for girls whose railroad-worker fathers died in on-the-job accidents be maintained forever. But by the 1930s, when railroad accidents were far fewer than they had been when the gift was made a half century earlier, there were too few orphan girls for the money to be used wisely.

- Another donor, before cars were invented, created an endowment for watering troughs for horses.

- The donor of another endowed gift stipulated that the income it generated could *not* be used to benefit women or ethnic or religious minorities.[1]

The Dead Hand Should Loosen Its Grip

Those who accept the inevitability of change understand that contemporary society cannot be held hostage to someone else's time. In 1880, Sir Arthur Hobhouse, a British judge who gave a lot of thought to what we now call estate planning, vigorously railed against *manus mortua*. In, "The Dead Hand: Addresses on Endowments and the Settlement of Property," he argued, "Wealth, in order to be useful, ought continually to be used and controlled by those who have the greatest interest in it." Those with the greatest interest, clearly, are not among the dead and they should not have the power to arrange the world to their liking after they are gone. "There is no inherent right belonging to those who have played their part in this world," Hobhouse declared, "to dictate in what manner their former worldly goods shall be used." There is "no wisdom in allowing them to do so except to a very moderate extent."[2] And, more forcefully, "The grip of the dead hand shall be shaken off absolutely and finally."[3]

Hobhouse also thought much about the role of charity in society and brought compelling logic to the counterintuitive argument that a charitable motive is unnecessary to make charity work. "Charitable use is a lawful public use. Property given to uses in which the public are not interested is not given to charity. When property is given to uses in which a portion of society is interested, large enough and indefinite enough to be called the public, and those uses are lawful, it is given to charity."[4]

Of a donor's motives Hobhouse opined with conviction, "If people will not give freely and generously; if they will not really give; if they insist on only pretending to give, while all the while they are stipulating to remain owners themselves, then I say, 'Let their money perish with them!' It is such false gifts as these which have created the scandals and the demoralizing character of so many of our charitable institutions, or at least have prevented their improvement. They are like the gifts of malignant spirits of which old fairy tales tell us; they look like gold, but turn into something foul in the handling. They are fatal. Let us have no more of them."[5]

Not only was Hobhouse no sentimentalist for charity, he thought the very word to be inappropriate. "Because alms may be given from a motive of charity"—the emotion, not the organization—"and because many of these foundations have an eleemosynary object, therefore they have all been dignified with the sacred name of *charities*. It is, as I say, most unfortunate. There is a kind of sentimental halo about the name, which is singularly calculated to bewilder and mislead the judgment. I do not exaggerate when I say that, not only the populace, but legislators and even-headed judges have been dazzled by the beauty of the word, and have not seen the reality, often ugly enough, of the thing signified."[6]

The ugliness of charity might be a little hard to swallow for the tens of thousands of people who raise money on behalf of American-based charities, often with compelling, sentimental stories about how their work helps the world, or for the tens of millions of people in the United States, motivated as much by their heartstrings as by their crania, who donate money to countless causes every year. But today, as the eye of public scrutiny on the nonprofit world sharpens its focus, which requires more of the brain than emotions to defend against, Hobhouse's painful perspective continues to resonate sufficiently enough that everyone ought to take notice.

It could be argued that Hobhouse's counterpart in the United States was Fredrick Harris Goff, who in 1914 gave birth to the Cleveland Foundation, the oldest community foundation in the United States. Goff complained that too many trust funds were trapped in "the dead hand of the past," and wrote that fixed giving by trusts "blesses neither them that give nor those who receive."

He viewed with "disgust" the control deceased donors had over the affairs of the living. "How fine it would be," he once said, "if a man about to make a will could go to a permanently enduring organization—which Chief Justice John Marshall called an 'artificial immortal being'[7]—and say: 'Here is a large sum of money. I want to leave it to be used for the good of the community, but I have no way of knowing what will be the greatest need of the community 50 years from now, or even 10 years from now. Therefore, I place it in your hands, because you will be here, you and your successors, through the years, to determine what should be done with this sum to make it most useful for people of each succeeding generation."[8]

Even the timeless Jefferson might agree with that. While his ideas have lasted through the centuries, he would be the first to tell future generations to challenge them. Referencing the early 19th-century mortality tables available to him at the time, he opined that the life of constitutions and laws should be no longer than 19 years. "The dead have no rights," he wrote. "They are nothing, and nothing cannot own something." He was adamant that the powers to repeal and to amend were not the same— they are not as good—as simply ending things and starting over.[9]

Charities, one might imagine, could easily feel the same about their past donors who staked a claim on the future.

The Dead Hand Should Not Loosen Its Grip

It should come as no surprise that many donors like the idea of a dead hand. They feel they have the right, perhaps even an obligation, to reach into a future that exceeds their lifetimes. What's good for today will be good forever. Furthermore, their logic goes, organizations don't have the right to change things, even if they think it's for the better.

In 1911, William Allen, a British philanthropist, wrote in *Modern Philanthropy* that the "dead hand has a bad reputation among trustees," and listed a few suffocating restrictions that donors imposed on charities. Think horse troughs in the 21st century. But he was actually setting up a more nuanced argument, which at first seems to defend the dead hand.

"What is really objected to is not the deadness of the hand," he wrote, "but the deadening effects upon trustee, beneficiary and other donors," and, "a deadening effect is just as deadening from a live hand as from a dead hand. There is no kind of deadening that deadens more fatally than the sympathetic live hand, which from misinformation and lack of efficiency standards invites insincerity, evasion, waste, incompetence and incompleteness in the use of its gifts. Energy can be deadened by riches and freedom, as well as by restrictions."[10] Allen was saying that the future world would be better off if donors could be assured that their wishes could be honored than if charities took the liberty to use the money differently, even if just by a little bit, from what the donors intended.

That works, however, according to Allen, only when the charity asks several questions of itself to ensure that the donor's goals will be worthy in the future. He wrote of several concerns a charity must take into account when accepting an endowed gift to promote scholarships. "The problems that testators and beneficiaries must face or evade when given instructions or commissions by donors are indicated by . . . questions which I asked when invited to outline suggestions for making this fund (to send 50 men and women each year to college) really accomplish something worthwhile."[11]

It's the expected future feasibility of the donor's wishes, based on a rigorous and honest examination of needs and expectations, that validates the acceptance of a donor's wishes.

When the organization accepts a gift, it is entering into what could fairly be considered a legally enforceable, common-sense arrangement: *In exchange for your gift, we agree to do what you ask with it. We don't have to take it, but if we do we'll honor the terms.*

This way of looking at the matter is what drove the Robertson family to sue Princeton.

Even so, Bill Robertson said he was reluctant to take Princeton to court. The idea of generous people positioning themselves litigiously against an organization whose mission they love—or, the opposite of that; the idea of charities suing their donors—is jarring. It is particularly discordant when we take into account the benign birth that once created the joint venture: the donor's resources combined with the charity's expertise and mission.

Most of the disputes involving dissatisfied donors or their heirs have been resolved short of going to trial, but it is likely that most failures on the part of charities to honor their long-dead donors' wishes have never even been identified. Still, the list of philanthropists irritated with the charities they have supported is growing. The Princeton lawsuit is only the most expensive, most long-lasting, and most well-known of many complaints that one charity or another has deadened the donor's original energies by assuming more freedoms than were implicit in the gift agreement.

Donor Standing

Let's look at something fairly basic in the issue of donor intent: the donor. What right do donors have to take legal action against a charity when they think it is using the money in ways they didn't intend? You might think this is a softball question; the answer, you might say, is that since the donor gave the money he or she has every right to sue when things go awry.

But you would be wrong. In legal circles the demand is built on the word *standing*. Not just anyone can sue anyone else. The person taking the other to court must have a personal connection to the claim of what has gone wrong.

If Mary loans money to John and John doesn't pay Mary back, and they agreed to the terms in writing, Mary can sue John. She can sue John because she has been personally harmed. Mary's brother Tom, however, cannot sue John on Mary's behalf. This is because legally Tom doesn't have anything to do with Mary's predicament; unlike Mary, Tom doesn't have standing. Even if Tom is very upset at how John is treating Mary, generally only Mary can act in court.

In the arena of charitable donations, another important piece to the equation is that the donor has *given the money away*. By the time it's in the charity's hands, it's no longer in the donor's possession. In effect, by making a gift a donor gives up his or her right of control. Where John owed Mary money, the two of them entered into a contractual relationship. But, even though the donor-intent question is thought by many to involve a formal agreement, gifts to charities are often thought of *not as contracts*, but as transactions that most often fall into the realm of *trust law*. Think of a charity as a trust.

And that's where it gets tricky. Not only are there so many aspects to contract law and trust law—and this is not the venue to sort it all out[12]— the outcomes of legal disputes can be very different from one another.

Why trust law and not contract law? Think of it this way: Who owns the money after it's given to the charity? The charity.

But who owns the charity?

Unlike a for-profit corporation, a charity has no stockholders. That means no one person or group of people owns the charity—or the donor's gift. In fact, the charity is owned by the public. But because a mob can't bring a lawsuit, the attorney general in almost every state has the job of making sure things don't go badly at charities. And when things do go wrong, the attorney general's office is often the only place a donor can turn to make them right. Charities, like all entities, are permitted to enter into contracts, but when a donor makes a gift, the transaction, it turns out, is not so contractual, at least not in the same way as between John and Mary.

Before going into when a donor has the right to sue a charity, however—yes, that right does exist—let's get back to the idea of the charity being treated as a trust. To do that, let's look first at a non-charitable trust scenario. Harvey Dale, an attorney in New York and a professor at New York University who specializes in tax-exempt law, uses an example that he says is counterintuitive to most people, and different from most agreements between two parties.

"Suppose a man, X, sets up a trust for his children, A and B," Dale posits, "and X gives some assets to T, the trustee, for the benefit of A and B. There are four people in this situation: 1) X, the person who has the money and puts it into a trust, 2) T, the trustee, 3) A, one beneficiary, and 4) B, the other beneficiary. T undertakes to pay out certain amounts to A and B, as well as to undertake other responsibilities for A and B. Soon T begins to behave very badly, and so X goes to court to sue T. Does X win? Answer: No. X loses. In fact, X gets thrown out of court. *X has no standing even to be heard in court.* Why is that?"

Dale says, "The donor gave away the beneficial interests in the assets to A and B. And he gave away the legal title to T. If the transaction between X and T were a contract, and T misbehaved as a contracting party, X would certainly have standing. But in the case of trust law, it is perfectly clear that X may not sue. *The creation of a trust is not a contract,*" Dale emphasizes. "Of course, A and B—or, if they are young, their guardian—have standing. As you can see, in trust law the question of standing precedes the question of merit. If you don't have standing you can't get to the merits."

Not even charitable beneficiaries have standing.[13]

But *somebody* has to have standing. Charitable assets are intended to benefit the public, and so the attorney general is the entity appointed to protect them.

But should that office be the only entity with standing? As it happens, one goal in the arena of charitable giving has become the balance between the attorney general's exclusivity and the ability of anyone else to sue a charity. Because of the developments relating to donor-intent issues, at least some nonprofit law experts are beginning to think that there are situations where people other than the attorney general ought to have standing. "This is true," Dale says, "particularly when the attorney general's oversight abilities are inadequate." The reality is that, because of budget or political restrictions, not all government oversight offices are up to the job—which could be unfair to the donors. "At the same time," Dale points out, "for fear of extortion and harassment, you don't want to permit just anybody to sue a charity."

Thus, the dilemma.

"It is uncontested that the attorney general or the equivalent state officer has standing to sue T," says Dale in the context of charitable trusts, "but it is an open question as to when and under what circumstances anyone else can sue T. Whoever that might be, however, it can't be decided capriciously. The charitable class is large, and chaos would ensue if just anybody had the right to sue." Dale says it is a matter of best managing a set of tensions. "The law is all about competing public policy options. They include accountability on the one hand, and avoiding undue harassment on the other." The goal is "not to necessarily relieve the tension, but to find some way to balance it, and then to allow that balance to modify over time."

A big difference between private trusts and charitable entities, Dale says, is that the "state undertakes the responsibility to seek accountability. The state is directly engaged. The process to maintain charitable arrangements is not free. That's not true with a private trust, and it's certainly not true with a contract between two private parties."[14]

Dale points out that in the Smithers case the court balanced those tensions and ultimately permitted someone other than the attorney general to sue a charity.

R. Brinkley Smithers and the Attorney General

In 1971, R. Brinkley Smithers, a recovering alcoholic, and his wife pledged $10 million to St. Luke's Roosevelt Hospital Center in New York City to establish an alcohol treatment center. The idea was to provide a place for recovering alcoholics in "a free-standing, controlled, uplifting and non-hospital environment . . . a therapeutic community removed from the hospital setting."[15] In 1973, with the first installment of $1 million, the hospital opened the Smithers Alcoholism Treatment and Training Center in a newly purchased building in Manhattan's upper east side.

By 1978 Smithers was unhappy and wrote that the hospital had "not lived up to my letter of intent" and that he wasn't going to follow through with his pledge, about half of which had been paid. "Under the circumstances no funds or stock will be forthcoming from me," he wrote. In 1981, however, even though he had made no further gifts, Smithers agreed to a proposal that the building be sold. According to his wife, Adele, although her husband had no intention of completing the gift, he did want the center to continue.

The president of St. Luke's at the time, Gary Gambuti, continued to assure Smithers that the "hospital would adhere to the terms of the gift and carry out Smithers's intent in making it." It took an intense period of cultivation and stewardship, but eventually Smithers was "completely satisfied" and in October 1983 paid off the remainder of his pledge.

The 1971 gift agreement said, "The income is to be used exclusively for the support of the Smithers Center, to the extent necessary for current operations, and any unused income . . . is to be accumulated and added to principal." The principal was not to be used for anything other than capital improvements, and, in any case, was not to exceed half the fund's initial value. The hospital agreed to this.

The building was not sold in 1981, and for the next several years things went well, or at least it seemed they did, and in 1992 Mrs. Smithers agreed to the hospital's request to help organize a 25th anniversary gala, to be held in April 1995, by raising money for the restoration of the building and for scholarships to benefit patients who needed financial assistance.

Mr. Smithers died in 1994.

In March 1995 the hospital announced, to Mrs. Smithers's surprise— as the idea by then seemed to have died down—that it planned to finally sell the building and move the Smithers Center into a hospital ward. It also canceled the anniversary gala.

When Smithers agreed to the originally proposed sale of the building in 1981, his thought was that the center would move to another free-standing facility. After all, he was clear about that provision in his 1971 written gift agreement, which the hospital accepted. It never entered his mind, therefore, that when the possibility of a move arose that the new center would be moved into a hospital. By the time the hospital really decided to move the center, Smithers was dead, but the about-face upset the widow.

She also was taken aback by the hospital's reasoning: that it had to sell the building to become more competitive, as the leadership had all along assured the couple that the center was operating at a profit. Mrs. Smithers asked for a full accounting of the center's finances.

It turned out that the hospital had been misusing the money, "misappropriating monies from the endowment funds since before Mr. Smithers's death, transferring them to its general fund where they were used for purposes unrelated to the Smithers Center."[16] Mrs. Smithers informed the New York attorney general of this and he got the hospital to return almost $5 million to the Smithers endowment fund, although that amount did not include the lost investment income on the principal.

That was about it, though, as far as the attorney general was concerned. He did not weigh in on the move.

So Mrs. Smithers, who was named the executrix of her husband's estate, sued the hospital. She wanted to prevent the building from being sold, unless a court approved the sale, and she wanted all the money, which was more than the $5 million the attorney general's office got the hospital to agree to, put back into the proper fund, as well as any rental or sales proceeds from the building if there ever would be any. She also wanted a tighter accounting of the way the money was spent and the way the fund was administered.

Adele Smithers wanted the hospital to honor her husband's wishes as expressed in the agreement signed in 1971.

The hospital fought back, claiming that she lacked standing. The attorney general said the same thing. But the court reasoned, "it was only Mrs. Smithers's vigilance that brought" this whole issue "to light, since apparently the attorney general had no procedure in place by which to ensure compliance by the donee." More broadly, the court then said, "Nothing . . . has been brought to our attention which prevents a testator from leaving his money to a charitable corporation and having his clearly expressed intentions enforced."[17]

The Appellate Division majority essentially accused the attorney general of not doing his job:

"The desire to prevent vexatious litigation by irresponsible parties who do not have a tangible stake in the matter and have not conducted appropriate investigations has no application to Mrs. Smithers. Only a plaintiff with a genuine interest in enforcing the terms of a gift will trouble to investigate and bring this type of action. Indeed, it was Mrs. Smithers's accountants who discovered and informed the attorney general of the misdirection of gift funds, and it was only after Mrs. Smithers brought her suit that the attorney general acted to prevent the hospital from diverting the entire proceeds of the sale of the building away from the gift fund and into the general fund. The attorney general acquiesced in the sale of the building, its diversion of the appreciation realized on the sale, and its relocation of the rehabilitation unit, even as he ostensibly was demanding that the hospital continue to act 'in accordance with the donor's gift.' Absent Mrs. Smithers's vigilance, the attorney general would have resolved the matter between himself and the hospital in that manner and without seeking permission of any court."[18]

This was unprecedented. In a later decision relating to another aspect of the case, another court said, "The Smithers case makes new law, allowing a private cause of action to enforce the terms of a charitable gift." That court agreed with the Appellate Division by noting, "The conduct of St. Luke's-Roosevelt Hospital appears to be of such an egregious nature that it is conceivable that Mr. Smithers's gift was entirely frustrated and that the gift should fail."[19]

Bill Josephson argued the Smithers case in his capacity as the head of the New York State Charities Bureau at the Attorney General's office. The Charities Bureau has oversight of the activity of the almost 100,000 charitable organizations that are located in New York[20] and requires any charity, wherever it is located, to register if it solicits money from the state's residents.

During his tenure, Josephson analyzed issues facing nonprofits, including that of donor standing and donor rights. Also, as fraud and abuse, and even ethical misconduct on the part of charitable organizations, can attract the attention of Congress, he has been asked to provide analysis and opinion before the Senate Finance Committee, which often takes the lead when any type of federal investigation of the nonprofit community takes place.

"Standing is a complex issue that is very much in flux," Josephson says. The interesting thing about Smithers is that the court chose not to give the attorney general *exclusive* standing."

According to Josephson, Betty Weinberg Ellerin, one of the members of the Appellate Division of the New York State Supreme Court, and the primary author of the precedent-breaking decision, asked him, "We cannot always count on the attorney general to do the right thing, can we?" And he said, "No, Justice Ellerin, you can't."[21]

The State let Mr. Smithers down and the court let the widow, who was also the executrix of his estate, fight the battle on his behalf.[22]

The tension between accountability and undue harassment that Harvey Dale identifies, however, did not go away with this decision. The Appellate Division's dissenting justice explained that the issue was not whether "Mr. Smithers would have had standing, but whether his *estate* has standing," and pointed out that the estate was not the donor of the gift. He also said, in direct opposition to Justice Ellerin, that the attorney general did his job to secure the intentions of the donor.[23] Although his was a minority view in this historic case, the logic sways in many other cases around the country, as well as in other cases in New York State.

Dale doesn't feel strongly one way or the other. In fact, he notes, the Smithers case remains the only decision in New York that has allowed anyone other than the attorney general to sue a charity. "No other court has expanded it beyond that since the Smithers decision. So, if you're going to argue on a legal basis on what the law is in New York, it's still the attorney general exclusively, unless you have the surviving spouse who is the executrix of the donor's estate—not a child, not someone else—and that's a very narrow case."

Because others not so close to a donor have tried and failed to sue when the question of standing was at play, Josephson says, "It's important if you're remote to the donor to try to get a court to authorize you to sue." Since the Smithers case, New York has modified the law to clarify the process. But the donor, or the attorneys, must be aware of how it works. Josephson notes in a paper that he authored, "Donor" is now defined to include "a person designated in the applicable gift instrument to act in place of the donor." Also, he wrote, "Donors who wish to ensure that their restricted gifts can be enforced would be well advised not only to designate in the gift instrument a legal entity to do so, but also to fund the likely expenses of enforcement."[24]

Josephson uses the phrase "quite muddled" to describe the state of affairs in New York when it comes to the issue of standing,[25] and so the issue is likely to go back and forth a little. Dale says, "I would not like to see the tensions resolved in a fixed and mechanical way. I would like to see society continue to evolve, and so I am a fan of having standing, at least in some cases, when procedures are in place that avoid the risks of harassment and extortion as far as possible. And I would not like to have too much standing in cases where the attorney general is really active."[26]

Beryl Buck and Cy Pres

A well-known conflict in the donor-intent canon is the case of the Buck Trust, a drama where the San Francisco Foundation basically shot itself in the foot.

In 1935 Leonard and Beryl Buck moved to the city of Ross in Marin County, located north of San Francisco, just across the Golden Gate Bridge, and lived there the rest of their lives. They had no children. When Leonard died in 1953, he left his wife his entire estate, which consisted largely of stock in Belridge Oil, the company his father founded with two other people in 1911. John Elliot Cook, Leonard Buck's attorney whose acquaintances called "Doc," once described the beginnings of

Belridge Oil: "These three old fellows went to the San Joaquin Valley and bought some land that a coyote would have turned its nose up at. Then, they bought some more property that seemed equally terrible near Los Angeles. The second property became part of Beverly Hills and the first property some say is the richest oil company in the world."[27] The stock was valuable when Frank Buck bequeathed the stock to his son, and it was even more valuable when Leonard bequeathed the stock to his wife.

Before Beryl Buck died in 1975, she wrote a will that established a trust to benefit Marin County. Its language was clear that the funds were to be spent only within the county.[28] The trust was valued at approximately $250 million in 1979;[29] within a few years it had grown to approximately $450 million.

The San Francisco Foundation accepted the responsibility of distributing the income from the trust each year.

Assuming a payout formula permitting five percent of the corpus, the annual amount that would be made available to the people in this one county in the late 1970s was approximately $12.5 million, which would undoubtedly grow over time.

That vast amount of money, designated for just a tiny population,[30] led the people at the San Francisco Foundation, as well as many leaders in the four other counties the foundation served—Alameda, Contra Costa, San Mateo and San Francisco—to try to figure out how to spend the money on people who needed it more than those in rich Marin.

The perception was that a wealthy person, solely because she and her husband loved the county in which they lived, left gobs of money to help people who really didn't need it. Imagine walking along the street and confronting a beggar. As you get a $20 bill out of your pocket, you don't give it to him but instead hand it to the well-dressed person who happens to be passing by at the same moment. Accept for a moment that you would like to help that poor person on the street. Would ignoring the poor person and helping the other person seem fair? If it doesn't, you can understand the motive to modify the terms of the Buck gift.

Mrs. Buck, however, was gone and could not take part in the debate. And, as we have seen, an important consideration in the fairness issue is the weight given to the matter of what *she* wanted.

Largely the result of the dead-hand worries of Fredrick Goff, community foundations give themselves a power of *variance*, which means that a foundation is free, within limits, to modify the restrictions imposed on the gift by the donor. Even so, John Cook said he was not aware of the variance power and was "repeatedly assured" by John May, the San Francisco Foundation's director—the two, as it happens, were close friends—that "the foundation would be loyal to Mrs. Buck's wishes."[31]

But it wasn't. Even though the foundation initially agreed to the Marin-only restriction, its directors soon began to think the purpose of the trust should be broadened. The prevailing sentiment was that, with all that new money, something had to be done to better serve the five counties.

Here's the interesting thing, though. In its attempt to divert from Mrs. Buck's directives, the foundation did not employ its variance power. Undoubtedly that was because its rules required a unanimous vote to impose the variance, and, knowing that wasn't in the cards, the directors instead tried to impose *cy pres*, the legal route a charity can take to modify a donor's wishes if those wishes become impossible, impractical or illegal to carry out. *Cy pres* was the strategy the foundation used in 1984, when it applied to the court to change the purpose of the trust's income.

The reasoning went like this: "Due to the increase in magnitude of the Buck Trust, the relative affluence of Marin County, and the relative needs of the other counties served by the Foundation," it was impracticable, inexpedient and inefficient "to comply with the Will's provisions."[32] The foundation did not claim that the goals were impossible or illegal, so it had to rely on an expansive interpretation of the word "impractical."

In addition to serving as Mrs. Buck's lawyer and draftsman of her will and trust, John Cook was also an investment co-trustee and therefore had standing to bring the trust's case to court. And he did.

Ron Malone, who is today the senior litigation partner at the San Francisco law firm Shartsis Friese, represented Cook. "The foundation," Malone says, "brought together a great legal team, including a charitable trusts professional from Yale law school and a Nobel laureate in Economics, to figure out a way to break the trust and eliminate the Marin-only restriction. They felt that there was way more money in the trust than they could 'efficiently' spend in Marin, which had the second-highest per-capita income of all counties in the United States at the time. If only they could spend a sizable chunk of Mrs. Buck's money in the other counties that the San Francisco Foundation served, they would get a much more significant bang for the buck. They felt that they would do much more good by doing that than by spending the money only in Marin County, as Mrs. Buck directed."[33]

Although there was strong sentiment on the part of many influential people—including California's attorney general, who said that a condition of "a charitable surplus or saturation in Marin County might exist"[34]—the court ultimately said no.

The $20 went to the well-dressed person, but that's what the donor wanted.

"The Buck Trust case," says Harvey Dale, "was turned into a *cy pres* case and was then settled. It was actually a *failure* of the variance power. If it had been properly exercised or if the foundation had needed only a majority, as opposed to a super-majority, vote, we never would have had the Buck Trust case."

One of the reasons the court denied the *cy pres* petition might have been that the foundation didn't provide much specificity to support its argument. It's also possible that the court was worried that capriciously allowing the foundation to move money around against a donor's wishes would create concern among future donors about whether their wishes would be honored, which would dampen giving. Or the directors, who were running a large, established and benevolent organization with a good reputation, may have thought that they didn't need to explain themselves, that their understanding of what was best for the people in and around San Francisco was unassailable. In the end, however, we don't know.

In this regard, Malone thinks that many nonprofit administrators can get a little too righteous. "In the Buck Trust case," he says, "the people fighting for the San Francisco Foundation were really good people, high-minded . . . and they really believed this baloney. They sat in their conference rooms all by themselves and they convinced themselves what a great thing this would be." Good intentions alone, however, aren't enough for *cy pres* to kick in, and, according to Malone, "after a six-month trial they got removed as trustee and they went from 39 employees to four employees."[35]

Part of the settlement—the case was not decided by a judge or jury—was the creation of the Marin Community Foundation, funded by the assets in the Buck Trust. The agreement preserved Mrs. Buck's essential intention, stipulating that the money would "be spent within Marin County," even though "the benefits could flow outside of the county," says Dale. "It was not to be used, as the San Francisco Community Foundation had argued, for the greater needs of the San Francisco Bay area."[36]

As it happens, Ron Malone and Harvey Dale would each play a role in *Robertson v. Princeton* a decade and a half after the Buck Trust case was settled: Malone as the lead trial lawyer for the Robertson family and Dale as an expert witness for Princeton.

Albert Barnes and the Judge

In both the Smithers and the Buck cases, the donors' intentions were eventually upheld. A case where they were overridden involved the Barnes art collection, one of the most spectacular in the world.

When Albert Barnes, at the age of 79, was killed in 1951 outside Paoli, Pennsylvania, after running a stop sign and crashing into a truck, another death, slower and as painful, began: that of the wishes he had for his private art collection. That demise took its course over a period of 60 years.

Many today, however, call it a rebirth: finally, a public outing of paintings collectively valued at around $25 billion. And so it was a big deal when the Barnes Foundation opened its new museum in downtown Philadelphia in 2012. And it should have been. It houses one of the most extensive collections of European and American masters of impressionism and post-impressionism—with Renoir, Cezanne and Matisse weighing in heavily—all gathered under one roof, all acquired personally by the eccentric, unpleasant, and wealthy Albert Barnes. He was often called "de Medici of Merion."[37]

Still, a lot of people thought that the new museum's grand opening, regal as it was and as magnificent as the galleries are, represented the legal theft of a person's *manus-mortua* right to dictate how his wealth is to be used in the future.

For decades Barnes kept his growing collection in a modest location—a large home, really—in Merion, Pennsylvania. His idea, after he established a foundation in 1922 and acquired nonprofit status for it, was to permit students to view and study the art and for classes to be conducted. He instructed that, after his and his wife's deaths, the gallery would be open five days a week and available only for the use of students and teachers from organizations that enjoyed the trustees' blessing. The public would enter on Saturdays only between 10:00 a.m. and 4:00 p.m. He directed the trustees to "ensure that the plain people, that is, men and women who gain their livelihood by daily toil in shops, factories, schools, stores and similar places," would be the type who gained admission.[38] He did not want the art elite wandering around, for he despised them. Admitting the public, however, would take place only *after* his death. While he was alive, in addition to students, only people who were personally granted a card of admission, after applying for it from Barnes himself, would be permitted inside.

Also—and this was the significant issue—he ordered that the collection *never* be moved. The foundation's by-laws said, "All the paintings shall remain in exactly the places they are at the time of the death of the donor."[39]

One might wonder how a charitable organization could be so anti-public. How was Barnes able to maintain the foundation's nonprofit status if practically no one from the public was able to enjoy the art? He loved his art but he didn't like the type of people—the snobs, as he thought of them—who most wanted to view it or were most qualified to assess it.

As early as 1934, among the first of many legal battles the foundation would encounter over a period of almost 80 years, the Pennsylvania
Supreme Court ruled that the nonprofit exemption was born of the foundation's mission to promote the "educational and cultural development
of young men and women."[40] So it was an educational organization, not
a museum. Despite the quality of the artwork, the "artistic nature of the
Foundation's educational goals, the limited hours for public admission,
and even the unrecognized theories taught within the institution's walls,"
according to Ilana Eisenstein, a legal scholar, the place was entitled to
nonprofit status. "The Barnes Foundation's qualification as a charity," she
wrote, "is a good example of the proposition that so long as a trust generally fits within one of the six categories of charitable purposes, it 'will be
regarded as charitable unless its objective is wholly irrational.'"[41]

Even so, a quarter-century later, the court re-visited the question.
"Although the Barnes Foundation has been judicially recognized as
an institution of public charity," the court said, "and, therefore, enjoys
exemption from taxation, the public as such has been denied access to the
gallery housing the canvases and other works of art. Because of that fact,
the Attorney General of Pennsylvania filed on April 17, 1958 . . . a petition . . . calling upon the Barnes Foundation and its trustees to show cause
why they should not unsheathe the canvases to the public in accordance
with the terms of the indenture and agreement entered into between
Albert C. Barnes, the donor, and the Barnes Foundation, the donee."[42]

In response, shortly afterward the foundation agreed to open its galleries for two days each week to 200 people, and then, after Mrs. Barnes's
death, three days per week. The foundation argued for an entrance fee of
two dollars, but the state objected. It was eventually decided that members of the public would each be charged one dollar to get in.[43]

The Barnes Foundation by-laws also required that the endowment be
invested only in federal, state and municipal bonds. As a result, the endowment didn't grow very much over the years. According to one report,
"The Barnes [foundation] had $9 million or $10 million when Barnes
died, and when [Violette] de Mazia died, some 40 years later, through
one of the greatest stock market booms in history, the foundation had an

endowment of . . . $10 million."[44] Violette De Mazia served as the Barnes Foundation president after Barnes's death.

That restriction alone may have led to the demise of the donor's wishes.

The details of the Barnes collection saga—the attempts by some of the Philadelphia establishment, including the Pew and Lenfest Foundations, to control the foundation and to make the collection more available to the public; the deteriorating condition of the building in which the paintings were housed; the strange and surprising revelation that a small, black, financially struggling liberal arts college would gain control of the foundation; the dwindling endowment; efforts to sell some of the pieces to raise money; a world-tour of the art, in direct violation of Barnes's wishes; turning the peaceful, leafy Merion street where the art was housed into a tourist attraction, as well as the neighbors' reactions to that; and the ensuing legal threats and battles at almost every step of the way—are chronicled elsewhere.[45] Suffice it here to say that Merion, Pennsylvania was the home of one of the world's great art collections, and the person who set up the foundation that owned the art tried to make sure almost no one would be able to see it.

But even with all the planning and specificity captured in writing by his lawyers, Barnes didn't get what he wanted. The pressure from influential businesspeople and foundations in Philadelphia to move the collection was enormous. And it wasn't just the local elite who thought the art should have a bigger audience. No less a national figure than Supreme Court Justice Antonin Scalia said, "This was one of the few productive lawsuits in modern times."[46] Scalia made that remark in 1993 while visiting the Barnes collection at the National Gallery in Washington, DC, when the exhibit was on the world tour authorized by a court to raise money.

What about Barnes's directives? Not only does it take conceit to dictate such detail—the exact placing of paintings, the suffocating investment restrictions—interpreting a person's attempt to so fully control things into perpetuity also requires just a little bit of imagination. Indeed, in the last gasps of the legal effort to keep the collection where it was, one attorney had the chutzpah to make this claim: "The collection should not be moved because it is intricately arranged to command his foundation and the Merion mansion itself in every age to seek the just and the courageous, those qualities of the archangel Michael, in each of us who enter the foundation from the garden landscape of Pennsylvania."[47]

What of the argument that such a treasure should be as accessible to the public as possible? While we can understand the importance of a donor's intentions, doesn't the idea arise in this most extraordinary state of affairs that a donor's directives could once have been *too* restrictive? Is there a time after the owner dies when such a uniquely emotional, historic and valuable treasure should belong to the public? Or, because violating the donor's wishes is akin to desecrating a grave, does that time never come? Does the dead hand, no matter what, *never* loosen its grip?

The issue, as far as Judge Stanley Ott, who ultimately decided to permit the collection to be moved to Philadelphia, was concerned, was one of balance: Barnes wrote out a valid desire, yet that desire, in part because it was so specific, was overtaken by the realities of time.

The judge, as one observer saw it, "ruled that given the dire financial straits of the foundation," moving the collection "was a reasonable solution. It kept the collection intact, which the court believed was as true to the spirit of what Dr. Barnes had wanted" as could be accomplished. "It was better than selling off parts of the collection or letting the collection just sit there in Merion and ultimately have the foundation go bankrupt and then have the paintings sold off to pay off its creditors."[48]

The judge felt that to save the Barnes, it had to be moved, even though the donor had been adamant about not moving it. Ever.

In Search of a Better Lexicon

But *ever* is a big word and encompasses ideas and actions that will take place well past our lifetimes and the lifetimes of everyone who will be born in the future.

Surely, therefore, donors exaggerate. They cannot really mean to go that far. They mean to go out only so far, some decades or perhaps a hundred years at the most, right? Or perhaps not. Harvey Dale says, "Donors can be very procrustean." Perhaps donors really do mean that they want their strict wishes obeyed into the unimagined beyond. Countless gift agreements to nonprofits use the phrase *in perpetuity* to define how long donors want their dictates to reign. If the donors don't mean that, perhaps their lawyers, as well as charities, need to consult the dictionary more frequently. And if, practically speaking, the way *in perpetuity* is often used can't mean the unforeseeable future, perhaps it doesn't mean even the foreseeable future. A line is in there somewhere, but no one knows where it is.

"Congress," Dale remembers, "once had a proposal before it that would limit the time within which donor intent could survive." (In the run-up to the 1969 Tax Act, which placed restrictions on foundations, there was some discussion of limiting the amount of time a foundation could exist. The limit that received the most attention, 25 years,[49] was not adopted as part of the legislation, however.) "The dead hand problem," says Dale, "is a real problem. Donor intent, unfettered and in perpetuity, can certainly come in conflict with the needs of society."[50] That long-understood conflict is why *cy pres* relief exists.

But *cy pres* is itself a matter of some interpretation. In the Smithers, Buck Trust and Barnes cases, no one disputed what the directives were. Some people didn't like the directives, but there was little or no uncertainty about what the donors had in mind. Sometimes there is uncertainty, and so the meaning itself of the directive is unclear or disputed. "Princeton, I'm sure," says Dale, "would not say it could do whatever it wanted with the gift. They're saying, 'Listen. This is what the Robertsons wanted, and to the degree there's been any change, we're doing as close to what they wanted as possible. They're just saying that they're adapting to current circumstances."

This creates a problem. If the donor, or the heirs, and the charity can't agree on what the intent actually was, then it does no good to bicker about whether it was actually adhered to. Dale isn't sure whether the issue at Princeton can, in fact, be boiled down to donor intent, as the phrase is so broad. "How do you ascertain donor intent? Is it possible that Bill

Robertson thought his parents had one thing in mind while they didn't have that thing in mind at all?" Of course, the same question should be applied to Princeton's argument. "His father and mother aren't around," says Dale, "and so talking about the dispute in terms of donor intent—only donor intent—makes it tough. The very phrase implies that it's clear what the donor wanted and Princeton wasn't doing it. And if the question is, 'What in God's name did the donor have in mind?' that could be about donor intent, but it means something different."

Clearly, we need a better vocabulary to deal with this.

"Let's call it *Donor Intent I,*" offers Dale. That would be the first stage, that of understanding what the donor meant. *"Donor Intent II,* once intent is unassailably known and understood by all, would be about whether the institution is actually doing what the donor meant, what the two parties agreed to in the first place." Dale thinks that an important piece of the Princeton case is *Donor Intent I.* "Was Bill right about what his father had in mind? Or was Princeton right about what his father had in mind? They both were saying they were honoring donor intent, but, as we've outlined it here, *Donor Intent I* and *Donor Intent II* are different inquiries."[51]

Distinguishing between the two and then addressing each may be the most important part of the process. It's hard for an institution to clearly know a donor's desires, but it is unlikely that the institution would intentionally acknowledge violating it.

Susan Gary, a professor of law at the University of Oregon, thinks of the issue in much the same way. "Even words in a carefully negotiated and written gift agreement may not have plain meaning, especially if circumstances change," she says. And even in the most well written documents, the effort might be doomed to fail. "A foolproof answer to the question of how to establish donor intent should remember that, in many situations, donor intent simply cannot be determined with certainty."[52]

Donors and Heirs Are Going To Court More Often

The courtroom is becoming the remedy of choice for those donors or their heirs who become uncomfortable about how donated money is being used. But it's not a good remedy, not in the sense that finality can be found; often, donors or heirs reach out-of-court settlements. And when finality can be found, the result does not always support what contemporary interested parties think the donor wanted.

In February 2011, after five years, much of which was spent trying to find a person with standing, Tulane University won its battle to absorb the all-women's Newcomb College, a school that was part of the Tulane community but an entirely separate entity. In the aftermath of Hurricane Katrina, the university's trustees decided to combine the college with the rest of the university. Those opposed to this consolidation charged that the decision "relegated Newcomb College to the realm of memories and denied the future of a perpetual, living memorial to Sophie Newcomb as Mrs. Newcomb so clearly intended."[53] The court disagreed. "The donor's will," it said, written at the end of the 19th century, "which established Newcomb College, did not require Tulane to continue operating it as a separate degree-granting institution."[54] Although a lot of people were upset with the decision, at least it was based on a full judicial review.

Decisions can go the other way, as well. In early 2012 singer Garth Brooks won a $1 million settlement after a jury believed his testimony over that of the president of Integris Canadian Valley Regional Hospital in Oklahoma, the hospital to which Brooks had donated $500,000 so that it would build a women's center in his mother's name. Brooks's agreement with the hospital was oral—not written—and so the jury had to determine who was telling the truth.

It may be that a jury is likely to sympathize more with an individual or family than with an organization. That sympathy might also be measured in how much money is awarded. The Brooks jury said the hospital had to give back the donated $500,000 *and* pay an additional $500,000 in punitive damages. One juror said she thought the hospital went back on its word. "We wanted to show them not to do that anymore to anyone else."[55] The Newcomb case was determined without a jury.

Consider the plight of the Hershey School. Upon his death in 1909, Milton Hershey, the candy tycoon, established a trust that would run the school as "a permanent institution for the residence and accommodation of poor children," who would be "fed with plain, wholesome food; plainly, neatly, and comfortably clothed, without distinctive dress, and fitly lodged." The school would be free for all. "The advantages and benefits to be derived by the scholars . . . shall be in every respect gratuitous, and under no circumstances shall any charge be made."[56] Hershey donated his entire estate to support that directive.

Today the school has an endowment of over $10 billion and serves 1,800 students—a per-student endowment of $5.8 million, by far the most well endowed academic institution in the world, including Princeton, which has the highest per-student endowment of any university. Yet, is the money being used wisely? Are Milton Hershey's intentions to house and educate poor children being carried out?

"No," says F. Frederic Fouad, an attorney, a graduate of the school, and the president of Protect The Hersheys' Children, Inc., a group organized to fight what its members consider gross injustices on the part of the board, as well as the nonchalance of oversight officials. "For a sense of the misdeeds and culture of impunity surrounding this charity," he says, "consider how, in 2006, the charity purchased a failing luxury golf course frequented by the golf-loving board members. The $12 million investment was two to three times the appraised value of the course. The purchase bailed out as many as 50 local investors, including one board member, all of whom would otherwise have faced losses. The board added a $5 million Scottish-style clubhouse and has subsidized course losses to the tune of about $500,000 annually, all the while Pennsylvania officials failed to take effective measures."[57]

For years, Fouad says he has been trying to give voice to the children who should be served by the Hershey School, something he is certain that Milton Hershey would have wanted, and explicitly outlined in his Deed of Trust. "After Mr. Hershey's death," he says, "the Hershey story became disgraceful. The beneficiaries are needy kids, but they were thrown to the untender mercies of the world. Their champions, such as our group, have no resources, no legal standing, and no public support, which is why we have been crushed despite the glaring misconduct. In Hershey, there is no dispute whatsoever that wrongs were committed."

Still, Pennsylvania's attorney general found in 2013 that the trustees did not "violate their fiduciary duty by buying a golf course" for well above its appraised value or by "spending $5-million to build a club house and restaurant on the property, or by purchasing an adjacent roadside market for $8.6-million."[58] Trustees are, however, now subject to a compensation limit.

Fouad was not happy. Real reform, he said, was absent in the decision. "None of the present board members were removed for past transgressions. Because they didn't remove board members, the composition of the board hasn't changed. There's absolutely no change in the board. The same self-selection process remains in place. It's basically old wine in an old bottle."[59]

Fouad notes that the Princeton story is about "a wealthy family, with standing, that could take action and obtained redress over their concerns. Hershey presents a stark contrast to the Princeton matter. They are both about donor intent, but in the Princeton case the remedy was supplied by the donors' family who mounted their own legal campaign, without being forced to rely on the kind of compromised officials that we have dealt with in Pennsylvania."[60] Nevertheless, the Robertson family faced immense obstacles.

The history of the Bishop Estate, which controls two schools in Hawaii, might be considered even more egregious than the Hershey School mess. In 1995, the *Wall Street Journal* described the Bishop Estate as "the nation's wealthiest charity." At the time its endowment was approximately $10 billion. The trust in the Bishop Estate was established at the death of Princess Bernice Pauahi in 1884, and its mission is to "erect and maintain in the Hawaiian Islands two schools, each for boarding and day scholars, one for boys and one for girls."[61]

The trust operated for over a century without much controversy, but over time political and business pressures emerged to be so strong that no one was able to keep the charity in check. An article in the now-defunct

Honolulu Star Bulletin said of the charity, "The community has lost faith in the Bishop Estate trustees, in how they are chosen, how they are paid, how they govern," and detailed the problem: "Trustee appointments, which paid nearly a million dollars a year, were rigged by politicians and judges; trustees lined their pockets at the expense of the institution's bottom line; the supposed protectors of the trust, the attorney general and the courts, looked the other way; investment results were manipulated to mislead, with no accountability; and the Kamehameha Schools, the core of the trust's mission, were being scandalously shortchanged at every step."[62] The IRS said the trustees were treating the trust like "a personal investment club," and investigators "eventually compiled a list of 47 Bishop Estate investments that each lost at least $2 million between 1994 and 1996."[63]

The Hershey School and Bishop Estate cases make clear that mismanagement of charitable funds is often linked to ignoring a donor's wishes. While Princess Pauahi was not specific about what kinds of investments the trustees should avoid, the intention could not have included allowing cronyism to outweigh prudence. In the same way, although Milton Hershey was not specific about investment guidelines, it would defy logic to think he would permit his future trustees to violate such a common-sense issue as whether the school should purchase a golf course, while ignoring so many deserving kids who needed a place to live and learn.

Milton Hershey and Princess Pauahi both died a long time ago and didn't have children to ensure their wishes would be fulfilled. That's one big difference between many donor-intent cases and Robertson's fight at Princeton.

One Court Speaks—Loudly

In what may be the clearest vindication of Bill Robertson's quest, at least in taking his complaint to a legal setting, a New Jersey Appellate Court in August 2013 harshly analyzed the facts in a lawsuit involving donors' intentions.

The case involved a couple, Bernard and Jeanne Adler—of Princeton, by the way—who had given $50,000 to a charity called SAVE, A Friend to Homeless Animals, a no-kill animal shelter. They sued the organization because the money did not, as the donors were assured it would, go toward building new and spacious rooms for large dogs and older cats, animals that have difficulty being adopted. Instead, after SAVE merged with another charity, A Friend to Homeless Animals,[64] it decided to build a smaller facility than what had been advertised in the fundraising literature prior to the merger. The new facility would be one-tenth the size of what was originally proposed and the space would be inadequate for the dogs and cats for whom the Adlers wanted their money to provide.

The Adlers' attorney was Stuart Polkowitz, a member of the law firm Brach Eichler in Roseland, New Jersey. Polkowitz characterized SAVE as an organization with a track record serving animal welfare needs in the Princeton community through its operation of a rescue shelter. SAVE's fundraising practices came into question when the organization abandoned the capital project promoted to the Adlers, no longer honoring the express condition of the gift, and then refused to return the donation. "My clients," says Polkowitz, "received a letter explaining that SAVE was moving its facilities after the merger. When they contacted SAVE to learn more about what was going on, the response was not satisfactory. They met with a board member to secure the return of the donation, but that was unsuccessful."

No one disputed the facts—the *Donor Intent I* hurdle was passed—so what was SAVE's rationale for not returning the money? "The board's makeup changed after the gift," says Polkowitz, "and the members made an economic decision. They didn't have the same vision as the prior board or the same commitment to raise funds during the economic headwinds of the time to pursue the project further." That's all well and good, but why not give the money back if the shelter wasn't going to be built as promised? "They said they were 'going to build a new shelter,'" according to Polkowitz. "'It's just not going to be as big as the one we planned.'"[65] Which, of course, flies in the face of the essential point.

SAVE, which was founded in 1941, was not financially stable. To build the new facility, the organization began a capital campaign to raise $7.5 million but raised only $1.3 million. Also, SAVE's base of support diminished from 600 people to 200 people, and the dwindling donations forced the organization to begin spending its reserves. According to John Sayer, a board member and the one person who testified for the defense, there was "a serious financial problem with respect to operating funds."

Even though SAVE's attorney denied it, she seemed to offer up its unfortunate financial picture as a reason that it should not have to return the money.

Defense Counsel: "This is a charity, your honor. The issue that's going to be ultimately decided involves whether it would be against public policy to . . . require SAVE to return $50,000 in donations. I think your honor is entitled to hear about the history of the struggle that they had raising funds."

The Court: "So are you saying to me that my decision should be based on the financial stability or instability of this organization?"

Defense Counsel: "No, but I think all the background you have . . . is useful."

Then Polkowitz weighed in for the plaintiffs. "While I appreciate there may be other economic issues involving SAVE," he said, "that's not part of why we're here today. We're here because my clients were presented a particular program and an opportunity to fund a portion of that program. SAVE is not following through with that program and plaintiffs are seeking the return of their money, because plaintiffs believe that they donated the money on the basis of what was proposed to them, not on the basis of the strength or lack thereof of SAVE, outside this particular capital program."[66]

One benefit the plaintiffs had in this case was that the donors and the charity's fundraiser, who in the case of talking with the Adlers was SAVE's executive director, were all alive and able to testify. "In researching various other cases," Polkowitz says, "I saw that in almost every situation the donors were long deceased. In those situations, the court had to infer the donor's intent."[67]

Whether it was because live people were able to testify or whether it was the specificity of the gift's condition, or a combination of the two, the court, whose decision was unanimous, held back nothing.

When the defense attorney asked if the proposed new, smaller facility would "have room available of the type that the Adlers had indicated they found important," the court said, "Mr. Sayer answered emphatically: 'Absolutely.' However, the extensive narrative amplification Mr. Sayer gave as a follow up to this one-word answer did not, in any meaningful sense, corroborate or otherwise support his testimony."

In finding that the Adlers were entitled to a refund, the court sent stinging rebukes to several of the defense's arguments. The main thrust, however, could be found in the essence of the way charities raise money and, akin to one of the main pillars in *Robertson v. Princeton*, the expectations they create for donors. After outlining the ways SAVE communicated, both orally and with written materials—the court called them "sophisticated weapons of persuasion"—the decision took note of the donors' feelings. "Their moral commitment to these animals was so strong that they were willing to donate $50,000 to make this a reality. In the words of Mrs. Adler, 'That's what we do. That's who we are.'"

Then, the language grew from "sophisticated weapons" to "fraud": "The record makes it clear that plaintiffs expressly announced their conditions at the time they made their gift, and defendant expressly acknowledged those conditions at the time it accepted plaintiffs' gift. Indeed, some of the most salient of plaintiffs' conditions . . . were offered by defendant as promotional incentives to entice donors like plaintiffs to give generously to its campaign. Under these circumstances, it can reasonably be argued that returning the gift is the most lenient sanction defendant may receive from a menu that includes breach of fiduciary duty and civil fraud."

SAVE also invoked the safety net of *cy pres*, the doctrine that might provide some desired wiggle room, but the court would have none of it.

"SAVE's argument in this respect crumbles under the weight of its own logic," it said. "As emphasized repeatedly by the court in McKenzie,[68] in the law of charitable trusts, where the gift has been made for a charitable purpose, and either originally or in the course of time cannot be literally executed, the gift will be administered, as nearly as may be, *according to the donor's intentions.*"

In this case, there was no confusion about the donors' intentions. "It would be a perversion of these equitable principles," the ruling said, "to permit a modern charity like SAVE to aggressively solicit funds from plaintiffs, accept plaintiffs' unequivocally expressed conditional gift, and thereafter disregard those conditions and rededicate the gift to a purpose materially unrelated to plaintiffs' original purpose, without even attempting to ascertain from plaintiffs what, in their view, would be 'a charitable purpose as nearly possible' to their particular original purpose."[69]

If a charity wants to invoke *cy pres*, it must have a reason and it must go through a process. It cannot simply drag out the doctrine for its defense with tortured logic after the fact.

The court also spoke to the legal bond between charities and donors. "The essence of a fiduciary relationship is that one party places trust and confidence in another who is in a dominant or superior position. Here, plaintiffs placed their trust in SAVE to meet the conditions of their gift. By virtue of their control of the funds, SAVE was in a superior position to determine to either meet plaintiffs' conditions, request their consent to rededicate the funds to another purpose acceptable to plaintiffs, or return the gift. By opting to disregard plaintiffs' conditions, SAVE breached its fiduciary duty to plaintiff."[70]

He won, but Stuart Polkowitz describes the process of working the case as one of "flying somewhat blind, since there was a lack of clear precedent in New Jersey regarding conditional gifts. I was hopeful that there would be a published decision in *Robertson* to provide some guidance to us because there was basically a lack of published law in New Jersey, and for that matter nationally, in this area."[71]

The unsparing rationale behind the decision in the Adlers' case might serve as a warning to all charities.

Bill Robertson, upon hearing the news, said, "It's too bad this wasn't decided before our case. We could have saved a lot of money."[72]

Rolling Over in Their Graves?

For all public charities and foundations, the question of donor intent—whether it is examined over just a short time, as in the Adler case, or a long time, as in the Bishop Estate case—is linked to the messy, unpredictable issue of how things inevitably change over time.

The biggest American foundation of them all, the Bill and Melinda Gates Foundation, however, will probably never confront the issue. In a move that may set a precedent for future benefactors, it has scheduled its own demise. "Because Bill, Melinda, and Warren [Buffett]," its website informs us, "believe the right approach is to focus the foundation's work in the 21st century, we will spend all of our resources within 50 years after Bill's and Melinda's deaths."[73] Similarly, another major philanthropist, Charles Feeney, is also winding down his multi-billion dollar foundation, Atlantic Philanthropies. His philosophy: "When you've got the money, you spend it. When you've spent it all, let someone else get going and spend theirs."[74]

But the Gates Foundation and Atlantic Philanthropies, at least for now, are highly unusual, and many foundations are the objects of much ire from those who write about donor intent. One of those objects of ire is the Ford Foundation, among the largest in the country.[75]

In 2012 Adam Meyerson, the president of the Philanthropy Roundtable, opined in the *Wall Street Journal*, "The Ford Foundation is one of the best examples of donor neglect." He first quoted Ford's philosophy: "I do not believe in giving folks things. I do believe in giving them a chance to make things for themselves." He then referenced a letter Henry Ford II wrote in 1977 that described why he was resigning from the board. "The foundation is a creature of capitalism, a statement that, I'm sure, would be shocking to many professional staff people in the field of philanthropy. It is hard to discern recognition of this fact in anything the foundation does."[76]

Marta Tellado, the vice president for global communications at Ford, took issue with Meyerson's editorial. She didn't think that the 39 words Meyerson quoted represented the essence of the 1,141 words that Ford used to write his letter. She noted that Edsel Ford, who started the foundation (Edsel was the son of Henry Ford and the father of Henry Ford II), gave it a broad charter. Tellado quoted the charter, which said that the foundation was created " . . . to administer funds for scientific, educational and charitable purposes." Then, Tellado went to what she thought was the heart of the matter: "In the thoughtful and constructive resignation letter that Mr. Meyerson quotes only part of, Mr. Ford concludes, 'The foundation already has a magnificent record of achievement. I'm confident that it is capable of still more significant contributions to the world in the years to come . . . The future of the foundation is in capable hands.'"[77]

Meyerson replied to that response by saying, "Marta Tellado's letter confirms the wisdom of our recommendation that donors clearly define the charitable mission of their organization."[78] This fits with what Martin Morse Wooster, in his book, *The Great Philanthropists and the Problem of Donor Intent,* acknowledges. "It is true," he writes, "that Ford left no explicit instructions on how the money should be spent."[79]

But here's the thing. What if Edsel Ford would say today that his instructions *were* explicit? Just because the words that describe the foundation's mission—"scientific, educational and charitable"—are not ultra-tangible does not mean that they are poorly written goals. And just because Henry Ford was entrepreneurial does not mean Edsel Ford applied his father's outside-of-philanthropy thinking to his foundation. Just because a person is conservative does not mean that his or her philanthropy, especially if it is a directive to future generations, must be conservatively oriented. Of course, it's fine if it is—that's the benefit of starting a foundation, or of setting up an endowed fund—but if the instructions don't provide for that, then shouldn't future boards feel free, even obligated, to pursue the foundation's mission as they attempt to best interpret the founder's goals?

Andrew Carnegie, whose foundation is inexplicably among those often criticized for being far more liberal than he ever was, made things easy, at least in the context of interpreting his wishes. His "vision for the work of the Corporation," the foundation's website says, "was unique in that he understood that as the decades passed, the issues of his day would be incorporated into or supplanted by concerns that more immediately affected future generations. Acknowledging the certainty of uncertainty, he wrote, 'Conditions upon the [earth] inevitably change; hence, no wise man will bind Trustees forever to certain paths, causes or institutions.' Therefore, he gave his trustees . . . 'full authority to change policies or causes hitherto aided, from time to time, when this, in their opinion, has become necessary or desirable. They shall best conform to my wishes by using their own judgment.'"[80]

Philanthropists might also want to consider the advice of Julius Rosenwald, an early president of Sears, Roebuck & Company, who felt that foundations, as well as the imposition of a donor's intentions, need a short shelf life. "I am opposed to gifts in perpetuity for any purpose," he once wrote. According to his grandson, Rosenwald reiterated the view that "donors of tightly restricted endowments were essentially insulting their trustees by displaying a lack of confidence in those trustees to manage the funds wisely."[81]

Meyerson is right about advising donors to be clear about what they want—in Harvey Dale's way of thinking, that would be conveying *Donor Intent I*—but today's criticism of organizations that don't follow their donors' intentions is not limited to addressing unbiased confusion. While it is true that philanthropy encompasses the idea that donors want to make the world a better place, not everyone agrees on what *better* means, a disagreement that is habitually born of ideological differences. Much of the disapproval is closely connected to the violation of a particular point of view—a conservative point of view.

Conservatives who have written about donor intent allege that many established charities are liberal, and that the donors whose intentions the charities are said to have violated would be upset if they were alive today to see how their money is being misspent. In this context, sentiment and ideology can trump informed, serious judgment and interpretation, and so much of the complaining about where charities are going and what old so-and-so really would want today is little more than polemical rhetoric.

In 2006 an article in the *National Review*, John Miller said, "In 1961 Charles and Marie Robertson gave one of the largest gifts ever made to higher education. Today, their heirs are trying to take it back, in an unprecedented lawsuit that carries major implications for conservative philanthropy." Miller continued, "Over the years, violations of donor intent have caused conservatives great harm. The Left has captured billions of dollars in financial resources by seizing control of philanthropic foundations and ignoring the wishes of the people who endowed them."[82]

In addition, Martin Morse Wooster, dissatisfied with the restrictions inherent in binding documents, has invoked a similarly sweeping interpretation. Foundations, he has written, whose donors did not leave explicit instructions "do not follow the spirit of their donors' intent. All these abrogations," he claims, "are characterized by a shift away from traditional forms of charity to left-wing advocacy and from a respect for free markets to redistributive political action."[83]

Why is conservative ideology a part of the discussion of donor intent? There are no parallel invectives coming from those who espouse a liberal point of view. The answer may be within the value system that calls for the supremacy of individual liberties, an extension of which would be protecting the rights of a property owner, even after he or she dies.

Ron Malone, the attorney who represented the Robertsons, thinks that donor intent is not a political question. "This is not a liberal issue or a conservative issue," he says, but points out that the people who are most upset about the issue of a donor's intent being trampled are usually conservative and moneyed. "A lot of charities are run by very liberal, well-intentioned people, and their typical attitude is: *We're the professionals. We know what's best, we know what efficient philanthropy is, and we know how to spend charitable dollars better than donors. Just give us the money*, they say, *and we'll take care of the rest.* Experience teaches us that the more time that passes after a donor is dead, the less correlation there is between the terms of the gift and what happens with that gift. When they give money for a specific purpose, they want it spent for that purpose."[84]

Anne Neal, the president of the American Council of Trustees and Alumni, a group located in Washington, DC, whose website describes its mission as "committed to academic freedom, excellence, and accountability at America's colleges and universities," sees the problem in unbiased terms. "There was nothing conservative or liberal, nothing even remotely political, about the Robertson lawsuit at all. It goes to the issue of institutional and academic integrity. This is about holding institutions to the pledges that they make."[85]

Nothing is set in stone in this landscape of good intentions, and much has yet to be answered. The Smithers, Buck, Barnes, and the Adler cases, while only a tiny sampling of how benign intentions can be transformed into what many see as malignant actions, were energized by the essential issues: determining standing, establishing what a donor's intentions are, determining whether a charity violates those intentions, and how we deal with the more elusive, although very real, feeling that a charity's trustees think they know better than the donor.

It was into this arena that Bill Robertson and his sisters and brother journeyed when they felt strongly enough that something wasn't right at one of America's elite educational meccas. "All of these issues, Robertson says, "were on my mind when I decided to sue Princeton."[86]

Chapter 4

The Gathering Storm

The seeds of destruction were planted early and tensions were high from the beginning.

Charles Robertson and the IRS

In late April 1961, several weeks after the Robertson Foundation's governing document was signed, but before the IRS signed off on the deal or any money was transferred, John Myers, Charles Robertson's attorney, met with a Mr. Hatfield, the Assistant Director of the Tax Rulings Division at the IRS. In a memo to Robert Goheen, Princeton's president, Myers described just how unsure the tax agency was about granting tax-exempt status to the foundation. Hatfield, according to Myers, said that "his division . . . was examining carefully the question of whether or not they could rule that . . . this gift was *for the use of* Princeton." Although Myers conveyed that concern, he was upbeat with Goheen. "In my opinion," he wrote, "there is no reasonable doubt on that score."[1]

Even so, the question needed to be answered with clarity. Myers had told the IRS, "Unless a ruling as to a deduction for gift tax purposes was forthcoming, the donor could not make the gift in view of the possibility that one-half of the $32,000,000 might be dissipated in taxes."[2] If Princeton couldn't guarantee that it would control the foundation, the IRS would not grant it tax-exempt status. Without tax-exempt status, there would be no deduction for the Robertsons. Without the deduction, there would be no gift.

In 1961, the marginal federal income tax rate was over 90 percent.

The optimism of Robertson's attorney was based on the proposed board's makeup. With a permanent majority, he reasoned, Princeton would always be in control, a fact that should satisfy the IRS.

But the IRS apparently wasn't content with that. Uncertain but wishing to be helpful, Hatfield suggested that the foundation wait a year.[3] This is where the tax law is different today from what it was in 1961. Victoria Bjorklund, a partner at Simpson Thacher & Bartlett LLP whose specialty is nonprofit law, and legal counsel for Princeton during the lawsuit, says that, unlike today, in 1961 "a private foundation couldn't get a deduction unless it was in operation for a year—or unless it was attached to an already existing charity."[4]

One of the reasons waiting a year would be a problem stemmed from Charles Robertson's concerns about A&P's stock. He didn't want to wait too long after the family trust dissolved because he thought the stock's value would decrease. Time was of the essence.

Since waiting a year wasn't feasible, the question was just how subservient the foundation would be to Princeton. "Princeton has as full control and ownership of the property in question," Myers told Goheen, "as if it owned all the stock of a corporation or the entire assets of a business. This follows from its possession of four out of seven member-trustees … We advised Mr. Hatfield that in fact Mr. Robertson had virtually given up to Princeton every right except the right to witness his money being spent and an opportunity to speak with respect to operation (but not to exercise any control)."[5]

Even that didn't do it for Hatfield, however, and he told Myers, "It would be helpful for the President of the University and for Mr. Robertson to submit joint statements that the Foundation was in fact subject to Princeton's control."[6]

Goheen then made his case directly to Mortimer Kaplan, the Commissioner of Internal Revenue. In response to Hatfield's concerns, Goheen tried to assuage any doubt as to whose influence would reign at the foundation. "The prospective donor has fully understood and agreed that the University must have the responsibility for the direction, maintenance and operation of the School in all its aspects. Indeed, the Trustees of Princeton University would not have agreed to accept this gift . . . if they had not been advised and believed that the University controlled the Foundation through its majority representation."[7]

But that optimism might have been misleading. The donor remained silent at the time, and Myers predicted as much to Hatfield. "Under the circumstances, Princeton felt the whole gift might be lost" if that "request were made to Mr. Robertson."[8]

Why would Robertson's attorney say that? Why, given the certainty Myers was reporting to Goheen and to the IRS that Princeton would control the foundation, was he concerned that Robertson would not accede on the issue of control? We will never know for certain because everyone close to the matter at the time is deceased, but it seems odd that, in a meeting during which a donor's attorney is arduously arguing the case for the legitimacy of a charitable gift, the attorney would acknowledge that the donor would be reluctant to write a letter to that effect.

Four decades later, Goheen remembered "a certain amount of skepticism, whether the university would really control it [the foundation] or whether the family would run it." He referenced the letter he wrote to Kaplan, whose background, Goheen believed, included a stint as a professor at the University of Virginia. This, he thought, would provide two avenues of approach to the IRS. Kaplan might look favorably on the application because, as a professor, he might relate to how the gift would help the university, and because, as Goheen put it, "This was a tremendously significant gift not only for Princeton but for the nation." He told Kaplan that he "respectfully felt the federal government should grant it favorable tax status." The foundation, he thought, would respond to a national need by "enabling" Princeton to develop "a new and substantially enlarged graduate school."[9]

That seems to have worked. In September 1962, the IRS approved the Robertsons' application, writing, as it does for all foundations and public charities it sanctions, that the foundation was "not required to file Federal income tax returns as long as you retain an exempt status."[10] A legal expert described how the arrangement was mutually beneficial: "By using the foundation, rather than giving the money directly to Princeton, the donor's family would continue to oversee the use of the gift. And by giving Princeton control over the foundation, the donor would be able to obtain deductions for gift and income tax purposes."[11]

That might sound understandable on one level—benefits for all—but the structure actually acted as a conduit for, and perhaps even provided the rationale, for the enormous animosity that was to come.

Princeton Is In Control

Princeton contends that there was never any doubt, on its part or on the part of Robertson, about who was in control of the foundation. Victoria Bjorklund says that, regardless of what one might infer from Myers's statement about Robertson's reluctance to send an unambiguous statement to the IRS, Charles and Marie Robertson knew full well what they were giving up. Charles made it clear, straight away, and she submits three documents as proof.

The first was the Certificate of Incorporation, which Robertson signed. "He was very involved and he was a very active leader," Bjorklund says, referring to Robertson's never missing a board meeting and to his involved chairmanship of the foundation until his death in 1981. "To portray him as having been taken advantage of or as having been led around by Princeton . . . I believe is just inaccurate."

The second document is a letter that Robertson wrote to his attorney in August 1970, in which he states, "It seems to me entirely clear that the foundation was organized . . . exclusively for the benefit of . . . Princeton University. Actually it is operated and supervised by its Board of Directors but under the charter and by-laws it can I think be shown that Princeton at all times has and must have control of the Board of Directors."[12]

That letter was written not only because Robertson wanted to clarify his understanding of the gift. That year, 1970, was particularly important and busy for the IRS and for all the foundations that had been established in the United States before then. The letter was actually a run-up to what the IRS would soon require Robertson to sign.

By the middle of the 1960s, it became apparent that the domain of private foundations needed significant Congressional reform. The non-profit landscape of the time was littered with wealthy people who had figured out how to use charitable entities to primarily benefit themselves, which was not in keeping with Congress's intent on the matter of the charitable sector. As a result, the most sweeping tax reform legislation ever, as it relates to public charities and private foundations, was enacted in 1969.

At hearings earlier that year, Texas Congressman Wright Patman—who in the 1930s had led the price-fixing charge against large chain stores, such as the A&P—began the barrage of criticism. "Today," he said, "I shall introduce a bill to end a gross inequity which this country and its citizens can no longer afford: The tax-exempt status of the so-called privately controlled charitable foundations, and their propensity for domination of business and accumulation of wealth. Put most bluntly, philanthropy—one of mankind's more noble instincts—has been perverted into a vehicle for institutionalized, deliberate evasion of fiscal and moral responsibility to the nation."

Patman blamed Congress for not examining the cost of permitting donors to establish foundations that, as he saw it, primarily helped only the donors. "The onerous burdens on 65 million taxpayers demand that Congress curb the tax-exempt foundations which, in unwitting good faith, it helped to create." The taxpaying public, Patman thought, was subsidizing too many personal, individual activities. "If the rich care to fritter away their dollars in senseless frivolity, that is certainly their privilege—but Congress has no obligation to give them tax-free dollars at the expense of the rest of the country. Mr. Chairman, my bill is by no means a vindictive measure; indeed, by encouraging the foundations to return to the original purpose for their existence—that is, philanthropy—they should emerge stronger, not weaker."[13]

One of the provisions in the new law was to determine which organizations were private foundations and which were public charities.[14] To ascertain which groups belonged to which category, the IRS sent out a form that required donors to validate the organization's status as a private foundation. This Robertson did in August 1970.[15]

"The sole objective," he wrote, "is the establishment, maintenance, and support of a Graduate School program in the Woodrow Wilson School at Princeton for the training and education of men and women for government service. The sole recipient of the Foundation's income, funds, and property . . . is Princeton University." Then he said it: "The Robertson Foundation is controlled by Princeton University. The University made it clear from the outset that it could not undertake the long-term commitment involved in the project (e.g. faculty contracts, student fellowships, etc.) unless it had effective control of the Foundation. This was agreed to by the donors."[16]

The completed IRS form was the third document.

Early Frustrations

Actually, the tensions that eventually led to the lawsuit were not so much about whether Princeton controlled the Foundation but about whether Princeton exercised its control properly. Clear-headed managers know that being in charge does not entitle them to do whatever they want. In fact, control should ideally inspire a strong sense of responsibility: in this case, a solemn approach to fiduciary duty—the kind of enlightened understanding that the family felt was absent.

Before he made the gift, Charles Robertson expressed his disappointment with the quality of the Woodrow Wilson School's program and the heft of its director. "The W.W. School does not enjoy a particularly favorable reputation with a majority of the men with whom we talked. They did not seem to be aware of any substantial contribution by the School to the Federal public service." Robertson also disparaged the leadership. "Although liked, the present Director of the School is not considered qualified for the job of directing the contemplated new school."[17]

His and his wife's gift was evidence that Robertson had confidence that the infusion of new money would change things.

Five years in, however, Robertson was unhappy. He didn't like the direction of the Woodrow Wilson School or the results.

In 1966, Richard Allen Lester, an economist at Princeton, wrote to

Marver Bernstein, the dean of the Wilson School,[18] that he had been hearing this criticism: "The school has not developed a new, distinctive type of curriculum, faculty and research orientation but instead has tended to follow traditional teaching methods and to be dominated by departmental and academic values to the neglect of stress on the problems of policy determination in a realistic atmosphere of democratic processes and creative compromise of interests."

Lester then explained his own take on that. The school's curriculum did not deal with the "lower level problems and practical kinds of solutions that professionals in government must wrestle with. The selection and advancement of faculty are too much in terms of scholarly reputation, academic values, and reputation in their discipline, and not enough in terms of understanding of and contribution to public affairs, per se. Excellence in a discipline, especially in scholarly publications, takes precedence over public service and knowledge of the actual problems and complications of policy formulation and implementation of policy on government."[19]

Although scholarly reputation and excellence are desirable commodities on a campus, that's not what the Robertsons were talking about when they gave their money. And that's not what Princeton agreed to when it accepted the money. Robertson wanted graduates to be sent into a world where they would actually work in the federal government. To that end, Lester suggested that the school free itself from traditional university thinking by developing a distinctive battery of courses, a different and separate faculty, and its own values.[20]

Scholarly theory was trumping practice.

Something had to change or the whole point of the gift would be defeated.

Where Are the Graduates Going?

By 1970 Charles Robertson was even more worried about the results than Lester had been about the curriculum a few years earlier. In a memo to John Lewis, who succeeded Bernstein as the school's dean, Robertson explained how he had studied the graduate school alumni directory and calculated the number of people who actually entered the government since the gift was made. Those entering "government service or in private organizations concerned with public affairs" averaged about ten per year. "On the other hand," he noted, "the number of MPAs[21] who failed to enter public service and turned to academia, private business or the law averaged . . . about eight MPAs per year."

He asked, "Might not the above figures suggest the need for a very hard look at admissions? During the sixties 44% of the graduates failed to enter public service. I would certainly hope that during the next decade this percentage could be sharply reduced." He then listed a number of for-profit entities where graduates were employed. Not only did he generate the list to express his displeasure with so many people going off to places other than the government, he also wanted to take another jab. To high-light what bothered him, Robertson wryly wrote that the Continental Illinois Bank, among the several on the list, "likes the School's graduates but keeps a tight rein on its corporate giving as far as the W. W. School is concerned."[22]

Six months later, Robertson openly mocked the school's failure to place graduates in the federal government. "I've grown accustomed," he wrote, "to hearing the remarkable progress of one of our MPAs—the son-in-law of a well-to-do neighbor in one of Manhattan's prestigious financial institutions, and from my regular links partners his complete satisfaction with three of our grads in his business consulting concern. Sure, they're in 'public service' but so is our electrician and innkeeper and train conductor and lifeguard." Robertson denounced the school, saying that if people think it is strengthening the government by sending graduates off to other organizations, it is also true that the same thing is being accomplished by the "dentist who removes an abscessed tooth from the President's jaw."

He then wondered why his gift, which had grown to $45 million by 1971, shouldn't be able to buy something that followed the original idea. "I'll be damned if I know why this cannot be done," he wrote, and then reiterated the original idea for the dean. "The 'X' Foundation's purpose is to strengthen the United States government—*not* the faculty of X university, *not* the First National City Bank, *not* the Atlanta Symphony Orchestra, *not* the Mobil Oil Company—but the United States Government."[23]

Frustrations of the Consultants' Group

Around that time, several prominent public servants—the Consultants' Group—whom the Foundation had assembled, asked the Wilson School to conduct a self-evaluation. When Robertson read the report, he was able to confirm to himself that he wasn't the only one who felt things weren't going well. One member of the group, George A. Lincoln, the director of the Office of Emergency Preparedness at the White House, complained in a letter to another member, William Marvel, the president of the Academy of Natural Sciences, "Clearly, any outcome which places more than half of the graduates" in areas other than the federal government that are concerned with international relations and affairs "can hardly be called successful 'emphasis.' It seems obvious that the school has thus far failed to come close to achieving the stated objective."

Lincoln was reading the same statistics that Robertson read, but Robertson had—generously, to Lincoln's way of thinking—lumped together those entering federal service and those taking public affairs positions outside of the federal government. The number for federal service, the stated goal in the original document, was 56, out of a total of 229 graduates during the 1960s. Using that as a benchmark, the success rate was not 44 percent, but 24 percent.

That the self-evaluation misleadingly labeled the low numbers as a success was one thing, but the Consultants' Group also thought it wasn't well conceived. "The report is centrally deficient," Lincoln wrote. It does not "seem to attempt to measure anything against known and accepted yardsticks." The group found the report to be little more than an exercise in self-congratulation with blandly worded suggestions for improvement in what was otherwise asserted to be a successful program. Lincoln noted that the report lacked the most useful tool to evaluate the school:

a cost-benefit analysis. "Put bluntly," he said, "how much has the donor provided per graduate actually put in the Federal Service?" Put even more bluntly: Was Robertson getting his money's worth?

The implied answer was . . . no. "Three years ago, I was concerned about the drift of the school related to the objective," Lincoln wrote dispiritingly. "Over the three years, it seems to have set a more definite course away from that objective." Still, he was optimistic. "Now that we have gotten the riot period over with (I hope), and Vietnam is about to be wound down, maybe the responsible people will be willing to turn back to their commitments."[24] Vietnam wouldn't be wound down for another four years, and the "responsible people" at the Woodrow Wilson School, according to Bill Robertson, never did get their commitments in order.

With this negative feeling floating around, Roger Jones, the chair of the Consultants' Group, sent a hard-nosed inquiry to John Lewis, the dean. Jones served under seven presidents in various capacities and was a deputy secretary of state under President Kennedy. In a five-page memo written in October 1971, he asked Lewis to respond to several issues.

Jones noted that one part of the report stated, "Certainly there is reason to recall that no on-going academic institution of consequence—no good faculty—can be centrally programmed into patterns of effort substantially at odds with its own interests." He asked the dean, "Does that mean that the composite interests of the WWS faculty are now substantially different from what they were a few year ago? Are they inconsistent with the spirit of the gift's premises? Is this, if so, a matter of concern to the School and to Princeton?"

Another issue the report brought out was "the definition of public affairs articulated at the beginning of the 'X' Foundation document," the part that said students should be prepared for careers in government service "with particular emphasis . . . on international relations and affairs." Jones noted that, although that wording "clearly subordinates non-governmental activities," the self-evaluation claimed that "the appropriate span and diversity of this concept remains an issue today." Jones felt that the mandate was a fact, not an issue, and should not have been open to discussion.

In a strongly worded effort that drew attention to the problem as one of not following the donor's intentions, Jones noted that a whole chapter of the self-evaluation "contains statements about which factual questions could be asked or discussion carried on in terms of the relationship to the announced purposes of the Foundation's gift."

Jones was asking tough questions because the group saw so many things going on that were discordant with what the general understanding about the Robertson Foundation's intentions had been. After outlining several other concerns, Jones asked Lewis for a five-year plan, an outline of an educational strategy, a review of the obstacles that would need to be overcome, and periodic progress reports.[25]

Four months went by before Lewis responded. The dean explained that he was "stalling" because of the "uneasiness" he felt in dealing with the question "in which you place the greatest stock," which was why so many students weren't entering government service. He also acknowledged that he knew he had "better get some answers on paper" as the Robertson Foundation board and its advisory group would soon be meeting. But, although the stalling might have been warning enough by itself, being late wasn't the big problem. The content of the dean's response was disappointing.

First off, it was brusque, irreverent, and defensive. "Your request for the strategy statement is premised on an exaggerated view of the extent to which our present situation needs repairing." Given all the "trauma" of the 1960s, the school "did a pretty effective job of keeping faith with the 'X' purposes." Jones also took the opportunity to express pride in "the higher percentage of federal government placement" the prior year.

When John Lewis had recently written a report summarizing the placement of the prior year's graduates, he noted that of the 47 students in the class, 10 received jobs in the federal government and four went into the Foreign Service. This was, as Lewis said in his memo to Jones, a higher number than the year before. But was this cause for celebration? Such was the dean's spin. Lewis noted that 1971 was "the worst job market since the Depression," but that "the high caliber of our graduates resulted in the outcome that no one needed to go unemployed."[26] He was happy, and he may have had reason, but the low placement numbers in the federal government were what the Consultants' Group and the Robertson family board members were concerned about.

Much of the tension that was building would hinge on conflicting interpretations of this kind.

But there was further disconnect in Lewis's response to Jones.

As for producing an actual strategy statement, as Jones requested, Lewis explained that such a plan "must be shared by a substantial majority of the faculty, and that is not the simplest thing to arrange." The characteristics of academia and the bureaucracy at Princeton, apparently, would keep strategic thinking from happening. Besides, as far as Lewis was concerned, "The School is in pretty good shape." He did acknowledge, however, that it "can strengthen its supply of personnel to the federal government," and offered to "continue to attach a heavier weight to work, especially governmental work experience."

But, if his leanings weren't already clear, the dean made a truly bold assertion to drive home his point that there should be a hands-off policy for his school. Although he noted the magnificent generosity of the gift, he said, "You would not think us worth our salt if we did not remain highly protective of academic autonomy."[27]

Academic autonomy is one thing, and it is something any university needs to protect, but, as Bill Robertson says, "These guys were simply trying to change the game. Suppose the autonomy," he asks, "departs from the mission? Mom and Dad said they wanted to create an institution that would be on par with the great medical, law, and other professional schools."[28]

John Leslie, another member of the Consultants' Group, told Charles Robertson, "My basic conclusion—and I regret having to say this—is that the University and the School have failed to follow a *positive* course of action calculated to carry out the wishes of the Donors as expressed by them and as publicly accepted by the University. I do not suggest that there was a deliberate evasion," only that "a positive determination to push the School in the indicated direction was lacking."

Failing to recruit the right students with the right message seemed to be part of the problem. Leslie worried about the lack of gravitas with some of the people in the admissions office. "An illustration of this point," Leslie said, was the newly appointed Graduate Admissions Director, a person who had graduated from the school only the year before. That would put him at about 25 years old at the time. Leslie sardonically asked "how a man of such late vintage could possibly understand and carry out the long-stated goals of the School," and if the young man was actually only a "chief clerk with no effect on recruitment or admission." He then took note of a change in the admissions process that he felt should have been implemented from the beginning. "This year for the first time . . . the selection of candidates included consideration of the applicants' career goals and interests as related to the stated purposes of the School."[29] This was 1972, more than ten years after the Robertson gift, and the Woodrow Wilson School finally thought it would be useful to ascertain that students who would be studying to enter government service actually had an interest in government service.

In addition to the lack of proper applicant screening, Leslie thought that the school wasn't doing enough to persuade the federal government that it needed formally trained professionals to enter its service.

He also felt that the "School appears to be extraordinarily expensive." Not to the students, for admission was free, but to the foundation.

Basically, in Leslie's view, things were a mess. And nobody at Princeton cared.

His most critical observation, however, was that while the university was well aware of all these issues, they generated almost no reaction. "Even a good, strong rebuttal or rejection would have been more helpful than the barely audible sounds which come from the bottom of the deep well into which we have dropped our criticisms and suggestions."[30]

Leslie twice corresponded with Charles Robertson to this effect. Robertson's reaction: "John Leslie's two letters go directly to the School Administration's jugular. I endorse both 100 percent."

William Marvel began a letter to Charles Robertson with an attempt to find something positive. He began by saying he felt that the Woodrow Wilson School was in "a fundamentally healthy state" and that a "lot of good work" was taking place.

But the body of his comments, which centered on the communications between the School and the Consultants' Group, was dispiriting. His "most profound dissatisfaction," Marvel wrote, "results from the nearly total blackout of communication, sharing of ideas, liaison and relationship between the two parties. This goes to the heart of the role originally conceived for the Consultants' Group, wherein as advisors to the 'X' Foundation, they would help to interpret and communicate. But this role cannot be effectively performed unless we are given a regular flow of information from the Woodrow Wilson School."

Marvel said that his concern was born of a deeply held conviction: *"This is that the uniqueness of the 'X' Foundation gift*—its tremendous size and the limited, although most important, purpose for which it was made—laid a particular kind of obligation on Princeton and the Woodrow Wilson School: that of developing a response that was fully commensurate with the gift." To that end, the group some years earlier called for a study—the self-evaluation—to be conducted by both insiders and outsiders. But, he said, "The idea was not favorably received by the University administration." When it was conducted, he says, "it was done exclusively by 'insiders.'" Marvel's most serious reservation about it was that it did "not seem to me to address the central issue: the need to develop a picture of what a truly *great* graduate school of public affairs in the 1970s should look like."

That negative assessment was viewed even more harshly in the context of John Lewis's reaction to the report. The dean had said that things were basically okay, which prompted Marvel to write to the other consultants and to Robertson, "This question"—the one John Lewis brought up about needing a number of faculty and administrators to sign off on a five-year plan—"relates to a larger issue that arose repeatedly, namely the need for assertive leadership by the Dean rather than the passive approach of moving ahead only on the basis of near-total consensus." Marvel too called for "a factual, hard-nosed study of the economics of education at the Woodrow Wilson School."

As for the concern of following the donors' intentions, Marvel suggested that the school keep tabs on the total number of years each graduate spends in government service. "The resulting composite picture of man-years would be greatly superior to the present data." He asked that everyone sit down, "with our Princeton friends dropping the defensive stance they usually adopt," to clear the air so that the school could "go on to new heights and greater glory." Important to Marvel were the donors' intentions. Concluding his letter to Robertson, he said, "Much more important is the tremendous thing Marie and you did over ten years ago. To honor Marie's memory and to give you the reassurance and satisfaction you have so richly earned, we *must* get things back on track."[31]

Even John Gardner, the legendary and fair-minded founder and chairman of Common Cause, was disappointed. The question, he wrote to Robertson in 1972, "is whether the university has performed as one might have expected, given the expressed wishes of the donors and President Goheen's statement of August 6, 1961." This was a question he said he could address with objectivity, having no dog in the fight. "My answer would be in the negative. In fact the gap between expectation (as expressed by President Goheen as well as by the donors) and reality is very great indeed."[32]

How difficult it must have been for Charles Robertson. He and his wife had given $35 million to fund what they hoped would be a route to strengthen the federal government with smart, ambitious graduates of the Woodrow Wilson School. Robertson was explicit about retaining a family voice in the process—not in the programmatic details, but in the broad direction and goals—all the while ensuring that the money would be used for the Wilson School specifically and not for Princeton generally.

Yet, even though he knew and acknowledged full control of the Foundation had to be retained by Princeton, the worries that had been on his mind from the very beginning had not gone away. The poor evaluation of the School's progress, as well as the tenor of the meetings he had been in with Princeton, only served to make those worries more acute.

Robertson Replaces "X"

Robertson Hall, as it was later named, turned out to be a spectacular building. In 1962 Robert Goheen said he wanted a building as "a fit embodiment and expression of the high aspirations we hold for the enlarged school. We wanted a building which would speak to all people, in dignity and beauty, of the unprecedented opportunities for national and international service."[33] Designed by world-renowned architect Minoru Yamasaki, the building was intended to express "the nobility of public service." Yamasaki was also commissioned, in what *Time Magazine* said would make him "the country's most hotly disputed architect," to plan the World Trade Center.[34] The 15 acres where the World Trade Center was located were adjacent to the spot where, little more than a century earlier, George Hartford and George Gilman gave birth to the A&P.

"When President Johnson flew up from Washington to speak at the dedication" in 1966, Charles Robertson wrote to his children, "your mother did not attend the ceremony." At the time, it was called the Woodrow Wilson Building because Marie Robertson didn't want any publicity. Only Robertson and his daughter Anne represented the family. "Your mother was a very shy person and the reason she remained away from the ceremony was that she did not wish to be associated with the gift of thirty-five million dollars."[35] Marie Robertson's desire for anonymity was the reason the foundation was known as the "X Foundation" for more than a decade.

But the anonymity wouldn't last.

There were two reasons that the Robertson name eventually was made public in connection with the gift. The first, and the lesser important, was the growing political tumult of the times. By the 1970s, Vietnam was getting to be too much for Americans, young draft-age Americans in particular, who were angry about a war whose objectives were unclear yet whose outcome was growing clearer every day. The consensus was that the United States would lose if it didn't pull out. Congress was feeling left out of decisions about the war, decisions that it felt were not the President's to make unilaterally, and so was trying to exert more authority over the executive branch.

Add in Watergate.

As part of that executive-legislative turf war, the country's involvement in foreign affairs was being questioned; it seemed to many that foreign relations was nothing more than one big clumsy, chauvinistic attempt to overthrow Communism everywhere, even in countries with popularly elected leadership, even in countries that seemed to have scant ability to threaten the United States.

One target of the restlessness was the CIA, the government's most secret agency.

In the middle of the decade, Congress held hearings that exposed the CIA's efforts to assassinate selected foreign leaders and to conduct illegal surveillance on thousands of United States citizens, most of whom opposed the war, many of whom were college students, some of whom were studying at Princeton. In hindsight, it is easy to understand why the foundation that paid the bills for the graduate program at the Woodrow Wilson School came under student scrutiny.

Questions were asked: What is the "X Foundation"? Who gave the money for it? Why? Was Princeton a tool of the increasingly unpopular government? At some point in those tumultuous years it became obvious, in the way it does for people who are generally clueless, that the X Foundation, which was supporting the school that was sending its graduates into the world of foreign affairs, was actually a front for the Central Intelligence Agency, that the whole purpose of the school was to subvert actual academic inquiry by dogmatic doctrine to support American foreign policy.

This was nonsense, but Princeton's hands were tied. The donor requested anonymity and, as long as the donor was alive, that request would be honored.

The second, and deciding reason, for publicizing the Robertsons' connection to the Woodrow Wilson School was that Marie Robertson died in April 1972. The following year, in the midst of the anti-war fervor and suspicions about who was behind the X Foundation, Princeton wanted to know if it would it be possible to go public with the family's name. Charles Robertson was permitted to consider that the children were grown, the memories of the Lindbergh baby's kidnapping had faded, the ghost of Louis Reed could no longer embarrass Marie, and no harm could come to the family. In addition, much good could come of letting the world know about the two extraordinary people who bestowed upon Princeton an endowed fund no other university that was training future members of the foreign service enjoyed.

In June 1973, with Charles Robertson's permission, Princeton lifted the veil: the veil of secrecy—which quieted the "campus radicals," as the *New York Times* called them—and a more literal veil, as newly painted portraits of Charles and Marie Robertson were publicly introduced in a ceremony in the university's library.

Robert Goheen said of the gift, "It is really quite remarkable that we were successful so long in protecting her desire for anonymity. Any alert reporter—even a *Princetonian* reporter—could quite easily have pierced that veil of anonymity if he had tried. So could the SDS, if it had truly wanted to. The iniquitous network of intrigue and irresponsibility that bears the name of 'Watergate' is today a strong reminder that, all in all, openness is a better thing than secrecy in public affairs when large amounts of money are available. So, it is especially gratifying that all shadows of suspicion about the origins of the 'X Foundation' can now be dissipated."[36]

Although going public with the gift had his approval, on balance Charles Robertson wasn't happy. "The family wanted to emphasize the importance of the school and not the family," he was quoted as saying at the time. "But the public demanded to know who the hell's money it was, even though it was none of their damned business."[37]

"Turn Around and Start Over Again"

In November 1972, seven months after his wife died, in a letter to his son, Robertson had something positive to say: "The School has attracted a strong faculty, has produced an appropriate curriculum with the highest academic standards and has attracted a student body consisting of well qualified university graduates, foreign students, military officers, and mid-career government employees."

But that pretty much exhausted his good feelings, as, in the same letter, his exasperation re-emerged: "Princeton has failed in its attempt to meet our goal. It has failed to place very many of its degree holders in the Federal government service!"[38]

His desire was simple enough, but, as we have seen, the academics at Princeton saw it differently. They saw the gift not as about putting graduates into government service but about developing the erudite process that would play out in the classroom. Why else would the dean of the school opine that the problem of not getting graduates into the government was exaggerated, or that providing a written five-year plan would be too difficult? It is not difficult to imagine this going through the dean's mind: *This isn't a crass business. This is an academic institution, a highly regarded one at that, and academic autonomy must be protected.*

The clash was outlined succinctly in a lucid letter John Gardner wrote to Charles Robertson. On Princeton's ability to make decisions he said, "I do not think any donor should ever be in a position to dictate the intellectual path taken by the university faculty. The faculty must be free." Then, regarding Princeton's gift agreement with the Robertsons, he wrote, "But unless a faculty explicitly asks the university administration to accept in its behalf nothing but unearmarked gifts—contributions to general funds—one must suppose that it is prepared to make commitments with respect to the use of the funds. And considering the extraordinary freedom the faculty enjoys—and must continue to enjoy—it would surely want to be particularly scrupulous to avoid a situation in which it had—no matter how innocently—breached a commitment."[39]

Robertson had long been aware of the seriousness of this culture clash, how the lack of the family's influence on the board might be instrumental in destroying his and Marie's dream. The idea, he wrote his son, was that he and Bill's mother wanted "each one of you and your children and your children's children" to be "concerned with and involved in furthering the growth and development of the school." The three family members of the foundation's board were to "keep an eye on things generally and be heard when the occasion required it." Robertson once again acknowledged that Princeton controlled the foundation, but added, "We family members can and do make suggestions, voice criticisms and call attention to goals unachieved."

Almost presciently he outlined the issues that would drive his children to court three decades later. While he acknowledged that the family members were not "entirely free to act and speak and to advocate policies which are substantially in opposition to those held by the University faculty," they also "will not stand in awe of the President of the University nor any of his distinguished colleagues on the Foundation Board." He thought the divisions were so strong already, to say nothing of his concerns that they could grow, that he asked the family members to think of themselves as "his majesty's loyal opposition. They must speak out loudly and clearly," he said, "when they have justifiable criticisms or constructive suggestions to make."

Then this admonition to his heirs: "They must always take a firm stand in support of the Foundation's original purpose and objective."

He also pointed out that the foundation's endowment—about $50 million by 1972 and annually generating about $1.5 million of income—was separate from the university's funds. "They should watch the pennies and study the budget with care and ask penetrating questions," he said of the responsibilities of the board's family members. "Universities are not holy places and Princeton should come broom clean with the School's annual budget, its annual expenditures and its balance sheet. They must keep a sharp watch on the per-graduate student cost."

More generally, he worried that Princeton would try to ignore the family members. He asked that they "keep their ears carefully attuned for a sweet talking member of the faculty" because they might "find themselves afloat in a sea of rhetoric which doesn't purport to reply to the question but which has the objective of putting them to sleep or of boring them to distraction. This is a frequent ploy of academia which can turn what might have been a worthwhile meeting into a slumber session."[40]

Yes, this is how Charles Robertson felt about Princeton.

Although Robertson admonished himself, admitting that as the donor he "has not lived up to his early promise," he wanted to double down. "I have hammered away at the failure of the University to live up to the objectives of the Foundation and of the acceptance of its goals by President Goheen in 1961—and I will increase my pressure from here on out until I succeed in bringing those responsible to heel or acknowledge defeat." He asked his heirs to "go for the jugular if they are quite sure of their ground."[41] Such an admission of failure may sound odd, coming from a man who, as we have seen, had been keeping a close eye on things, but he thought his efforts had not been enough.

These were fighting words. What began as a partnership had turned into an ongoing confrontation. Who could have imagined that things would turn so sour, especially in light of Robert Goheen's public comments shortly after the gift was made? "The magnificent action of the donors in establishing this foundation enables Princeton University to do what it and many other universities have long wished to do: establish professional education for the public service at a level of excellence comparable to the country's best schools of medicine and law. The donors wish to provide gifted students and governmental officials with the finest possible preparation for careers in the public service, with particular emphasis on foreign affairs. Their generosity challenges the University to measure up to their confidence that Princeton can do the job."[42]

The people at Princeton undoubtedly hoped that Robertson's dissatisfaction would be fleeting. After all, criticizing is easy, and the re-energized program at the school had yet to really gain traction. The tumult of the 1960s, unpredicted at the beginning of the decade, actually did result in a growing dissatisfaction with the government. When the Robertsons made their gift, public trust in government hovered around

75 percent. When the decade ended, the trust level dropped to about 55 percent. By the end of the 1970s, it eroded to about 25 percent.[43] The war in Vietnam, the Watergate scandal, the oil embargoes, and the hostage crisis in Iran all contributed to a feeling that government service was not the place to be.

Still, in a country where millions of students are graduating from college every year, interest in serving the government could not have entirely waned. General Andrew Goodpaster, who served as NATO's Supreme Allied Commander in Europe and who was one of the Robertson Foundation's family trustees, said in 1972, "The need for well prepared young people of the highest caliber to serve the United States in the international field is of the highest order of importance, and will grow rather than diminish in the future. If anything," he added, "I would say that the need is even more acute today than I could foresee—partly because of trends toward lessened interest in, and commitment to, foreign affairs among many young people. It seems to me . . . that a great university has a unique capability to contribute toward fulfilling that need." Perhaps however, if the need were made clear, the students would come. "I acknowledge, Goodpaster continued, "that the actual achievement in this regard has been less than I, for one, hoped for—and less, in fact, than implied by the terms on which the gift was offered and accepted."[44]

Livingston Merchant, a diplomat and another of the advisors in the Consultants' Group, also acknowledged the challenge. "Certainly this field has not loomed large in the recent classes' choice of careers," he said. "Concern with our internal life is of course only the other side of the concern for our security from dangers without and our displaying a responsible role in a world shrinking daily in time and distance. But the proper balance between the two areas of concern has been badly skewed—and the skewing encouraged by the intellectual and academic fads of the day." Remember, among other diplomatic and government posts, Merchant twice served as the United States Ambassador to Canada under Presidents Eisenhower and Kennedy, and was Under Secretary for Political Affairs under President Eisenhower. "To me," he said, we "must swim against the tide and strive to right the imbalance."[45]

Those who questioned the direction and success of the Woodrow Wilson School were not filled with untempered passion or uninformed about government service. Livingston Merchant, George Lincoln, Roger Jones, and the others who were weighing in, each engaged in the success of the school, were all accomplished professionals in the diplomatic world.

And they had something else in common too: They all, at one time or another, invoked the donors' wishes as the basis for their critique.

Robertson also directly vented to William Bowen, the recently appointed president of Princeton. In a 1972 letter, after outlining the foundation's mission and then listing several non-governmental positions where Wilson School graduates were employed, he noted that the substantial income managed to graduate no more than ten people on average each year into careers in international relations. Wondering aloud if he and Marie were getting their money's worth, he pointedly asked, "Would I be very far off target remarking that the amount spent by the University to educate each MPA candidate exceeds by a very wide margin the cost of educating any M.D., L.L.B., Ph.D., in this or any other country? And would I be guilty of gross exaggeration were I to remark that the cost (total annual income divided by the number of MPA's entering the Federal Government service) is truly astronomical?"

He implored, "Simply ... turn this School around and start over again with the avowed purpose of living up to the terms and conditions in good faith. The time has come to face up to the obvious fact that the School has never come within shouting distance of achieving its goal and I personally doubt that it ever will as long as it continues on its present course."

These are not the sentiments of a happy donor.

He then made three suggestions. One was to hire a full time senior administrator with connections in Washington whose goal would be to identify qualified potential students interested in international relations. The administrator's "point of departure," Robertson thought, "would start with the White House and extend through the upper echelons of a dozen or so more Federal Departments and Agencies." The second was to provide an educational experience "designed specifically for the purpose of enhancing" students' "competence and dedication and to further their careers." Third, beef up the student body so that the school would confer "at least 100 MPA degrees annually." He pointed out that there was plenty of money to do that.

He asked Princeton's president to "learn from the past" and "not dwell on our past mistakes. The time for alibis is behind us." His suggestions, he said, "might well result in an annual recruitment of the truly outstanding younger men in 'Federal Government service concerned with international relations and affairs.' That was our original goal, it continues to be our goal, and it emphatically always will be our goal!"[46]

Despite the impassioned plea, however, things didn't change. An internal memo, written in 1996 by an external committee that reviewed the Wilson School, concluded that things were not going well. "The majority of the faculty," it said, "are generally oriented not toward the School and its mission or destiny, but toward their home departments and disciplines." The disciplinary emphasis, as opposed to the school's mission, "reduces the faculty's commitment." Even more disapproving, the report echoed Charles Robertson's long-standing criticism, one that his son carried on and made a key part of the lawsuit: "Practical skills and practitioners come a distant second after conceptual skills and academics."[47]

John Palmer, a former dean of the Maxwell School of Citizenship and Public Affairs at Syracuse University and a future advisory board member of the Robertson Foundation for Government, was one of the members of that committee.

Paul Volcker Weighs In

Yet another person added his voice to the growing number of dissenters: Paul Volcker. Although he says he is "most proud of being the grandfather of a Princeton alumna," he is the former president of the Federal Reserve Bank of New York and the former chairman of the Federal Reserve under Presidents Carter and Reagan, as well as chairperson of the President's

Economic Recovery Advisory Board in the Obama administration.

He knows a thing or two about public service.

Volcker's criticism grew beginning in the 1990s, first with an essay he wrote and culminating in a 2001 letter to Shirley Tilghman when she assumed her responsibilities as Princeton's new president. "I am not alone," he wrote, echoing an earlier version of the Pew Research Center's poll measuring the public's declining trust in government, "on being dispirited by the clear evidence of steady erosion of the public trust in public officials and in government generally in recent decades." His letter also echoed one of his earlier essays, in which he wrote, "In all the Western democracies, there has been a truly alarming erosion of faith in government—faith in its ability to define the public interest, to achieve consensus, to act with competence and honesty."[48]

He put this question to Tilghman: Is the Woodrow Wilson School playing a role in solving the problem? "To put it bluntly," he told her, "my answer is a resounding no."[49]

Volcker's observations were separate from the dissatisfaction growing within the Robertson family. He thought the naming of a new president at Princeton would be a good time to write and to say that the Wilson School ought to "shape up. I actually have a strong loyalty to Princeton—I'm an alumnus and my grandchild was graduated from there as well—and, when the lawsuit came, I didn't want to get caught up in that. My real concern," Volcker says, "is that Princeton just stonewalled the suit."

Volcker remembers, "When Ann-Marie Slaughter came in as the new dean," in 2002, "she was making real progress and refocusing it, and I thought they had a credible case to make that they were on their way to being consistent with the Robertsons' wishes. But what Princeton did not do, I suspect, was to reject the terrible advice from their lawyers. The lawyers probably said, *'Don't give an inch. Don't do anything to show you're doing anything in response to the complaint, because then you'd be deluged by your other donors. So never—never—do anything but stonewall the Robertsons.'* And that's what they did. They thought they'd win in court in any case, and they thought this Robertson was a rabble-rouser."

Then, after a moment of reflection on that point, Volcker says, "Imagine Princeton going to trial against their biggest donor. I doubt they would have won in court."

The irony, he thinks, is that, by the early 2000s, "in substance the school really was trying to do a better job."[50]

In his letter to Tilghman, Volcker said, "What hurts is that the Woodrow Wilson School is far and away the most richly endowed school of public policy in the country. The endowment specifically dedicated to the graduate program—some 130 students or so—is a significant part of the University total. I believe it is also larger than the endowment of all the other schools of public policy and public administration put together, with the exception of the Kennedy School at Harvard. The great bulk of that money was provided by a single gift decades ago."

"As I understand it," Volcker said, "the stated purpose was to enhance education for the public service. Yet, what is Woodrow Wilson School's reputation in that field? *A missed opportunity for leadership . . . a great disappointment . . . going nowhere,*" phrases he said others in public administration used when describing the school. He asked that Princeton not take his word for it, but to look at the most recent evaluation by academic peers. "The words were polite, restrained, and respectful, as befits the prestige of Princeton and academic courtesy," he said. "But what they added up to was a damning sense of disappointment."[51]

Volcker thinks that Princeton's motto—*In the Nation's Service*—means something that, of all the centers of academia at Princeton, should be most clearly manifested at the Woodrow Wilson School. But in that regard it was failing miserably. "Those words can be, and I guess sometimes are, interpreted so broadly as to cover almost anything the University—for that matter whatever any university—does. But then the meaning would be gone. To me, the School performs superbly well at the undergraduate level, adding an important extra ingredient to the liberal arts program."

But the graduate program is "something else—frankly something of an intellectual hodgepodge despite all the resources committed, without clear focus or *professional* mission. It has almost no faculty that it can call its own. The curriculum is diffuse, and little directed toward the management of government as opposed to vague public policy. 'Watered down' would probably be the description of even those giving the courses. But the fact is the School is run mainly as an adjunct to other faculties, with their own sense of a particular discipline, professional rewards and status, and preoccupations. And, sadly, (from the standpoint of public policy and management) the 'payoff' in those disciplines lies more and more in theoretical abstractions, further and further removed from public policy, and far more from management."[52]

Volcker highlighted another growing criticism, one that would play a major role in the lawsuit: the bleeding of resources to other departments—a third rail in the litany of accusations that Princeton was using the Robertson money wrongly. "The initial spirit and enthusiasm engendered by the Robertson gift has long since dissipated. The great majority of the economics and political science faculty"—who were essentially riding on the financial waves generated by the foundation—"is content with the present arrangements." While that arrangement served their priorities, he wrote, those priorities "are increasingly far removed from the practical world of government and administration. That abstract, theoretical bent is simply not what the Wilson School was supposed to be about."

And then, after noting the irony that the university's president when Volcker was a student had been a professor of public administration, which "isn't even a tiny part of today's curriculum" at the Woodrow Wilson School, Volcker wondered if Princeton should have accepted the gift in the first place. "Perhaps. But how much better if the University decided to put its shoulder to the wheel. Why not bring together the prestige, the talent, and, yes, the money at Princeton to stimulate renewed interest in public service, to encourage disciplined study and to provide sorely needed fresh leadership to a really critical area of American life? It's a tough, possibly ultimately, undoable challenge. But isn't it worth the effort—doesn't it really *demand* an effort that so directly fits into the vision and lifetime vocation of Woodrow Wilson himself, who bridged the world of practice and academe?"[53]

Forty years into the game, and things were seen to be so bad that one of the university's most acclaimed alumni—one of America's most influential public servants at that—had to wonder if the original gift should have even been accepted.

In 2006, in the middle of the lawsuit, Bill Robertson took the university to task on that point. In an advertisement in the university magazine, he referred to a 1980 memorandum from Bill Bowen. Robertson said the university had always "chafed under the restrictions of the gift" and had "never once approached the foundation's board to legally broaden the mission. Instead, they have secretly spread the funds to other departments." Bowen's words that incited Robertson's ad included, "I have had enough experience with Charlie and Bill to know that they hold tightly to the original promises. Indeed, even to raise questions with them would seem to me to be counterproductive in the extreme. I think that we should encourage the School, and that we can do so, to undertake appointments and responsibilities that will benefit other parts of the University as well as the School itself."[54]

Charles and Marie Robertson wanted a school with a specific discipline, a success rate that beat the band, and ongoing input from the family. Instead, the Robertson heirs found themselves with a decreasingly influential voice, in their minds talking to people who weren't listening, who thought the school, instead of being a first-rate resource for the national government, was something more akin to a slush fund from which other departments could help build their academic glory, a mere delivery mechanism to pump up the rest of Princeton.

The question was not only whether Princeton should have accepted the gift, but whether the Robertsons should have offered it.

Investing the Foundation's Growing Assets

Bill Robertson's complaints about the way things were going at the Foundation fell into three categories. One was the lack of placement results; another, the egregiousness of which was to be learned only after the lawsuit was filed, was the financial outlay outside of the mission, including the construction of a new building, Wallace Hall; the third was the investment oversight of the foundation. Although it had not dominated the increasingly antagonistic back-and-forth, it was the investment oversight issue that ended up igniting the lawsuit.

While he was alive, Charles Robertson was constantly concerned about how the endowment's income was being spent. In a 1971 memo to Eugene Goodwillie, his close friend and advisor, and one of the original foundation board members, Robertson said, "My peasant instinct suggests that we should take a hard look at what Princeton does with the difference between what it earns and what it spends." He calculated that it was earning close to $1.5 million and was spending just a little more than $1 million. "What happens to this excess income?" he asked. "I would like to see it carried on the University books as a distinctly separate account which restricts use for the WWS and not be made available to the University even on a loan basis."

And he didn't approve of the dean's autonomy to spend money. "I certainly would like to establish some brake on John Lewis's right to budget the entire income, particularly in view of the fact that the School has no intention of increasing enrollment."[55]

The amount of income, which grew dramatically over the years, was a function of how the endowment was being invested.

"In the beginning, says Bill Robertson, "my parents actually shared the investment responsibilities with the university. My father wanted to be in on the investment meetings and wanted some say as to who would actually be the investment advisor." Princeton, however, to make the investment process more efficient and reduce costs, wanted to commingle the assets of the foundation with those of Princeton's endowment. "But that's where my dad drew the line." Even though the administration of the money was likely more expensive, keeping the assets separate represented the foundation's independence from Princeton.

In the early 1970s, during the bear market of 1973 and 1974, the fund's value dropped from about $50 million to around $28 million. That prompted Charles Robertson and Princeton to change managers. Those managers, however, also recommended commingling the assets. So, as the question persisted, Bill Robertson, who had joined the foundation board around that time, interviewed people at the Rockefeller Brothers Fund, the Carnegie Corporation, and several other foundations, to find out what they thought of having a separate fund. "Every one of them," Robertson reports, "said that if you want to maintain some sort of influence over this foundation, you must have separate management." After Robertson wrote this up in a report, he says, "Bill Bowen, the president of the university, basically backed down. My dad was adamant, especially after I wrote my report on what other foundations were advising."

Robertson says that, by this time, which was coming into the late 1970s, his father was "sick with Alzheimer's and so Bowen didn't want a fight with him." [56] Even though at about that time Charles Robertson wrote, in a letter filled with accolades, that the Woodrow Wilson School was "first rate,"[57] Bill Robertson says he knows the sentiment was not true and attributes a failing mind to his father's unfounded hope that things were turning around. In any event, in 1978 the father told his children that he was confident that if Bill had his way, "the Foundation will maintain its present independence from the University and not be swallowed whole."[58]

Princeton tried again to take over the investments, but again to no avail. Roger Jones, chairman of the Consultants' Group, told Bill Robertson in early 1979 that he understood that the "negotiations with the Princeton hierarchy" on this matter were "long and difficult," as well as "tough and unpleasant. I congratulate you," he said, "on a superb piece of diplomacy. From here on out there should be no more of the kind of insensitivity which the University people showed in making their recommendations for comingling. I find it difficult to understand how they could have advanced the idea if they had taken the trouble of reading again the original documents."[59] Jones was referring to the Foundation's Certificate of Incorporation, which said that the assets "shall be considered and administered as a separate and distinct endowment fund."[60]

Jones buoyed Robertson's feelings further by telling him, "Please do not think that I am being sentimental in an overly personal way when I tell you that I believe implicitly that your mother's spirit was at your right hand. You have been true to her concepts, and, of course, those of your father, who, for many reasons, could not take on the task you so willingly assumed."[61]

The foundation created a new investment committee in 1979 to manage its own assets, and "the portfolio did extraordinarily well on its own," says Robertson. "The performance was considerably better than PRINCO's for many years."

In the summer of 1998 Harold Shapiro publicly expressed his appreciation. "The committee that oversees" the foundation endowment," he said, "has been led for the past two decades by the donors' son, Bill Robertson '72." Shapiro also noted the contributions of the other two people on the committee, John Beck and Jay Sherrerd, both of whom sat on the university's board of directors and were highly experienced in managing money. "Through the exceptional skill and dedication of these individuals, the original gift has grown to $365,600,000. On its own, it would rank high among the endowments for institutions of higher education. The annualized return on the endowment for the period 1979 through August 1998 is 16 percent. This compares favorably with the 14.4 percent return for the same period on the standard benchmark." Although Shapiro did not say this, the foundation's returns also outperformed Princeton's during that time. "For this," Shapiro commended, "we owe a great debt of gratitude to the Robertson Investment Committee."[62]

Because of that, over a period of 20 years "Princeton never overtly tried to take over the investments, although I always knew they wanted it," Robertson says. "Look, it's normal for an institution. They're big and strong and they didn't want little loose ends out there influencing what was happening in their endowment."

The PRINCO Dispute

An entity called PRINCO—the Princeton University Investment Committee—was established in the 1980s to oversee Princeton's investments. Ever since its founding, Robertson feels, that group wanted to take over the money management of the foundation. "John Beck was pissed off. He must have been wondering: *Why can't we do as well as the*

Robertson Foundation?" "We" was the Princeton endowment. Finally, after many years, in 2001 PRINCO earned a higher return than the Foundation's. That's when Beck proposed the change. "But I'm waiting for it," says Robertson. "I wrote a note to Jay Sherrerd telling him that I hope you do not agree with John Beck. I told him that my family and I will never agree to allow the Robertson Foundation to be managed by the university exclusively. My dad was adamant about that."[63]

Nevertheless, despite the foundation's long record of good investment results, the unambiguous language of the originating document, and a clear understanding that the family did not want this to happen, the board's Princeton majority still wanted to move the assets to PRINCO. Bill Josephson, the former head of the Charities Bureau, said Princeton did this "notwithstanding the fact that the endowment, as managed chiefly by Bill Robertson, had performed over the entire period of time better than the Princeton endowment had performed."[64]

"So, the spring of 2001 rolls around," Robertson says, "and John Beck formally proposes that the fund be taken over by PRINCO. They"—the Princeton members of the Robertson board—"then went to work on me; phone calls back and forth telling me it's a great idea."

Although Robertson thought a move to PRINCO would be upsetting, he soon discovered something else that was as upsetting. The timing of Beck's proposal came just before the next meeting when the foundation's balance sheet showed that the foundation had spent $45 million. "In previous years," says Robertson, "it had been $12 million or $15 million, something like that." The foundation, without the knowledge of any of the Robertson family representatives on the board, had committed $15 million for new construction, Wallace Hall.

As a result of the foundation's strong investment performance during the 1990s, at a meeting in late 2001 the board took up the question of expanding the Woodrow Wilson School. Robertson says he had no problem voting to expand the school on the basis of educational goals, but he explained to the board that he didn't want to feel compelled to expand indiscriminately just because investments were going well.

That remark led to some resentment from an unexpected source.

Robertson remembers, "Andy Goodpaster," one of the family-member trustees, "said to me after the meeting, 'You just don't want the school to spend your precious money.' And that was before I realized that the real plan was to spend the money on something that had nothing to do with the Woodrow Wilson School." It turns out that the new building would not be used exclusively, or even primarily, for the School.

The Princeton-appointed board members would take note of the division in the Robertson ranks.

"They said that they would try to raise the money, but that if—*if*—they couldn't, they would like to use foundation money to help build the building. The idea was to house Woodrow Wilson School programs in Wallace Hall." But Princeton promised they would raise the money, and so the expectation was that nothing would be needed from the foundation. And even in that event, "not much, just some, would have to be provided by the foundation."

Robertson was in regular touch with the school's dean, Michael Rothschild, who told him that the fundraising was going well. So well, Robertson remembers Rothschild saying in an email, "that we won't need to use any money from the Robertson Foundation. We have raised $10 million from one donor—the Wallaces—and it's going very, very well right now." Robertson was told not to worry. "But then, all of a sudden, there was this expenditure out of the foundation for more than $20 million. Why was that? "Because of Wallace Hall," Princeton told Robertson. "Wait a minute," he said. "Not only did the board not approve this, we didn't even discuss this."

"They had a majority. They didn't care," he says.

With the discovery of the Wallace Hall expenditures, the sore subject of PRINCO grew even more contentious. Robertson responded to a personal appeal from Shirley Tilghman, who asked him to meet with PRINCO's senior staff. "She said I really should reconsider. 'It's so obvious, so much easier, more efficient,'" she told him.

"PRINCO was doing well and by around then they'd had a couple of good years," Robertson acknowledges. So, even though he didn't like the idea, he began to wonder if perhaps some accommodation might be arranged. Some of the money in some asset classes, maybe, might be handled by PRINCO, with the understanding that the investment committee would maintain control over major decisions. Thus, despite all the disagreeable history on this topic, in January 2002 Robertson met with the PRINCO people.

He didn't like what he heard.

They told him about the magic of going heavy into alternatives and private equity, where, although the money was at high risk, the potential was sky-high.[65] To a traditional—some might say old-fashioned—investor, like Robertson, this was heresy. "I didn't buy it," he says. "The whole thing was smoke and mirrors and it wasn't to be trusted. And we were already doing well enough because we had picked great managers to begin with."[66]

Bill Josephson adds this perspective. "For a number of important reasons, the Robertsons did not agree that Princeton should manage the endowment. Princeton had, in the management of its endowment, gone over to what some people call *modern portfolio theory*, where the emphasis was not on traditional endowment investments yielding interest, dividends, rents and royalties as income, and publicly traded stocks and bonds as principal investments. Princeton had gone into some relatively illiquid investments, like real estate and hedge funds, investments that entailed new degrees of risk; for example, foreign securities, which also presented the question of exchange rate risk as well. The Robertson family felt that consolidating the Robertson endowment with the Princeton endowment would not only be inconsistent with the donor's intent and structure, but also in fact would diminish the availability of income."[67]

The *New York Times* reported in 2012 that it was "hard to find a college or university that stuck with the customary and far simpler allocation between stocks and bonds." As of 2011, the National Association of College and University Business Officers, a group that tracks investment results for higher educational organizations, found that endowments of all sizes "underperformed a simple mix of 60 percent stocks and 40 percent bonds." Timothy Keating, president of Keating Investments, was quoted as saying that many investors would be better off with the simpler strategy, and not have very much of their endowments, if any at all, in alternatives, which have high fees and are often illiquid. Simon Lack, another financial advisor, calculated that "the hedge fund industry as a whole lost more money in one year (2008) than it had in the previous ten years. If all the money that's ever been invested in hedge funds had been put in Treasury bills instead, the results would have been twice as good," he said.[68]

It didn't help when Robertson, during his visit to PRINCO's offices, analogized PRINCO's plan to one touted by Long Term Capital Management, the famously failed hedge fund with two Nobel Prize winners leading the team. "The failure of the highly leveraged fund almost brought down the whole international financial system," Robertson remembers. "That was an explosion. Nuclear. So I asked if they remembered that, now that we're talking about quantitative investment strategies. And do you know what the head of PRINCO told me? He said, 'Well, they"—Long Term Capital Management—"almost made it. They almost hit a home run.' And I said, 'Yeah, but they didn't.'"[69]

The tortured defense of Long Term Capital might have come directly from Robert Merton, one of its two Nobel laureates. To him, it seems only to have been a question of degree, not of philosophy, that caused the firm's collapse in the late 1990s. "The solution," Merton said, "is not to go back to the old, simple methods. That never works. You can't go back. The world has changed. And the solution is greater complexity."[70]

But even that nonsense wasn't the whole problem. "For them, the people at PRINCO, it was all about getting this money where they could get a grip on it," Robertson says of the foundation's assets. "And then, we'd be out. Our influence would be gone."

In 2003, the year after the lawsuit was filed, the board, over the objections of Robertson and the foundation's two other family-appointed trustees, voted to move the assets to PRINCO. The foundation was conducting a study on other investment firms that might do the job, but Robertson strongly suspected that the process was just a front, a suggestion to appease him and buy some more time. "There was never any question that they were salivating over getting that money to PRINCO," Robertson says.

"Bill was very upset about the decision," says Ron Malone, Robertson's lead attorney for the lawsuit, "because it was directly contrary to his father's understanding of the original deal." Malone points out that intelligent people can do dumb things. "You can have a debate about who should manage the money and how it should be managed," Malone says, taking note of how well PRINCO was doing, although it isn't invincible, as the market would later show. "In theory it wasn't a dumb idea to have Princeton manage the money," Malone acknowledges, but he also says that he "couldn't believe how the university ran roughshod over the family, people who believed it was a matter of principle and a matter of commitment."[71]

Paul Volcker also thought the move was ill-advised. "In the middle of this conflict"—the one about the school's direction, and which, by the way, Volcker felt Princeton was beginning to address to the satisfaction of the Robertsons—"they insisted and outvoted the Robertson family to move the funds into the Princeton endowment. Why was this so important? I mean, I can understand why it would have been administratively cleaner, but why raise more hackles with the family? I just didn't understand why they wanted to scratch at that scab at that point. Perhaps they thought of Robertson as a pest and that this was a way to get rid of him," says Volcker. "It had nothing to do with the substance of the real issues."[72]

The final indignity to the family may have been when, at the April 2002 board meeting, Robertson asked, "Oh, by the way, how's it going with placing our graduates in the foreign service of the federal government?" When the answer to that question was disappointing, he asked, "Do you ask applicants if they are interested in working for the United States government? The admissions director said, 'No, no I don't.'"

"He admitted it right there in that meeting," Robertson says.[73]

A few months earlier, the *New York Times* published an analysis of the Woodrow Wilson School in the aftermath of 9/11. The school "finds itself in something of a bind," the newspaper said. "At a time when the United States is embroiled in a war against terrorism and needs experienced operatives on the ground, the Woodrow Wilson School—by its own admission as well as those of academics at other schools—is heavy on traditional scholarship and teaching." One Princeton professor quoted in the article said, "the school had lost some of its strength in international relations over the years and had become 'dominated by economists and by an economic view.'"[74]

Charles Robertson felt from the beginning that the school wasn't living up to its mandate. By the turn of the 21st century, things looked even worse.

An Absence of Collegiality

Bob Halligan, the former employee of the Agency for International Development and former Wilson School student who joined the Robertson Foundation in 1982 as one of the three family-appointed trustees, said another issue loomed large: the absence of trust between the family and the university. "The board would meet once a year. We would get the materials for the meeting, sometimes the day before the meeting, sometimes the evening before the meeting. And we complained about that quite a bit. This was in the 1980s. We didn't have time to review the financials and we didn't have time to review the placement problems about graduates going into government service. We didn't have time to think about it. We just had to react to it."

Even so, Halligan says, he didn't look for problems. "I was glad to be on the board. I owed a big debt to Charlie. Without his advice and help, I wouldn't have gone to the Woodrow Wilson School. He got me in there."

Halligan had been unaware of the growing discontent—or perhaps predisposed to not see it. "I couldn't imagine Princeton doing anything wrong," he now says, "and that was part of the problem. During the '80s and '90s the conversation about spending wasn't taking place. We were trying to make sure they were placing people, making sure they looked at females and minorities. I remember asking whether they ever dropped a program, and not only added them. That's the kind of focus we had then."

So, when Robertson told Halligan in 2002 that he wanted to sue Princeton, Halligan asked, "What the hell for? Then he explained what had been going on—things I had no idea about—and I supported him."[75]

After Charles Robertson died in 1981, the disagreements got more personal. "I always suspected they were downplaying us, especially after my father died," Bill Robertson says. "During his life and during my mother's life, when we had the annual meeting, it was at the president's house, a rather grand occasion, with dozens of Princeton officials and board members and God only knows what. It was a red carpet VIP affair." He remembers that there was a time the meetings would be at the president's house, lunch would be together, and the air was filled with camaraderie. "But after my dad died, we never had another meeting in the president's house. It was clear to me that there was a definite effort to downplay the family, looking probably towards the future when we would eventually kind of go away."[76]

Not surprisingly, Princeton remembers it differently. Doug Eakeley, Princeton's trial counsel for the lawsuit, says, "The annual board meetings would continue. Faculty would make presentations. Bill Robertson would usually say something complimentary." He says that with the new president—Shirley Tilghman began her tenure as president just ten months before attending her first Robertson Foundation board meeting—governance reforms were undertaken.

Peter McDonough, Princeton's general counsel, and Eakeley, explain the problems in the foundation's governance, as well as Bill Robertson's perception that Princeton wanted the family to go away. "After Shirley Tilghman became president," says Eakeley—but after, and most likely because, the lawsuit was filed, according to Robertson—"the board began to meet every two to three months, minutes followed promptly, many more materials were coming in to the board members, formal votes were more often being taken, an independent auditor and an independent treasurer were retained. A whole raft of governance reforms took place."

Tilghman also put forth "a welcoming hand to Bill, that's captured in the minutes of that first meeting" after Tilghman became president. "But," both Eakeley and McDonough remember, "it was rebuffed."[77]

McDonough reflects on the changes over the years. "In the early days, Charles Robertson is chair and he's interacting with Bob Goheen and Bill Bowen, and it wouldn't shock me at all that there are dinners in the president's house and that there's a very close collegiality. And maybe after they get through the rough patch in the '70s—I'm surmising here—it wouldn't shock me at all if there's an effort to smooth over those rough patches." Eakeley points out, "Bill Bowen regularly visited Charles Robertson in Florida and Long Island."

"So now," McDonough continues, "let's fast forward to a moment when Harold Shapiro comes in, having been the president of the University of Michigan. Now, he's new and has a university to manage, and one of his responsibilities is to serve on the Robertson Foundation board. It's not shocking to learn that he might view this as an obligation. And that might be taken as an affront to . . . now Bill, not Charlie. Now let's also replace a dean who is schooled in stewardship"—"Donald Stokes," Eakeley clarifies—"with one who's more pragmatic and who lacks some social graces." Eakeley: "Michael Rothschild." "It's easy to see," surmises McDonough, "how Bill can fairly come away with a sense that things have changed."[78]

Robertson responds, "An independent auditor and an independent treasurer? That's not true. And the governance reforms? They were pretty much window-dressing during the suit. They didn't do much to address the issues we were facing. And no, I didn't rebuff anything." After some more thought, he says, "Things didn't *seem* to change. They *did* change."[79]

Imagine all the bad blood flowing back and forth, the two warring sides forced to sit in each other's company, in the same room at the same table, to make decisions about the future of something each felt was important. What might come to mind is the image of divorcing parents reluctantly brought together to jointly determine the fate of their children. But if the people at Princeton thought of Robertson as a pest—the high school ne'er do well, a gnat on a great university's enormous and tough hide—they ended up dealing with someone far more formidable.

Up until just before the lawsuit was filed, Robertson's attorneys were fairly sure it could be avoided. When Robertson described the situation to Ron Malone and then asked for his help, Malone's initial reaction was that it sounded as if the only thing that needed to happen was for someone to sit down and talk with the people at Princeton. "You don't treat donors this way. Let's give a little, take a little, and we'll work it out."

That's what his advice was at the time, says Robertson. But he was wary. Despite the tension that Princeton surely understood, he says he was not able to obtain a copy of the foundation's books and records, which, as a trustee, he was entitled to. He wanted them because he wanted to know how the money was being spent. "They kept stalling. There was never any give with these guys. And it was getting pretty obvious they weren't going to cooperate. On anything. There was simply no give."

Enough Is Enough

Was there, at this point prior to filing the lawsuit, any soul-searching? Some introspection, aside from all the rancor, that might avert going down so damaging a path? "I asked myself this," Robertson says: "What would my father say? He loved Princeton. I wondered if I was just so far off the tracks on this. So yes, there was some soul-searching. But I knew he would have said, '*Enough is enough. Go for it.*' The real issue," Robertson says, "was trust. The question for me was this: *Do I trust these people?* It was getting bad enough, but then, after they stonewalled us on the documents . . . I could see it. And I could see there was no other option. Something was really wrong. To say, *screw yourself on Wallace Hall*? They're a multi-billion dollar institution. Couldn't they have put some money into that building themselves?"

Had the Wallace Hall nonsense not been so secret, had there been more give and take, had there been some understanding that part of the money, if not all, could find its way to PRINCO, or had Princeton been more communicative about the direction of the school, the lawsuit might have been avoided.

"There were all kinds of ways this could have been different," Robertson says. "But this, in my heart of hearts, is what I was hearing: *We're Princeton University, and you're not. We know what we're doing. We don't get dragged down by the likes of you. Who are you people, anyway? Nobody. You're not even the people who have the money. You're just some irresponsible trust-fund kid who inherited money. You didn't even work for it. You have nothing else to do and this is just entertainment for you.* They didn't want to give, even a little, because they just thought they couldn't possibly be wrong. Princeton's characteristics were deception, disrespect, and cowardice. They could have discussed all the issues, but they were . . . devious. They thought they were so smart they would never have to confront this. They thought they would just outsmart us."

Robertson, echoing Paul Volcker's sentiments, also places some responsibility on Princeton's lawyers. "I'm sure they said not to give an inch."[80]

The acrimony that developed over the years had become unbearable. Robert Durkee, the vice president and secretary at Princeton who served as the university's public voice throughout the lawsuit, said Robertson "never had a real role in life," that he "grew more bitter"[81] over time.

In addition, four votes would always beat three.

Taking into account both the unfavorable math and the ongoing, increasingly insufferable condescension, Robertson came to realize that he would never win the battle for his parents' memory in the boardroom. So he decided, by incautiously shaking a formidable tiger by the tail, to take his chances in the courtroom.

Photos

Marie Robertson

Charles Robertson

Bill Robertson

The Hartford family's A&P Food Markets were the source of
wealth for the Robertsons' gift to benefit Princeton University. The
store above was at 41 Main Street, Norwalk, Connecticut.

Courtesy of the Hartford Family Foundation

The Robertson home on Banbury Lane

Woodrow Wilson, 13th President of Princeton University (1902-1910). In his inaugural address, he reiterated his theme "Princeton in the Nation's Service."

Nassau Hall, the oldest building at Princeton University (1756). On its steps in 1896, when he was a faculty member, Woodrow Wilson delivered his "Princeton in the Nation's Service" speech, to which "and in Service of All Nations" was later added.

President Dwight D. Eisenhower, Princeton University President Bob Goheen, and Charles Robertson

Photo by Elizabeth G. C. Menzies, courtesy of the Robertson family

Wilson Hall was built with funds from the Robertson gift to house
the Woodrow Wilson School of Public and International Affairs.
It was designed by architect Minoru Yamasaki.

Courtesy of Wanda Kaluza from her YouTube video
"Circle of Animals/Zodiac Heads by Ai Weiwei"

Remarks were given by President Lyndon B. Johnson at the Wilson Hall
dedication in 1966. The building was renamed Robertson Hall in 1988.

Ron Malone   Seth Lapidow

Frank Cialone

The Robertson Legal Team

A Courtroom Scene
Bob Halligan, Bill Josephson, and Bill Robertson
© *New Jersey Star-Ledger, with permission*

Chapter 5

Robertson v. Princeton

The time-honored gentleman's code of conduct associated with an Ivy League boardroom quickly disintegrated as the Princeton family feud that had been brewing for decades went public. On the morning of July 18, 2002, *New York Times* readers, including many Princeton students, administrators, and alumni, woke up to a prominently placed article with the headline, "Princeton University Is Sued Over Control of Foundation." In it, Bill Robertson was quoted as saying, "My family believes the trust my parents placed in Princeton University when they gave this generous and well-meaning gift has been betrayed."[1]

Princeton's Robert Durkee said, "The first salvo is always fired by the plaintiff."[2] By this he meant that the accusers own the first shot at defining the legal narrative, which in turn often gives them the lead in the race to capture the public's sympathy.

The university responded by blowing off the allegations, claiming that the plaintiffs had nothing, that the charges had essentially been invented: *Hey guys, you're making things up and you may even be lying; in any event we want you to stop wasting our time*. Bill Robertson was finally demanding the attention he felt his family was entitled to—in a court of law and, by extension, in the court of public opinion. He wasn't making things up and he wasn't going to go away. As the dispute developed, one newspaper would write, "In higher education circles, *Robertson vs. Princeton University* is the kind of epic lawsuit that could make Ivy League history."[3]

"It's important to understand," Bill Josephson, the former head of the Charities Bureau in New York State, remembers, "that the genesis

of the lawsuit was with Princeton's effort to take control of the investment of the endowment."[4] Ron Malone, the Robertsons' attorney in San
Francisco, agrees. "Without any question, that was the trigger."

Malone attributes the moment to something personal for Robertson.
"Bill was very upset about the PRINCO decision because it was directly
contrary to his father's understanding of the original agreement. It went
back to Bill, as a young man, being put on the foundation board by his
father when Eugene Goodwillie died, and his father specifically cautioned
Bill to be wary of any attempts by the university to take over management
of the foundation's endowment."[5]

In addition to outlining the PRINCO problem, the lawsuit also
claimed that many of the foundation's expenses over the years were
improperly incurred, including those associated with the construction of
Wallace Hall. The Robertsons requested a full accounting of the foundation's books and records, as well as repayment of whatever was found to
have been improperly spent. The family also accused Princeton of breach
of fiduciary duty, *ultra vires*[6] acts, the violation of a restricted gift and
promissory estoppel.[7]

Robertson demanded an end to the marriage. He wanted to substitute "another school of public administration at another university" that
would "conscientiously and unselfishly dedicate itself to the purposes
of the Robertson Foundation."[8] Things were so off track, he thought,
Princeton no longer deserved the privilege of spending his parents'
money. After more than 40 years, a divorce—packing up the foundation
and leaving Princeton behind—was the only solution.

The Allegations

In lawsuits, the original complaint is only the beginning. A process
called *discovery*, where each side provides information requested by the
other, opens up the doors to see if anything other than what was already
known or highly suspected needs to be investigated. During the two
years following the initial filing, the Robertsons got their hands on materials that before then had been seen only by university officials. Much

of that information, the family felt, was incriminating, and, two years later, armed with a mountain of newly discovered evidence, they filed an amended, more robust set of accusations that would define what was to be argued in court.

The 70-page amended complaint, filed in November 2004, charged, among other things, that Princeton failed to fulfill the foundation's mission, had spent its assets on programs and projects that did not serve the mission, had withheld material information from the Robertson family, and had attempted to disenfranchise the family trustees from participating in the foundation's management.[9]

Specifically:

- "In the 1970s and 1980s, Princeton officers secretly discussed dissolving the Foundation or 'broadening' the purposes it would support in a series of internal memos."

- "In 1993, Princeton began diverting over $200,000 a year to the Office of Population Research (OPR) and the Center for International Studies (CIS), while representing that the Foundation paid '$0' for OPR and CIS."

- "In 1998, Princeton committed over $1 million in Foundation funds to support Ph.D. students in the Economics, Politics, and Sociology departments. Princeton officers conspired to conceal this funding from the Family Trustees."

- "In 2000, Princeton committed over $1 million a year 'in perpetuity' to the Program in Law and Public Affairs ("LAPA"), without disclosing the commitment or the funding itself to the Family Trustees. LAPA has received over $5 million, mainly to teach undergraduate and non-Wilson School 'fellows' to work on independent research projects."

- "In 2003, after this lawsuit was filed, Princeton decided to charge the Foundation an additional $3 million per year for 'overhead,' far in excess of actual costs imposed by the Foundation programs. Princeton used the money to pay for more Ph.D. students in non-Wilson School departments and to provide a 'discretionary fund' for the Wilson School Dean to spend without Foundation oversight."[10]

The theme of misspent money emerged from discovery. One snapshot: "Princeton has improperly and systematically diverted to its own use and benefit more than $100 million from the Robertson Foundation and fraudulently concealed its wrongdoing." Another: "For decades, Princeton has abused its control of the Foundation and has betrayed the Donors' trust by diverting the Foundation's assets, which are now approximately $600 million, for Princeton's own objectives." And another: The Woodrow Wilson School had "taken more than $260 million of the Foundation's funds since 1961, including $230 million since fiscal 1990, but" the school had "done little to accomplish the Foundation's mission."

The complaint also spoke to the structure of the foundation and the intentions of the donors. "By establishing and endowing such a separate entity, Mr. and Mrs. Robertson sought to insure that their intent as Donors would be respected." The plaintiffs characterized the money they said was being misused, as "Princeton's own private slush fund."

But the problems, the family claimed, weren't solely at the foundation. In an effort to show that Princeton was not a good and honorable keeper of donor-restricted assets, the complaint maintained that "Princeton has a pattern and practice of violating donors' conditions and improperly spending restricted gifts in ways that benefit the University's own general fund."

The goal of the lawsuit was to "end Princeton's abuse of the Foundation." The family asked for a "reversal of Princeton's takeover" of the investment portfolio"—the PRINCO issue—"and for the reimbursement of over $100 million, a number that would more than double after an audit, representing what the family said were improper expenditures.

The plaintiffs also wanted another foundation to be established "with all of its Trustees appointed by the Robertson Family and all of its assets dedicated to graduate training for government service."[11] That move, linked to the original request that the foundation simply be removed from the university's oversight, would reduce Princeton's endowment by the lion's share of a billion dollars.

The charges morphed from the legally oriented to the more personal. Peppered throughout the complaint were words and phrases, such as *secretly discussed, diverting,* and *conspired to conceal.* While large corporations entangled in legal battles might not take offense at being snookered—it's just business—individuals often see it far differently. To Bill Robertson, Princeton committed no less an offense than betraying everything his parents stood for.

Princeton: It's Not About Donor Intent

In 2006 the *Wall Street Journal* ran a front-page article that said, "Though the lawsuit originally was sparked by a dispute over who should manage the Robertson gift money, it has produced a trove of documents raising broader questions about Princeton's fidelity to its donors' intentions in this and other cases. *Robertson v. Princeton,*" the newspaper said, "may be the most important case higher education has faced over the question of honoring the wishes of a donor."[12]

Not so, asserted Peter McDonough, Princeton's general counsel. "This is not a donor intent lawsuit."[13] Doug Eakeley, Princeton's counsel for the lawsuit, puts it this way: "People *assume* that Charles Robertson's intent is dominant or should be controlling, but the intentions of Robert Goheen," Princeton's president at the time of the gift, "are just as important as Mr. Robertson's." The reason "was that the Certificate of Incorporation is more in the nature of a *contract* than a restricted gift." The university, Princeton's logic went, had just as much say about things as the donor did.

"The gift had only one restriction on it," Eakeley says, "and that was that the trustees of the foundation should comply with the Certificate of Incorporation. Bob Goheen literally, in several writings—in particular, one presenting the gift to the board of trustees at Princeton for acceptance—had his own way of describing the purpose of the graduate program and how the money was to be applied. Interestingly," Eakeley notes,

"20 years later, Charles Robertson, in another letter, quotes Goheen and says 'mission accomplished.'"[14]

Victoria Bjorklund, legal counsel for Princeton during the lawsuit, follows on that logic in her own analysis, written in 2008, in which she argued that characterizing the dispute as one of donor intent was misleading. "Contrary to suggestions in the press, the terms governing this generous gift were not unilaterally dictated by the donor."[15] In a later interview she said, "It was not a case of donor intent because Princeton was *a party to* the negotiation." The document "was written in a way that makes it such that Princeton's views have to be taken into account as equally as we take into account Marie Robertson's views. It was a negotiated transaction where the parties agreed jointly to undertake responsibilities, which Princeton carried out for all these years until the organization was dissolved."

That the document establishing the foundation was jointly agreed to is no mere nuance, Bjorklund says. "The Robertsons and Princeton negotiated," for example, "who would be on the board of trustees. Nobody denies that Princeton had views that were expressed" in the founding document as well as in later correspondence. "They were both represented by counsel. Princeton's intent matters just as much as Marie's intent in giving the money." Furthermore, "it's important to note that Charles Robertson chaired the organization for twenty years, until his death. He was an extremely active participant, as his correspondence shows. This was not a person who sat on the sidelines. He was actively engaged, and there is much correspondence to show that. His son Bill was also very active once he joined the board."

The difference between the Robertson gift and a donor-intent situation, Bjorklund says, is that "this was not an instance where a donor writes a gift instrument, hands over a check, disappears and then comes back later to say, 'Oh, but I wanted you to do X with my money.' No. This was a *participatory* engagement between the two parties. So to say that only the intent of Marie Robertson matters here and that she was somehow not given her due by Princeton is not accurate when you look at the historical record of this supporting organization."[16]

Eakeley also emphasizes the importance of the historical record. "If you accept the concept of the Certificate of Incorporation as a contract between Robert Goheen representing Princeton and Charles Robertson representing the donor, then a very frequent and reliable way to add specificity to language that might be ambiguous is to look at the behavior of the parties to the contract afterwards. What did they do? Granted, we had this two- or three-year period where Mr. Robertson is unhappy with the relatively low number of graduates going into federal government service, but right from the beginning, after the gift was made, the leadership of the university started building an expanded graduate program."

"And," says Eakeley, "Charles Robertson gets every sequential blueprint of what the expanded graduate program is going to look like. It includes domestic policy, urban policy, international affairs, economics . . . and he's present at the creation." Eakeley notes, as an example of why the lawsuit was out of sync with the father's wishes, that Bill Robertson took exception to classes on population control in third world countries. "Interestingly enough," Eakeley says, "there was never any criticism of the curriculum or the faculty" on the part of Charles Robertson. "The litigation was focused only on outputs."[17]

That raises a question, however: Does the presence of a robust input process obviate the need for questioning the lack of output? Charles Robertson may not have complained about the input, although Bill Robertson disputes even that assertion, but we know he was upset about the output.

As for Charles Robertson being unhappy for only a couple of years, his son says, "That's a lie. Two or three years? Try 15. More. My father was unhappy from the beginning. And they know it. And no, I never took exception to classes on population control. Specific academic decisions were Princeton's, as they should have been. My concern was where the graduates were going and the misspending of money."[18]

Interpreting the Original Document

Who owned the intentions was a critical question to resolve because the validity of the accusations that not enough people were going to work for the federal government depended on the answer. If Princeton could persuade the court that it had equal say in how the gift could be used, it wouldn't need to defend its graduate employment numbers.

Wresting the meaning of words would be a helpful strategy, too. As part of her defense of Princeton, Bjorklund pointed out, "A review of the Certificate reveals that Plaintiffs' interpretation . . . cannot fairly be reconciled with its text. For example: Paragraph 3(a) provides that the Graduate School should be a place where men and women dedicated to the public service "may prepare" for careers in government service. The use of the permissive '*may* prepare' as opposed to '*shall* prepare' or '*must* prepare' is critical."[19]

Ron Malone, the Robertsons' attorney in San Francisco, thinks that sort of logic is weak and misleading. "They were using a clever, after-the-fact lawyer reading of the document to claim that it said the Woodrow Wilson School is a place where people *may be* prepared for government service. So"—Malone continues to interpret Princeton's interpretation of the mission—"*we provide a place, and the students may prepare to do anything. That a small percentage of the students go into government service is not our problem.* It's disheartening," he says, "to see intelligent people make linguistically based arguments that they know are contradicted by the clear understanding of both parties at the time the gift was made."

Also, as long as we're on the meaning of words, the founding document also employs the phrase *with particular emphasis* to describe the donor's aspirations, yet only twelve percent of the School's graduates entered the Foreign Service upon graduation between 1962 and 2002. "Other graduate programs," Malone says, "with one one-thousandth of the funding did better."

"The truth is," Malone says, "any language with clever lawyers on either side can be ambiguous." Using Bjorklund's and Eakeley's line of logic but to a different effect, he says, "That's where the extraneous evidence of the discussions is relevant. If you look at the depositions and the contemporaneous internal documentation, it is clear that the university knew exactly what the deal was. One of the deans at the time acknowledged to the donors that Princeton's job was to recruit students who were interested in government service, spend two years with them, educate them and then funnel them into government service. They knew very well what their job was. To claim that this was not a donor-intent case is the ultimate untruth. It reflects a lack of integrity for the university to argue, long after the donor is dead and cannot defend himself, that the charter means something entirely different from what Princeton under-stood—*and acknowledged*—at the time the gift was made and up until the donor died."[20]

Bill Josephson is similarly confident. "The purposes are not broad," he says. "The foundation's mission was to strengthen the government of the United States." To emphasize the point, he repeats: "*Strengthen.*" He then counters the claim that fewer people than was imagined by Charles and Marie Robertson would want to enter government service, a trend strongly linked by Princeton to the political unrest in the 1960s and 1970s and that was used in part as the justification to expand the mis-sion. "It cannot be," Josephson said, "that the demand for this level of education has abated."[21]

As there aren't that many graduate schools in the country with strong, focused programs on international relations, it is hard to imagine that one of the most well known—and one whose tuition was free at that—would have difficulty attracting a sufficient number of candidates who anticipated careers in government service.

This point, however, would be disputed.

Within the question of how many graduates would enter federal service, there were two levels where the lawsuit focused: 1) not enough students were being recruited who had the right career ambitions, and 2) not enough emphasis was given to ensuring that the school's graduates were actually going into that field.

In addition to mounting a defense, Princeton played some barbed offense. While family members and their supporters understood Princeton's actions to be a violation of the donors' intentions, the people at Princeton took the position that not only were they following those intentions, but that the family's second-generation members were actu-ally guilty of the very crime that they accused Princeton of committing.

Shortly after the settlement, Robert Durkee wrote, "One of the great iro-
nies of this lawsuit is that the press bought into the family's assertion that
the case was about Princeton's adherence to 'donor intent.' While it may
have been about whether Princeton properly carried out" the terms of
the agreement, "the question of 'intent' raised by this trial was precisely
the reverse: whether the descendants of a donor can overturn the donor's
intent—as expressed in a carefully negotiated written document agreed
to by the donor and the university—with respect to both the purpose of
the gift and the mechanism by which it would be administered. It was
the Robertsons," Durkee contended, "not Princeton, who were trying to
overturn the donor's intent."[22]

Bill Robertson characterizes this comment as "nothing more than
Princeton's hijinks, a big lie designed to confuse the reader."[23]

A Former Princeton President Struggles

In his deposition during the lawsuit, an 84-year-old Robert Goheen
took the position that students' view of government service had transformed over the years. While he acknowledged that the primary idea at
the Woodrow Wilson School was to give priority to training students
committed to careers as executives in the federal government over those
in other areas of public affairs, he also said that the situation "changed
over time as one found that partly there wasn't the appetite in the federal
government anymore for some of these young people. Attitudes of some
of your best young people toward public service were changing, taking on
a more domestic character, often more of an international character outside of government. Holding true to your principles, you have to adjust
to changing circumstances."[24]

Goheen also responded to questions about the nuances of obtaining
permission from Princeton's board to accept the gift under the pressure
of time, while still honoring Marie Robertson's strong wishes that her gift
remain anonymous. Goheen didn't want "another academic year to pass
by" without being able to use the money at the Woodrow Wilson School.
He was also worried enough to immediately confer with the board's

executive committee—but, at that point, only that committee—because, while "the whole board was a group of wonderful people, they were not known for being terribly secure sometimes. Things would slip out that you wished hadn't."

Goheen was asked about a memo in which he wrote, "The objective is to develop postgraduate programs of instruction that will augment the flow of well-prepared people into positions of public responsibility and set new patterns of excellence throughout the nation for the training of men for the public service, with particular attention to international and foreign affairs." These words, practically mirroring the language in the original gift document, conveyed the purpose of the gift to the executive committee, whose members would then advise the rest of the Princeton board on whether to accept the money and the gift's restrictions.

In his deposition, Goheen confessed his frustration. "In hindsight," he noted, "we"—he and the Robertsons—"were very trusting of one another and we were not meticulous in our use of language. I think it was unfortunate that we allowed the Certificate of Incorporation to be phrased as it was in this limited sense of government service, because in all my discussions with the Robertsons, we were talking about public service and not simply government service, and that was well known. And, really, at the Woodrow Wilson School, that was accepted. This was a school for preparing people for the public service, not simply government service. And that ambiguity I think has haunted us ever since. It's just too bad it's there."[25]

This comment is why Ron Malone describes Goheen's testimony, under questioning—by Princeton's counsel no less—as validating the Robertsons' position on donor intent. "His testimony," Malone says, "100 percent supports what I'm saying." *Charlie was very clear about what he wanted* is the way Malone hears Goheen's testimony.

Goheen may have characterized his discussions with Charles Robertson as expressing a common understanding that public service meant something more than just government service, but, as we saw in the prior chapter, Robertson often expressed his dissatisfaction with the way Princeton was actualizing the objectives of the school.

In addition, the governing document, despite Goheen's portrayal, was not ambiguous. The language, referring as it clearly does to expected careers in international relations and affairs, was actually quite specific. Furthermore, his assertion that Princeton "allowed" the certificate to be phrased as it was makes it seem that some very smart people who were looking out for the best interests of the university had the wool pulled over their eyes. One of Bjorklund's defenses in the donor-intent question actually went in the opposite direction: Princeton was very much engaged in the process, she says, and knew precisely what it was doing and what it wanted to accomplish. If it was "too bad" the language "was there," as Goheen put it, it is also true, as the two were so "very trusting of one another," that there was ample time to fix the problem of the document's wording during Charles Robertson's lifetime.

Bill Robertson thinks that it "strains credulity to believe that those representing Princeton's interests were not meticulous in their use of language."[26]

What Does "Government Service" Mean?

The problem was actually worse, from the son's perspective. "The university," he says, "approaches a very wealthy family, where the husband happened to go to Princeton. They persuade him to make this donation. And almost immediately they start backing away from it. They told one thing to the faculty and they told something different to my parents. They told my parents that they had this mission of preparing students for federal service in the arena of international relations. But they didn't say that to the faculty. And Goheen admitted as much."[27]

That's not merely Robertson's memory talking. Goheen was asked about the interpretation of "government service":

Q: So the Princeton University Board of Trustees understood that the purpose of this foundation was to fulfill the objective of defending and extending freedom throughout the world by improving the facilities for the training and education of men and women for government service?

A: I explained to the board our interpretation of that ["government service"] as a less formal language. The objective in developing the Woodrow Wilson School post-graduate programs of instruction will augment the flow of well-prepared people in positions of public responsibility and set new patterns of excellence throughout the nation. And this broader interpretation was certainly a matter of discussion and understanding between Charles Robertson and all these people [faculty and administrators] and myself. I guess we were not careful enough about some of the language in here. I think that's regrettable, but we proceeded on the assumption of a broad interpretation of the language.

Q: You didn't include that broader language in your letter to Charles and Marie, though, did you?

A: No. I didn't. And I should have. But I didn't.[28]

James Trussell, the acting dean of the Wilson School, when the lawsuit was filed, didn't help matters on behalf of Princeton in his own deposition:

Q.   Did you try to direct foundation funds in such a way as to emphasize training people for careers in those areas of the Federal Government concerned with international affairs?

A.   I don't believe there was a particular emphasis on that.[29]

Even before the ink was dry, before the enterprise had even started, the school's administration and faculty behaved as if the purpose of the gift were far broader than it was.

As for Goheen's defense that things for the Woodrow Wilson School changed over time, Seth Lapidow, the Robertson family's lead counsel in New Jersey, minces no words. "The world may have changed but the gift did not. If there was a sea change at work, the university should have gone to the Robertson Foundation board and said so. Instead, they snuck around and did what they wanted to do in secret." As for Goheen's distinction between government service and public service, Lapidow retorts, "In 1961 public service meant only government service. There was nothing else."

Lapidow sums up the issue this way: "Goheen said one thing to Charles Robertson and another to his board. One was to get the gift and the other was to make sure that no one at Princeton raised an issue about taking on such a narrow purpose. His deposition bears this out. Goheen's intention is meaningless. He accepted the gift on the terms that Robertson set out, and the fact that he didn't want to scare the Princeton board by telling them what he agreed to was not our problem."[30]

There is other evidence that ensuring Princeton would adhere to the donors' intentions was of concern from the beginning. In 2002 an 87-year-old General A. J. Goodpaster, who served on the foundation board and who was one of the original confidants Charles Robertson called upon when deciding to make the gift, spoke in his deposition of how worried Robertson was about how his philanthropy would be put to use. "It was his observation, and I might say mine as well," Goodpaster testified, "that on occasion gifts were made to universities, and they were not applied in the way intended by the giver. And he said he and his wife really wanted to be sure that this gift, which is of magnificent size, would be applied in the way that they envisaged. So rather than make it outright—because of that concern of giving assurance that the intent would be fulfilled—he wanted to stay in considerable degree of contact with just what was done with the money."[31]

It would be fair to say that Charles Robertson had an inherent distrust of handing over so much money without ongoing supervision from the family. Toward the end of his life he wrote to his son, "The reason for the creation of the Robertson Foundation, as a separate entity from Princeton University, was the need for family and independent guidance as to the management and expenditure of Foundation income and assets. The founders felt that for the Foundation to achieve its stated objectives, family and outside, independent elements must be closely meshed with all phases of the management and spending policies of the Foundation. Moreover, they must enforce the official documents."[32]

Academic Freedom: A Defense

Princeton defended its authority to interpret the original gift document on another front as well: academic freedom. "It is perhaps more helpful," Victoria Bjorklund wrote in her 2008 analysis, "to characterize the Robertson litigation not as a case concerning a donor's wishes, but instead as an important case concerning, among other things, the scope of the *academic freedom* and *academic abstention* doctrines."[33]

By arguing the point this way, Bjorklund was invoking an important and cherished concept at universities.

Despite how donors craft their agreements and form their expectations when they donate money, charities need room to do their jobs. They must be able to rely on their own staff and trustees to make and execute the decisions that will further their missions. Donors, no matter the amount they give, cannot micromanage. This is true if for no other reason than that Congress wants to be sure that charitable tax deductions and an endowment gift's tax-free investment offspring are serving society generally and not just the whims of a few select people, such as donors and those close to them.

"Academic freedom," Bjorklund wrote, "although somewhat vaguely defined in the case law, refers at its most basic level to the First Amendment right of colleges and universities to be free from unwarranted interference from outside parties into academic and educational endeavors."[34]

In his own analysis, Peter McDonough cited a landmark United States Supreme Court case decided in 1957. "Every university has the 'essential' freedom," he said, quoting Justice Felix Frankfurter's words in the decision, "'to determine for itself on academic grounds who may teach, what may be taught, how it shall be taught, and who may be admitted to study.'" These are commonly known as the "four freedoms."

While taking care to confirm the importance of a donor's wishes, McDonough warned against ceding academic control. "Plaintiffs' requested relief—and, indeed, their very vision of the proper relationship between the Foundation and the University—would eviscerate these essential academic freedoms. Of course, the University recognizes its obligation to abide by the strictures set forth in the Foundation's Certificate of Incorporation. But the question of how to structure the Woodrow Wilson School's program to further this purpose is an academic one that is reserved to the University."

The Robertson view of the Foundation's mission, he wrote, "is so narrow and rigid, and their standards for *achieving* it so high, that they essentially brand every academic decision with which they disagree as an *ultra vires* act. Thus, they label as *improper* the use of Foundation funds to support 'public policy programs other than training for government service,' 'most kinds of academic research,' and programs focused on 'domestic issues.' They claim that the University has violated the terms of the Certificate through quintessentially academic choices, such as the School's decision to build its faculty through joint appointments in other scholarly disciplines."[35]

Bill Robertson counters this by saying the "foundation money was paying for those joint appointments as well as underwriting expenses in other departments" without paying attention to the original mandate and without any discussion with or even disclosure to the family members of the board.[36]

"This still makes me angry," says Seth Lapidow. "We were *never* trying to dictate what they could teach. They do have freedom in that regard. But they wanted that academic freedom to extend to using Robertson money for anything that they thought helped Princeton, rather than the mission. That is not what Justice Frankfurter was talking about. Nonsense."[37]

Celebrating the Woodrow Wilson School

There is no question that the Woodrow Wilson School is among the most highly regarded schools of international relations in the world. A brochure prepared in 2006, in commemoration of its 75th year and, incidentally, amidst the apex of acrimony in the lawsuit, explains, "Professionals from all areas of the discipline of public affairs play a vital role in the life of the Woodrow Wilson School program. Leading figures in national and international government are invited to give lectures and participate in classes, seminars, and conferences during each academic year."

Littered throughout the booklet are photographs of people who have spoken at the school, such as: Bill Clinton, Condoleezza Rice, and Lt. Gen. David H. Petraeus, who is a graduate of the Wilson school, as well as Colin Powell and Kofi Annan, and many others. "Students have the opportunity to meet with many of the speakers on a more personal, informal basis," the publication says. "Post-lecture dinners allow students whose academic focus is similar to the speaker's area of expertise to have one-on-one conversations where specific questions or points of interest not covered in the main lecture can be discussed. These and other kinds of opportunities at the School provide invaluable personal and professional development experiences to future generations of public service leaders."[38]

As for the employment issue, the brochure gives the impression that graduating students into the world of foreign affairs is a high priority for the Woodrow Wilson School. "The Office of Graduate Career Services... organizes preparatory sessions for the U.S. Department of State's Foreign Service Officer written and oral examinations and the U.S. Government's Presidential Management Fellows Program interviews. It also co-hosts job fairs and coordinates recruiting visits by prospective employers such as the World Bank, International Monetary Fund, U.S. Department of the Treasury, Central Intelligence Agency, U.S. Office of Management and Budget, U.S. Government Accountability Office, Congressional Research Service, Federal Reserve Bank of New York, RAND, and Catholic Relief Services."[39]

About two years into the lawsuit, McDonough had what he calls an "aha" moment, a jolt that provided him with a nail-hit-square-on-the-head response to the lawsuit's allegations. In 2004 Secretary of State Colin Powell was speaking at the School when a student asked what kept him up at night when he was trying to juggle all the problems of the world while focusing on how to apply his diplomatic skills to the task of keeping the

United States both peaceful and strong. In response, Powell said nothing about the threat of nuclear war or the bigger issues that most of us would think would worry him. "It's the softer things that don't make headlines," Powell said. "Rule of law, ending corruption, going after disease, clean water, food for people, teaching your people the skills they need in the 21st century. This is the essence of my work and my foreign policy."[40]

"The reason this was an 'aha' moment," McDonough says, "is that at this point we're still raw from 9/11, and here's the Secretary of State essentially identifying *every one* of the research centers at Princeton that are under attack by the Robertson lawsuit. Powell is saying that these issues constitute the essence of foreign policy." Two years later, David Petraeus, the four-star Army general, who would later serve as the director of the Central Intelligence Agency, arrived at Princeton to send the same message as Powell's—that it's a lot of the "softer things" that make up foreign policy in the 21st century.[41] "So," says McDonough, "if we were doubting the appropriateness about our academic judgments,"—and the lawsuit might well have planted plenty of seeds of doubt—"we had the Secretary of State and the nation's most prominent general, as well as a lot of others, saying we were on the right path."[42]

As McDonough celebrates the breadth of the program, the lawsuit has also required him to defend it, as well. He points out, "The gift has two purposes: one, strengthen the government; two, pay money to Princeton. And one informs the other." As for the complaint that not enough people enter government service from the school's ranks, he asks, "Does anybody presume that 100 percent of the students at a school come out doing the exact same thing as one another? That wouldn't be a very robust education. We can't get upset if one of our graduates is a writer."

Or, he might have said, a musician. The celebrated oboist, Joseph Robinson, a 1966 graduate of the Wilson School,[43] captured the attention of the plaintiffs as they were examining just where the alumni were ending up. Presumably, a professional orchestra is not the career destination Charles and Marie Robertson had in mind.[44]

This line of thinking was a lead-up to what McDonough calls his second "aha" moment.

"Think about World War II and how we did this in this country." By "this," he was referring to the educated professionals, already deep into their careers, who served the war effort. "We had leaders in industry and leaders in finance back then who were commissioned into the armed forces. They were the classic *in-and-outers*. They were called at a time of crisis. They served. And then they left. And they might have been called back." McDonough is thinking of the Korean War era here. "And one of the things this school was attempting to do was to prepare those people who might leave and go, for example, to U.S. Steel, who would be sufficiently educated to serve at a time of need. It envisioned *in-and-outers*." As for how that flows into today's mission: "*This* was the goal, as opposed to the first jobs taken."

Does this make any sense? The foundation's governing document doesn't say or imply anything to support an in-and-out concept.

McDonough is prepared for the objection. "The already-existing school"—the graduate program at the Wilson School was established before the Robertson gift made it financially sound—"was already contributing these people before." From that perspective, Princeton wasn't doing anything new, and felt that Charles Robertson, even though he wanted to emphasize that students would directly enter government service, didn't want to change that.

Princeton may have relied in part on a memo written by Robertson in December 1960, in which he offered several curriculum recommendations of the enterprise that was then gestating in his mind. Princeton no doubt took note of Robertson's desire to ensure that the course of study would *not* be "limited to areas pertinent only to foreign service," that there was a "need for an understanding of the problems and aims of labor," and an intellectual grasp of "the effect on policy of scientific (including missile) development." Pertinent to Princeton's defense on this matter in the lawsuit would be the senior Robertson's early recommendations to take into account the need for "a thorough knowledge of the history, political institutions, economy, etc. of the U.S."[45]

Seth Lapidow will have nothing of this. "McDonough's *aha* moment was finding a way to justify what they were doing for years without any thought at all. Finding a *post-hoc* justification for an action is not a substitute for doing what they were supposed to do in the first place."[46]

More specifically, then, on the topic of where the graduates were actually finding work, McDonough provides two reports with graphs, cumulatively covering the years from 2002 to 2007, which compared the program at Princeton with those at five other universities: Harvard, Johns Hopkins, George Washington, Georgetown, and American.

One graph showed the Woodrow Wilson School to be at the top of the category of graduates taking their first jobs in public affairs and the nonprofit sector; the school had a success rate of 85 percent during that period, while second-place Georgetown University had just over 72 percent. The other graph displayed the percentage of those taking their first jobs in the federal government, a foreign government, and state and local governments. Again, Princeton was in the lead with 44 percent, while second-place American University had just over 43 percent.[47] Moreover, in 2008 *U.S. News* ranked the school fourth overall of programs that granted a Masters in Public Affairs behind Syracuse, Harvard and Indiana.[48]

Despite the defensive dance, evidence shows that there was always an understanding at Princeton that the central idea was to get people into the federal government. The minutes of a 1965 board meeting recorded that the university-designated trustees recognized a need to do "everything possible to increase the number of graduates taking positions with the Federal Government."[49]

Charles Robertson often voiced his disappointment in the numbers while he was alive. Then, years later, John L. Palmer, a University Professor and Dean Emeritus of the Maxwell School of Syracuse University, the top-ranked school of public affairs in the United States,[50] was also unimpressed. In the mid-1990s, well before the lawsuit, Palmer was part of an external team that had, at Princeton's request, conducted a review of the

Wilson School, an update of the analysis conducted two decades earlier. The results weren't good.

A decade later, during the lawsuit, Palmer was again asked to assess the School's accomplishments, and that assessment was just as dismal. "Although the School has high academic qualities, it has had considerably less success than one would expect, given the resources it had available from the Robertson Foundation, in recruiting men and women with a strong commitment to careers in government service." Also, he says, "The school has had considerably less success than one would expect in channeling its graduate students into careers in government service. Plenty of evidence exists for that conclusion when the school's performance was put into both an historical and comparative context." Palmer's rigorous academic scrutiny supported the family's familiar refrain.

Palmer commented on the graphs that McDonough referred to showing how well the school was doing. Recall that the graphs showed the percentage of students who were offered employment in the government and the nonprofit sectors. "As soon as you throw in the 'and,' we're in a different ballpark," Palmer says.

As far as the improvement in the school's performance during the lawsuit, Palmer says that it only goes to show what they could have done earlier if they had tried.

"When I agreed to serve as an expert consultant to the plaintiffs in the case, I had only one preconceived notion; preconceived in the sense that it was based on my earlier experience with the external review team. All of us on the team agreed that Princeton could have had a lot more to show performance-wise for the resources it had been given. Once I understood the mission against the backdrop of Princeton's performance, I concluded the university was culpable, both for failing to abide by the mission and for concealing its failure."

Palmer doesn't know what the outcome would have been had the case gone to trial because of the inherent uncertainties surrounding the legal technicalities on which Princeton was beginning to base its arguments. "But," he says, "there was no doubt in my mind that they violated the spirit of the agreement. What Robertson wanted could not have been clearer." The family, Palmer concludes, "had every right to be critical of Princeton's performance."[51]

In a way, it's difficult to imagine. A world-class academic enterprise, with all its renown, finds itself at the center of a bitter controversy. Look at its accomplishments and position in the world of academia. Pause to acknowledge that the Woodrow Wilson School routinely convenes in the classroom so many of the world's leaders of international relations. Do that, and you might be tempted to wonder if this lawsuit was nothing more than a cruel, time-wasting, money-burning joke.

But Bill Robertson does not wonder or doubt. "The graphs combine a lot of things and are misleading," he observed when he saw the data. Also, for him, talking about the school's reputation misses the point, and the explanation that the tasks within the overarching goals of foreign relations have changed, or at least include the "softer things that don't make the headlines," is not a spot-on response to the question of whether Woodrow Wilson School graduates are performing those tasks.

"The question is," Robertson says, "how many students go into the Foreign Service or other areas that are included in what my father intended? And that number is dismal."[52]

With all the tensions growing, an observer might ask why somebody at Princeton didn't just pick up the phone to call Charles Robertson or, later, his son to talk about things. If the national mood had changed so drastically that too few people were interested in entering government service, why couldn't Princeton empirically prove it and make its case? If it was a good idea for other academic departments to benefit from the foundation's largess, especially if they would supplement the internationally focused education of students at the Wilson School, why couldn't Princeton have brought the family members together to explain how that benefit would actually have fit into the original expectations?

Maybe the arguments would not have worked. Or maybe they would have been persuasive. But we'll never know because, according to Robertson and Bob Halligan, who were on the foundation board for years, that kind of open inquiry and discussion never took place.

The general problem here, as is almost always the case when things go wrong—although these days it seems to serve as little more than a management pamphlet cliché—was a lack of communication. That's clear enough, but what many management pamphlets don't take into account is that communication isn't simply a lot of chatter. The quality of the conversations is the product of respect, and when respect is perceived to be absent, not much else matters. It becomes difficult to pick up the phone. As acrimony builds, the divisions grow more acute, real communication diminishes even further, and things inevitably erupt.

Paying the Robertsons' Legal Expenses

In addition to the general agitation brought on by the issues in the lawsuit, Princeton was upset because the family members weren't paying their own legal costs. This lawsuit was the most expensive in the history of nonprofit litigation—and it didn't even get to trial. The bill for each side was about $45 million—a total of $90 million going to lawyers and their expenses. Shirley Tilghman, Princeton's president, said, "It is tragic that this lawsuit required the expenditure of tens of millions of dollars in legal fees that could have and should have been spent on educational and charitable purposes."[53] Both sides lamented the expenditure of money, although each side, by expressing a confidence that it would win in court, apparently was willing to spend whatever would be required.

Peter McDonough was pointed on this matter in a presentation at the Georgetown Law Center. "This lawsuit dramatically impacts three charitable organizations: Princeton University, the Robertson Foundation . . . and the Banbury Fund." Undoubtedly, he crafted that sentence deliberately, as he wanted no one to misunderstand that a third party—the Banbury Fund, the charitable foundation that Charles and Marie Robertson had established in 1946—was footing the plaintiffs' legal bill.

"An unfortunate reality of this case," he wrote, "is that tens of millions of not-for-profit dollars have been redirected to lawyers and litigation expenses, with many millions more seemingly certain to be spent before the trial runs its course. The impact of these transactional costs on Princeton University is significant, of course. Their impact on the Banbury Fund is breathtaking. That private foundation's reported assets, which had topped $50 million, declined by nearly $30 million between 2002 and 2006, and it likely continues to endure an asset drain. The Banbury Fund's Form 990s[54] confirm that it is paying the . . . legal fees and expenses, as well as their public relations bills. Its 2004 submission, for example, lists over $5 million paid to . . . counsel, forensic accountants and public relations firms; its 2006 submission lists over $6.4 million paid just to the Robertson plaintiffs' counsel."

McDonough then expressed disappointment that real charitable causes weren't being helped as much as they could be. "During the first two years after this suit was filed, the Banbury Fund's charitable giving dropped by almost 89%, from a pre-litigation average of $2.42 million to just $271,500 in 2003. In 2004, after Princeton's lawyers made it clear that plaintiffs' use of charitable funds to pay for the litigation would be brought to light at trial in the context of a substantive issue, the Banbury Fund's non-litigation charitable giving rose to $1.59 million. In 2006, the Fund's non-litigation charitable giving declined again . . . to $1.15 million, as Banbury Fund payments to the Robertson plaintiffs' lawyers rose to an average of over $500,000 per month."[55]

With that ominous account, McDonough was teeing up this question: Why in the world was a charity permitted to pay for the lawsuit? Or perhaps something even worse: Was Bill Robertson fraudulently using the public's money for his own personal benefit? For his part, Robertson wonders if McDonough was "lamenting the family's ability to take on Princeton."

But using that $50 million number "is misleading," Robertson says. "The Banbury Fund was valued at that amount in 2000, which was two years *before* the lawsuit began." By 2002, when the lawsuit was filed, the drop in the markets, spurred by the tech bubble collapse, led to a decrease in the fund's value to $34.6 million. By the end of 2006, its value was $23.3 million. Princeton's general counsel, Robertson says, "exaggerated the effect of the lawsuit's costs on the Banbury Fund by about two-thirds."[56]

McDonough argued that the people sitting on the board of the Banbury Fund, all family members, were "disqualified persons" who may have been guilty of "self-dealing."[57] As did Victoria Bjorklund: "I do not understand why individual plaintiffs who were seeking individual remedies were not violating the self-dealing rules."

For nonprofits, an act of self-dealing takes place when a person close to the organization, such as a trustee or a major donor, personally and improperly benefits by the expenditure of the charity's income or assets. "There was more than an incidental benefit to them personally," says Bjorklund, "when they used the assets of this private foundation to pay their legal fees and their public relations fees. I don't know how they got advice—if they did get advice—that this was proper."[58]

Others, outside Princeton, agreed. "It's yet another egregious example of abusing philanthropy for personal gain," Aaron Dorfman, the executive director of the National Committee for Responsive Philanthropy, told *The Chronicle of Philanthropy*. "It shows why we need better self-regulation and better oversight and enforcement. How can they think that using the foundation to pay their legal fees is a legitimate charitable purpose?"[59]

Although the Banbury question ultimately did not figure into the lawsuit, McDonough today says that the issue was not dead. "At trial we were going to argue against the appropriateness of using the Banbury money. We were going to take this position, given how the family used the Banbury Fund." The money was being misused, he maintains, and "the Robertson Foundation would have essentially been turned into Banbury II."

Doug Eakeley says that the Robertsons "should have realized that they had a personal exposure to the IRS for a recoupment of all funds they caused to be expended by the Banbury Fund in an unauthorized way. They were personal legal fees."[60]

That was the position of Princeton's attorneys, but that's not how a lot of other smart people, including the IRS, saw it. If the issue wasn't dead going in, as McDonough contends, it may very well have been killed in court.

In 1962 Charles Robertson, as a director of the Banbury Fund, wrote to the other directors telling them to keep a sharp eye out on the success of the Woodrow Wilson School. "The objective and purpose of the Robertson Foundation is to do everything possible to insure that the program at Princeton achieves the goal which is envisaged for it: viz., that, in due course, the Woodrow Wilson School will become a truly outstanding professional School for the training of top-caliber men and women who are dedicated to the government service, and will . . . contribute in a demonstrable way to the strengthening of our government and to the defense and extension of freedom throughout the world." Robertson then presciently adds, "If substantial numbers of persons trained in the School do not go into government service, or do not remain in government service, or" for any reason "the recipients of the training are unable to achieve positions of major responsibility in the government, then no matter how excellent their training may have been, the basic purpose of the School is not being achieved."[61]

Robertson could not have been more clear or more emphatic about the role he wanted the directors of the Banbury Fund to play in monitoring the results at the Robertson Foundation.

Still, while that directive showed how seriously he wanted to protect the Robertson Foundation's mission, it might not have been sufficient to ensure the IRS's blessing for such a charitable expenditure. Something more would be helpful.

While preparing for the lawsuit, Bill Robertson sought guidance on the question from James Sligar, a partner at the New York law firm Milbank Tweed. In an opinion letter to the family, Sligar wrote, "Since the family-elected trustees" of the Robertson Foundation, "being in a minority, do not have access to the funds of the Robertson Foundation to support such a suit, they have sought assistance from Banbury and Banbury has responded by agreeing to pay" the fees. "By applying assets to pay the related legal fees," he wrote, "Banbury seeks to protect the Robertson Foundation from fiduciary breaches by the Princeton-appointed trustees."

Sligar noted that "Banbury's payments of legal fees promote the charitable and educational purposes for which the Robertson Foundation was established," and would not violate the self-dealing rules that prohibit payments to certain people close to a charitable organization. Then, because "Banbury was created with intentionally broad corporate purposes," he concluded, "applying assets to further the Robertson Foundation's mission is within Banbury's exempt purpose."[62]

In addition, at least four IRS Private Letter Rulings and one Revenue Ruling also supported the Robertsons' position.[63] Each document approved a situation where the directors of a nonprofit were reimbursed for legal expenses. One Private Letter Ruling said, "The Foundation's proposal to indemnify its director/co-trustees for the cost of any legal expenses associated with any suit related to their services . . . would not constitute acts of self dealing."[64] Another said that a foundation's trustees are permitted "reasonable financial protection" so they can conduct their activities "without unreasonable risk of personal liability for their official actions."[65] A lawsuit to protect the interests of a foundation's mission would appear to be an "official action." The even more applicable IRS Revenue Ruling came to the same conclusion.[66]

Marcus Owens, one of Princeton's expert witnesses and a former head of the exempt organization division at the IRS, said he conceptually had no problem with a charity paying legal fees if they are in accordance with its exempt purposes. The following is from Owens's deposition, conducted by Seth Lapidow:

Q:　　In your expert opinion, are the monies Princeton is expending to defend this action in accord with the exempt organization's purpose?

A:　　Yes.

Q:　　These are all perfectly fine?

A:　　Correct.

Q:　　Including the money they are paying you, right?

A:　　Correct. Absolutely correct.

Nevertheless, for Owens, the same idea didn't apply to the Banbury Fund. He said that the Robertsons would wrongfully benefit:

Q: Do any of the four plaintiffs in this litigation have any personal
       or private interest in the outcome of this litigation that you are
       aware of?

A: Yes.

Q: What?

A: If they win they stand a chance of avoiding some private founda-
       tion taxes.

Q: Explain that to me please.

A: If they win, and the Banbury Fund's involvement financing their
       participation is found by the court to be appropriate, then those
       expenses which the Banbury Foundation fund paid other than
       those in which they assumed an obligation of the individual,
       would be appropriate qualifying distributions and would not be
       acts of self dealing.[67]

This exchange seems like pretzel logic. Owens appears to be con-
tending that the payments constituted self-dealing because the Banbury
directors would receive a personal benefit if the payments were found *not*
to be self-dealing.

In his own deposition, Bill Josephson said that Owens's testimony
wrongly focused on the individual plaintiffs' non-existent personal benefit or private inurement by Banbury paying the legal and other fees.
"Marc's statements are riddled with personal, personal, personal. And I
don't agree with any of that. The family directors of Robertson are acting in their capacity as directors and officers. And I believe they have an
obligation because they sincerely believe the allegations in the amended
complaint are true, and they are doing it [pursuing legal action] for the
benefit of the Robertson Foundation. They are not doing it for any personal benefit to themselves. And I frankly am offended by the way Marc
has tried to twist the situation. It seems to me that in this respect, at least
in his expert opinion, he's acting as a hired gun."[68]

Ron Malone says attacking Banbury was nothing more than "a litigation tactic by Princeton to change the focus to Bill Robertson personally."

Referring to the 1962 letter by Charles Robertson, Malone says, "When Charlie and Marie ran the Banbury Fund, they made it clear that one of its purposes was to supervise the performance of Princeton. The Robertson Foundation and the Banbury Fund were sister organizations, founded and funded by the same people. During Charlie's lifetime, he made it clear that the Banbury Fund was empowered to conduct studies on how well Princeton was carrying out the Robertson Foundation mission."[69]

One basic question, also connected to how the Banbury Fund played into the lawsuit, was addressed early on. It is the first question asked by a court before a lawsuit can proceed: Did the Robertsons have *standing* to bring the lawsuit? For that matter, as the Banbury Fund was the client of Shartsis Friese, Malone's law firm, who was actually doing the suing? While it is true that the parents donated the money, did anyone else have the right to sue Princeton?

"The family trustees of the Robertson Foundation brought the litigation," explains Malone. "They were the only ones with standing. Just like with the board of directors of a corporation, the minority directors can bring a lawsuit for breach of fiduciary duty. The Banbury Fund would not have had standing to file the lawsuit."

So how does that square with the fund paying the legal fees? "The Banbury Fund is paying to enforce the charter of a sister organization. The wrinkle comes in because Banbury isn't the plaintiff, but some of the directors of Banbury are also directors of the Robertson Foundation." As Malone puts it, Princeton saw it this way: *"These people"*—by whom he meant the family members—*"had a legal obligation to pay the lawyers because they were the plaintiffs. And if that's true*—and they skipped over the if-that's-true part—*that means a charity that they control is paying a personal obligation for them. That's improper."* To that, Malone says, "I agree that it's improper for a charity to pay the personal legal obligations of an insider. But that's not what was going on. The individual plaintiffs never had a legal obligation to pay the expenses of the fund."

Malone made clear that he is "totally comfortable" with the fact that Banbury paid the legal fees to enforce the terms of the Robertson Foundation's gift.[70]

Seth Lapidow says, "Doug Eakeley was just spewing self-serving nonsense." In addition to the other IRS determinations on the subject, Lapidow refers to a 2002 Private Letter Ruling involving the Manhattan Eye, Ear & Throat Hospital. "There is ample authority that payment of fees in this context is perfectly okay. And they were not personal legal fees," as Eakeley had described them. "There is no basis for this claim," says Lapidow. "Not one of the family members was obligated to pay anything. The engagement letters were crystal clear."[71]

In any case, Princeton didn't push the issue, even though McDonough reiterates that it would have been brought up at trial. "That may be," Bill Robertson points out, "but the fact of the matter is that the judge allowed it."[72]

Whenever the lawsuit is discussed today, those closest to Princeton's side don't mind bringing up how wrong they feel it was for Banbury to have provided the funding. Even though the rules on self-dealing would have been the key attack weapon, Princeton's narrative now seems more personal than legal, as it tries to highlight what it sees as an essential unfairness when a family doesn't have to use its own money to pay for litigation its members initiate. "They had no personal skin in the game,"[73] said Robert Durkee, undoubtedly mirroring the views of others at Princeton.

But it is also true that no one individual or group of individuals at Princeton had personal skin in the game, either. In addition, insurance reimbursed approximately $15 million of the university's legal expenses. "Not only did we have the law on our side," says Bill Robertson, "we were able to financially level the playing field a little. Even so, Banbury's assets were a pittance compared to Princeton's. They hoped to strangle us with money. Too bad for them."[74]

Broadly Defining "Academic Freedom"

As unusual as the case was and as startling as the charges were, the Robertsons were certain their case was solid. "They most definitely had a case," Ron Malone says. "Princeton," was giving them and the foundation's mission "nothing more than lip service. I saw all the board's meeting minutes and the attachments, and it was obvious that Princeton knew exactly what Charlie Robertson and his wife wanted."

Malone says, "Princeton was doing an intellectual dance with them. They wanted to make the Robertsons feel like they were doing their best to carry out the mission when in fact what they were doing was reading *to themselves*," he says, "interpreting the mission much more broadly: *Build the best school that we can and do the best academic work that we can with your money. Sure, Charlie Robertson was clear about what he wanted, but this is Princeton University, and we do what we want, the way we want, because we are a great university blessed with academic freedom.* That's what they were saying to themselves, but didn't dare say to the donors."

It was what the attorneys learned during discovery, however, Malone says, that "blew the case open."[75]

Frank Cialone, a Shartsis Friese attorney who works with Ron Malone, explains that it got really interesting as he dug into the issue of how Princeton interpreted its leeway to spend money. "It started off where we thought they weren't doing a very good job. The results weren't very good. We looked at the staggering amount of money and the number of people going into government service, and it just didn't line up. So our initial thought was mission creep; that they wanted to do more around the edges of the mission," recalls Cialone.

"But then, when we looked more deeply—my job was to follow the money—we saw that it was more than that they wanted academic freedom. We found huge flows of money going to the wrong places." Cialone described what he called "the treaty." "It wasn't written down, but the treaty concept was an understanding that anyone affiliated with the Wilson School would get all of the expenses paid for by the foundation."[76]

For the Robertsons, the case moved from being about missed opportunities on Princeton's part to intentionally and secretly using funds in conscious violation of a donor's wishes.

Harold Shapiro was the president of Princeton from 1988 to 2001. "It was during his time at Princeton," Cialone, who took Shapiro's deposition, says, "when many of the improper decisions about using the foundation money were being made. I asked him—remember, he was president of the foundation for many years—what the purpose of the foundation is. I'm paraphrasing, but he said, *To do whatever directly or indirectly that which supports the graduate program at the Woodrow Wilson School at the dean's discretion.* So I asked him some questions about that. What about supporting the politics department? *Sure. If the dean thinks that will help the Wilson School, great.* What about supporting the undergraduate program? *That's a higher standard,* Cialone remembers Shapiro saying, *because the focus is on the graduate program.* Would the dean need to ask anyone else? *No.* No? So, the higher standard means the dean needs to ask himself . . . like . . . twice? Or what do you mean?" Cialone asked.

"Finally, I started using examples, some of which were real, such as paying the wife of a professor to work at the central administration office of the university. That is, she had nothing at all to do with the Wilson School."

In the following portion of the deposition transcript, Cialone is asking the questions and Shapiro is answering:

Q.   In your view, would it have been appropriate to use foundation resources to hire somebody to work in the central university administration in order to attract her husband as a professor?

A.   As with other issues like that, it all depends on whether that would work to strengthen the school or not.[77]

"The foundation," Cialone points out, "was *already* paying overhead charges to support the appropriate portion of the school's expenses at the central administration office. But, because she's married to a professor at the Wilson School they made a package deal—and the foundation was paying for it. Secretly." Bill Robertson, who served on the foundation board, was not told about this.[78]

Cialone continued to search for the elusive line dividing academic freedom and wanton spending:

Q.   So, in your view, for example, if you had a professor of public affairs who really liked football, would it be okay to use the foundation assets to hire a better football coach?

A.   It sounds like an exaggerated question, but the general principle is focusing on strengthening the school.

Q.   So, yes?

A.   Yes.[79]

When asked about this, Peter McDonough defends Shapiro's position. "This was about academic freedom and trying to be extreme and provocative in the context of spending." Doug Eakeley adds, "If you want an academic star to come to the program, you're going to try to find a job for that academic spouse." McDonough again: "This goes to the question of what the edges of acceptability are for achieving the mission."[80]

The plaintiffs and the defendants didn't see those edges in the same way. By this point Bill Robertson was seething at what he took as proof of unbridled infidelity to his parents' wishes. He had already called Princeton "an Ivy League Enron,"[81] and this new knowledge was only making things worse.

McDonough says that, as Princeton's general counsel, he was often asked questions, many of them along the lines of the hypothetical nature as represented by the question on football. "So here I am, the general counsel of the 'Ivy League Enron,' and my colleagues and friends are asking, *What's going on here?* And I respond that this isn't about a claim that the dean has a Mercedes that she's funding from the Robertson Foundation. No. This is a claim that we are doing *research* with Robertson Foundation dollars." McDonough pauses, and then says, "And we *should* be doing research."[82]

Because Princeton equated the mission with academic freedom, it defended the spending to support that freedom, even if it was only tenuously connected to the Wilson School. Many teachers who weren't at the Wilson School were being paid by the foundation in what was called a "joint appointment system," which, as it turns out, worked well for departments outside of the Wilson School. Don Stokes, the Wilson School dean, wrote in a 1991 memo that the joint appointment system "has been highly beneficial to the surrounding social science departments. The faculties of the Economics and Politics Department would be

no more than two-thirds their current size without the expansion of the
faculty made possible by the Robertson gift."[83] Stokes apparently saw the
expansion of 50 percent of other university departments, on the foundation's dime, as a good thing.

The claim of academic freedom was turning into one that came with
a practically blank check, with no oversight permitted the people who
cared most about how the money would be used, who cared most about
the Robertson legacy.

The Audit

Because of what they saw as so many unrelated financial expenditures,
family members commissioned a thorough forensic examination of all
the costs undertaken by the foundation. PricewaterhouseCoopers, the
largest of the big four accounting firms, [84] conducted the review and
found trouble.

"Internal controls are unreliable at best," the report began.
"Unrestricted and restricted expenses for the Woodrow Wilson School
were commingled." Money covering undergraduate faculty salaries
was mixed together with salaries for faculty at the Wilson School.
"Furthermore," the report charged, "Princeton has not established appropriate criteria for determining the allowability of expenditures charged
to the Robertson Foundation." On a five-level internal control scale at
PricewaterhouseCoopers, the foundation received the lowest rating:
"unreliable."

The accounting firm said that Princeton charged administrative costs
to the foundation "while it charged the same costs indirectly to the federal government." This practice "violates" the federal "Cost Accounting
Standards 502," and "is neither consistent with" federal requirements "nor
Princeton's Disclosure Statements." Princeton also transferred income
and assets from the foundation that "neither meet the expense recognition criteria under generally accepted accounting principles nor fulfill the
donor-imposed restriction in the Robertson Foundation's Certificate of
Incorporation."

One area of contention between the family and the university was something called the "Graduate Funding Agreement with non-Woodrow Wilson School Departments." During the 1990s, the Sociology, Politics, and Economics Departments at Princeton were having difficulty attracting enough students and were looking for ways to strengthen their programs. The school agreed to help. The finances of that commitment, however, according to the report, were improperly charged to the foundation. "The Robertson Foundation Board was not informed of the Graduate Funding Agreement, which was for fellowships" in departments not in the school. "Furthermore," the agreement was not separately disclosed in the financial tables provided to the Foundation Board."[85]

This prompts Seth Lapidow to describe his own "aha" moment. "I learned of the agreement when we won our first motion to compel discovery; Princeton, after stonewalling us for over a year, had to produce documents. In that first bunch of boxes, I found an internal document that showed the Graduate Funding Agreement. That was the first time I really knew they were secretly stealing money and that we could prove it."[86]

The PricewaterhouseCoopers report also tracked costs from 1996 to 2003, and found that while Princeton's total costs grew by 22 percent, the foundation's expenses grew by 193 percent—a rate of almost nine times faster. The school's growth in the number of students during that time was six percent. Even more dramatic, overhead costs went through the roof. "The average ratio of overhead over total program activities was 153 percent," the report calculated. "We are not aware that any other universities are charging indirect costs to sponsors at a rate of over 100 percent."

Indirect costs are overhead expenses paid for by the university and are deducted pro-rata from a program's budget to cover those costs. Each department or program then reimburses the university for those costs. At Princeton, the combined overhead costs significantly exceeded any other expense items exclusive of capital construction by an average factor of three times.

In all, the analysis—which took into account: 1) the lack of internal controls, 2) improper administrative charges, 3) improper income transfers, 4) the negative impact on overhead from non-assignable program costs, 5) the Graduate Funding Agreement, 6) the over-allocation of building construction costs, 7) double-charged depreciation, and 9) over-charged overhead—identified $217 million that was spent incorrectly.

PricewaterhouseCoopers also concluded that Princeton failed to ensure that donor restrictions were followed. [87]

Marcus Owens was asked in deposition about the diversion of funds unearthed by the analysis and how that relates to good governance. What follows is a portion of that testimony:

Q.   If Princeton, through its designated trustees, had diverted $200 million or more from the Robertson Foundation to purposes outside those within the foundation documents of the Robertson Foundation, would that comport with good governance, in your opinion?

A.   I think the relevant question before one can answer that would be: Why was the so-called diversion undertaken? In other words, the reason why would be an indicator of whether it was a wise decision or not a wise decision, whether it was good governance or not.

Q.   So if it was a wise decision to divert $200 million beyond the charitable purposes of the foundation, that would comport with good governance, in your opinion?

A.   If it was wise—if it was a result of a reasonable decision of the board because of compelling circumstances, then I believe that good governance would suggest that a decision of that sort would still comport with appropriate governance principles.

Q.   But that would be based on, as I'm understanding your testimony, that there would be discussion at the board level about doing so, correct?

A.   Correct.

Q.   So if it happened in secret, that wouldn't comport with good governance, right? If there was no board discussion about it, right?

A.   Correct.[88]

"It was nothing like that," say Peter McDonough and Doug Eakeley. "There was some inadvertent misspending, but only at the extreme margin," says Eakeley.

McDonough points out that the "most expensive experts on both sides were forensic accountants, and we had to essentially revisit every dollar paid since 1962 from the foundation to the University. *Every dollar.* One of the challenges is that we had a pre-existing graduate school and undergraduate program in the Woodrow Wilson School. And we had, by and large, a pre-existing faculty, who were jointly appointed in the Wilson School and academic departments."

McDonough then describes a mental schematic of four quadrants. "You have the Woodrow Wilson School, undergraduate and graduate programs, and then you have a faculty that teach in economics and also teach at the Wilson School. Now, you've got a supporting organization that funds only one quadrant—the graduate program of just the Woodrow Wilson School. The way spending was allocated, McDonough says, "was complicated to read but simple in concept. It was a rough justice formula,"—known as the Bowen Formula[89]—he says, by which he means that while no audit would be able to fully line up every dollar of what went to the school to support the graduate program, the formula would allow an auditor to follow the money plausibly enough. McDonough emphatically points out, "Charles Robertson, who was the foundation board chair when the formula was implemented, agreed to that concept."

"And that's what's in place up until the lawsuit," says McDonough. "But now we have to look back. They take this let's-audit-it approach. And hence this opportunity for endless complaints and endless revisionist history—and in some cases what we might call errors in accounting. It's just inevitable." McDonough also says that the lawsuit gave rise to "build a better mousetrap," by which he means a modernizing of the formula.[90]

Well before the lawsuit was settled, Princeton agreed to pay not $217 million, as the university denied that so much was misallocated over the years, but a little less than $800,000. Even though the sum was not large, the idea of retuning money made news. The *Trenton Times* said of Shirley Tilghman, "The President of Princeton University has admitted in court documents that $750,000"—it was actually $782,375—"earmarked by a foundation for the Woodrow Wilson School was diverted to other uses and that she kept the diversion secret from the family who had donated the funds."[91] The *Wall Street Journal*, noted, "The repayment marks a turnabout for Princeton; at one point last year, the school argued that university money—not Robertson funds—was used for the graduate student expenses."

Even that, Princeton claimed, was properly allocated. The money was spent on programs that were "closely related" to the Wilson School. The university said, in predictably protective but bland legalese, that it "was fully compliant with the purposes of the foundation and plainly authorized by its charter. The only 'error,'" Princeton admitted to, "was failing to disclose the payments to the Robertsons." The university also said that it had corrected the problem with "improved notification and governance procedures."

Robert Durkee was confident that the university would press on: "We continue to feel strongly we're on very solid ground in the case overall."[92]

Frank Cialone said, "It's about time."

As one might imagine, that relatively small reimbursement did nothing to assuage the feelings of the Robertsons.

An Arc of Embezzlement?

"In the quietude of their own offices," Ron Malone says, "these people asked themselves, *How should I spend this money?* knowing it all gets buried in reports to the family." And then, in response to McDonough's comment about the dean not buying a Mercedes from the foundation's bank account, Malone continues, "No, this is not about whether a person is a criminal, but it is very much about whether he or she has integrity." He says when people are confronted with important decisions, they should ask not only if the proposed course of action is legal, but also if it is ethical. "How would your answer that it wasn't legal or ethical read on the front page of the *Washington Post* or the *New York Times*? If you wouldn't like how your answer would read, you shouldn't do it because it is not right. If these people had followed that kind of moral guide, they would not have done what they did."[93]

Seth Lapidow speaks of the "classic arc of embezzlement" and describes it this way: "The first time an embezzler takes money, it's a very hard thing. Yet there's generally a reason. There's an illness or a debt or a gambling problem. Some externality that, in his mind requires him to take money he knows is not his. At this point he knows it is not his money. The second time is a little easier. The third time is easier still. And as the arc goes, it becomes easier and easier and easier. And then, after the embezzlement has been going on for some time, it's all of a sudden *his* money. The sense of entitlement has been building. And at the end of the arc of embezzlement, the person simply takes as much as he wants because it's his money. At this point he feels like he's entitled to it. The guilt and hesitation he felt at the beginning have long since dissipated." Lapidow then adds one additional step to the process. "While the embezzler is stealing the other person's or entity's assets, because he feels so entitled to them, he also wants to husband his own assets."[94]

Eakeley says that when Lapidow used the word *embezzlement* in court, "The judge would throw back at him the word *bloviate*, a word Lapidow had used earlier in the litigation. Lapidow acknowledges that he and the judge discussed that word, but only once, when, as he says, "to describe Doug Eakeley in action."[95]

"The money went to the intended purpose," Eakeley insists, "which was to maintain and support the graduate program at the Woodrow Wilson School. Embezzlement requires intent, and the deans were extremely cautious to husband the money of the foundation and apply it to the graduate program of the Woodrow Wilson School."[96]

Still, Lapidow is convinced that Princeton embezzled the foundation's assets—not for anyone's personal use, but that it was embezzlement nonetheless—and recalls how some years before the lawsuit, when the university was going through tight financial times, top university officials were asking, since there was so much money in the foundation, whether it would be possible to divert some of the Robertson money to other purposes at Princeton.[97]

Lapidow might have been referring to what Princeton president William Bowen meant when he was asked to do just that.

"I see essentially no possibility of receiving authorization to spend funds of the Robertson Foundation for purposes other than those for which they were given," Bowen acknowledged. "This would require a unanimous agreement of all those who serve on the board. In retrospect, it may well be that less restrictive language"—the language morphed from "ambiguous" in Robert Goheen's telling to "restrictive" in Bowen's—"should have been incorporated in the charter of the Foundation. But when Bob Goheen and his colleagues of that time were working all this out, circumstances were different and they proceeded as they thought best at the time."

The request had come to Bowen in an audacious memo, written in 1973 by Sheldon Hackney, the university's provost at the time. "In the very long run," he wrote, "it would be a good thing if the Foundation itself were to be dissolved and the funds given to the University earmarked for the same purposes for which they are currently being used." For Lapidow, this was proof of Princeton's perfidy. "The memo indicates that since the early 1970s, the University has had a long-term goal to subvert the intent of the donors."[98]

After explaining his response to the Hackney memo, Bowen said, "In any event, I have had enough experience with Charlie and Bill to know that they hold tightly to original promises. Indeed, even to raise the question with them would seem to me likely to be counterproductive in the extreme." He then ominously said, "I think we should encourage the School to undertake appointments and responsibilities that will benefit the University as well as the School itself."

The Robertsons then asserted that Richard Spies, Princeton's vice president for finance and administration, told the foundation's university-appointed trustees—but not the family-appointed trustees—that money was being siphoned off to help the rest of the university. They also discovered a memo in which Spies wrote, "The Foundation agreed to increase the amount of support it provided for faculty costs associated with some of the independent research units that are affiliated with the School. This enabled us to both expand the level of activity in those Centers, which benefits faculty and students to the School, and reduce the charge to general University funds for those programs."[99]

This was a smoking gun: as the Robertson attorneys saw it, a clear and secret directive to spend Robertson Foundation money outside the Woodrow Wilson School. It appears that while Robert Goheen claimed to be upset about the language in the governing document, William Bowen was more worried about the need to tell the family that Princeton actually didn't want to adhere to it. The message: *Don't ask. Just do it.* Did this complete the arc of embezzlement?

Seth Lapidow attributes much of Princeton's defense of spending the foundation's money to what came after the Bowen Formula was revised. After a review, it became the Slaughter Formula, named after Anne-Marie Slaughter, the dean of the Woodrow Wilson School during the lawsuit. What Peter McDonough characterizes as "building a better mousetrap," as he did when referring to the Slaughter Formula, Seth Lapidow characterizes as "a funding mechanism so corrupt that the judge entered an order forbidding Princeton to mention it at trial or use it in any way to show their good faith." Indeed, the order is unambiguous: "Neither the Slaughter Proposal" nor anything else relating to how the formula was derived is "to be offered as evidence at trial."[100]

Why? "Because," Lapidow explains, "Princeton refused to disclose how they came up with the formula and simply rammed it down the throats of the family and foundation. It was the apex of arrogance."[101]

Kenneth Logan, the other lead co-counsel in addition to Doug Eakeley, and now retired partner at Simpson Thacher & Bartlett, denies any "stonewalling on Princeton's part. The effort was to be quite transparent. "I'm sure," he says, "that any change"—in the formula—"was construed by Bill Robertson and his lawyers as either inadequate or an admission that there must have been something wrong before. It may have been contentious, but there was in no sense any effort to hide what was going on and why."[102]

Even so, the fact of the matter remained: If Princeton wanted to defend its spending decisions on the basis of the Slaughter Formula, it would have to permit the Robertson attorneys to learn precisely how the formula was derived—a level of transparency that Princeton ultimately thought would be too high a price to pay.

Lapidow furthermore insists that the intent behind the activities of the University members of the Robertson board was the kind that Princeton didn't want to own. "They knew that if they asked the family to extend the ambit of the gift, the family would balk. They decided to do it anyway after Spies asked if he could spread the money around."[103]

Shirley Tilghman defended the decisions to permit such diversions as part of the university's quest for, yes, academic freedom. From her deposition on that point:

Q.   I want to make sure that you understand my question, which is not whether the foundation board can say you can do it or not, but can the foundation board say you can do it, but not on the foundation's nickel?

A.   No.

Tilghman's response may have been driven her understanding that the quest for academic freedom was a higher ideal than the founding document's directives.

Q.   And isn't it true that the more broadly you define public service, the more academic freedom the university will have in shaping the program of the Wilson School; isn't that just true as a matter of logic?

A.   It is true as a matter of logic.[104]

Princeton would not back down. Peter McDonough says, reiterating his thoughts about how Princeton was not an Ivy League Enron, "The embezzlement was embezzlement, if you will, toward academic and intellectual pursuits—not embezzlement toward lining anyone's pockets or living in a bigger house. And so the word is provocative and misleading."[105]

Once the thread began to unravel, the concept of "academic free-dom," the plaintiffs' attorneys worried, could provide sufficient cover so that there would be no end to ignoring the directives expressed in the originating document. Even though it was brought up as only a hypothetical possibility, that the Robertson gift might one day provide the funds for the football coach's salary seemed alarmingly real.

A New Voice for the Plaintiffs

The hypothetical became more tangible when Jessie Lee Washington appeared in this drama. Her routine examination of an organ fund in the Office of Religious Life at Princeton turned out to eerily forecast what the Robertsons would later discover in the lawsuit.

After graduating from Bryn Mawr and a stint at Ernst & Young as an auditor and computer consultant, in the early 1990s Washington went to Princeton as a consultant in computing and information technology. She then left to earn an M.S. in nonprofit administration from Drexel and an M.B.A. from Dartmouth's Amos Tuck School. In early 1998 she returned to Princeton where she stayed for five years as a special projects manager and a research analyst. In the meantime she joined the Army Reserves.

"In the spring and summer of 2002," Washington says, "I was tasked to research a group of restricted funds—endowment accounts—for the Office of Religious Life." She discovered "about ten funds" in which she "found significant problems. The income wasn't going where it should." In her work, which soon after this time extended beyond that one department, she "discovered many cases where the university knowingly allocated or reallocated money to benefit another department or the general funds of the university." In August of that year, shortly after the Robertsons filed their lawsuit—but independently of that—Washington took her findings to senior members of the treasurer's office. She was asked not to make her report public. The people there, she said, "blew us off."[106] Apparently, Princeton was worried that this analysis, completed so proximately to the time of Robertson allegations, would harm its position in the lawsuit—and, no doubt, in the court of public opinion.

"When I read the article about the lawsuit in the *New York Times*," Washington remembers, "something sparked in my mind." She connected what she was finding in her work and what was being alleged in the dispute. "I saw Princeton deciding where money should go and ignoring donor intent, which is what I understood to be the general issue that Mr. Robertson was raising."

That worried Washington. "I felt that if they could do it to Mr. Robertson, then how easy would it be for Princeton to misallocate one lone woman's check to maintain a pipe organ in memory of her brother?" In her research she had discovered that a $5,000 donation toward the maintenance of the university's pipe organ had been diverted to the general fund. "The donors to many of the funds I looked into were deceased, and so I could see that Princeton could decide, for whatever reason, to allocate money for a different purpose."

Washington submitted her report again in February 2003. "I undertook an extensive review," she wrote, "of the endowment accounts established to support religious life at Princeton . . . I made several findings . . . including inadequate information systems, poor business processes, and questionable actions. I believe my findings suggest university-wide problems in the handling of endowment funds."[107] Washington knows how to interpret accounting numbers more than most donors do, and in her deposition she described problems with reports. "In the spreadsheet that had the inventory of accounts," she testified, "there was a mismatch between what the development system called the account and what the treasurer's office called the account. So they had the same account number, but different descriptions."[108] This confusion led to misallocating money.

She said she felt so strongly about the problems that she felt she "had to act as the breaker switch inside the cultural cycle across presidents, across provosts, across different treasurers, different general counsels, different vice-presidents, different directors of development, and different deans of religious life. The same kind of behavior," she felt, "was being carried forward; it was a kind of cultural phenomenon that was somehow being handed down. All of these things sort of evolved and became institutionalized."[109]

That restricted money does not always find its way to its proper destination is, unfortunately, not uncommon at nonprofits. Most of the time, however, as long as nobody is paying too much attention, managers and accountants are able to dig up the money from one source or another to balance the budgets and keep everyone happy. The money, it can be argued in this context, is *fungible*; that is, it is exchangeable. The concepts of fungibility and following the money in restricted accounts don't mix well together.

The intestines of the budget-driven body don't make for a pretty sight. Aside from the difficulty of following the dollars, problems arise when money that should be going to one program is siphoned off to another program.

The *Daily Princetonian* reported that Washington "discovered many problems with the university's endowed funds," and that they were "evidence of a systemic problem that warrants further review." Even so, despite the experience and credentials that attracted Princeton to Washington, Doug Eakeley dismissed her report as "essentially incorrect," and contended that she "didn't have the expertise to look into the issue and publishes her report as if it were the truth and written by an expert."[110]

But that assessment didn't square with the person who was most familiar with her work. In a letter giving Washington a raise, her boss wrote, "You have thrived in this environment of unpredictable events and circumstances, and demonstrated your excellent understanding of systems and organizations. I have appreciated your proactive, creative response to problems. I am also grateful for your endowment research, and your tenacious examination of our financial affairs."[111]

"I love Princeton," Washington says. Then, however, this analogy: "You see the uncle touch the niece inappropriately, and something doesn't feel right. But since it's the uncle, you don't say anything. You justify it by thinking he was being extra friendly or that he had a little too much to drink, whatever. So you excuse it away. And that's what was going on with what I observed at Princeton.

"I lived there, I proudly wore the Princeton sweatshirt, I was technically the chaplain to the Unitarian Universalist students, I was working for the vice president of campus life, I was there when the Internet was in its infancy and I helped bring it to campus, and I had access to all these wonderful experiences through Princeton. Everything about Princeton was wonderful. So, to see a bad thing . . . I didn't want to believe it. It took a while before I could come to believe it. The important point," she says, "is the denial that people put themselves in." This thought process leads her to mention Jerry Sandusky, the Penn State football coach who was convicted of acts of sexual molestation while others, who most likely had at least a sense of what was happening, looked away. "It's all denial," Washington maintains, as she speaks not of herself but of the institutional culture at Princeton that did not respond once she made her concerns known.[112]

This frustration must be balanced by Washington's own chronological accounting of her time at Princeton, in which she acknowledges that Peter McDonough had "reviewed her report and created a new committee, which would undertake an internal audit and report to the board." The commitment to that oversight, however, was not seen as timely. "Nothing happened. I got to the point," Washington says, that "I felt as if they were just giving me a pat on the head."[113]

For reasons unrelated to her inquiries, Washington left Princeton a few months after submitting her report for the second time. But she didn't forget about the issue. Although she loved the university, she says she knew "the culture around financial integrity there was screwed up."[114]

The minutes before 4:00 p.m. on Friday, September 17, 2003 were filled with angst for Washington. She knew she had to make the phone call. Over a year had passed since she discovered much of the money from endowment funds had not been spent according to the donors' wishes. Although three months had gone by since she left Princeton, the issue kept nagging at her.

Her time in the Army was instructive for this moment, she recalls. She joined knowing that many people who are progressive don't join the Army, and was aware of how limiting and damaging cultural behavior can be. "If good people aren't there to witness what we don't like, nothing will change," she says. "What I have learned about cultural behavior allows me to hold these two ideas in my mind at the same time: that Princeton is this awesome and amazing place *and* that there were bad things happening. Because of my skill set and direct experience in endowment spending, in some respects I felt that I was the only one who could tell this story. For these deceased people," she explains, referring to Charles and Marie Robertson, "I needed to speak up because they had no other advocate in this mix"—at least not someone who was once inside Princeton's accounting machinery where dollars and donor intent are supposed to merge.

A friend "who heard my worries in the spring of that year suggested that I reach out to the Robertsons' legal team." That suggestion, along with a great deal of soul-searching, finally drove Washington to act.

This is how she remembers that Friday in 2003. "Google wasn't as streamlined as it is now, but I knew I had to find that attorney for the Robertsons." She was thinking of Seth Lapidow, who was quoted in one of the newspaper stories she had read. She was determined and disciplined and finally found Lapidow's office number. The minutes were ticking by and a little voice kept nagging at her: *You are not going into this weekend until you make this call. It's four o'clock, so get going!*

"My name is Jessie Washington and I'd like to speak with Mr. Lapidow." The person on the other end of the line: "Are you press or counsel?" "Excuse me?" Washington asked. "Are you press or counsel?" By this time, many news stories had been written about the case. And attorneys were calling all the time as well. "Neither," Washington said. "I'm a former employee of Princeton University." A pause. "Okay. Hold on."

"When Mr. Lapidow got on the phone, he said, 'We've been waiting for someone like you to call.'"[115]

"I always knew," says Lapidow, "that there had to be some person who'd worked there, who'd participated in this nonsense and ran away screaming. If they did this to the Robertson Foundation, it only made sense that they'd done this to other donors in other funds. And I knew there had to be someone out there who had gotten sick of Princeton's attitude, someone who wanted to tell the story, someone who could help us prove that it wasn't just Bill and the family."

Washington remembers her "whole body relaxing. I felt beyond validated. I knew I had landed in the right place." She thought, "These people believe me." Washington's documents delivered irrefutable evidence. "Everything she said was valid," Lapidow says.

"Princeton's excuses were always the same. They said they could take the money for one reason or another"—he mentions the pipe organ—"and the pattern was always the same." Echoing Ron Malone's thinking, Lapidow says, "When there might have been a spending question, Princeton didn't give it to outside counsel to say, '*Look at this and advise us on what to do.*' They didn't ask, *This document says X, but can we spend it on Y? Give us your legal opinion.* No. They just looked at it, went into a room, locked the door, closed their eyes, and asked *themselves* if it would be okay to use the money on Y."

"And surprise! The answer always came back *yes*." Lapidow describes the mindset at Princeton. "If you don't already agree with Princeton, they say: *You may disagree with us now, but eventually you might be smart enough to agree with us. We're perfect.*"

Lapidow speaks of how the university wanted to try the case to "the glow." From his office, which is not far from the campus, he can see Nassau Hall, Princeton's signature and most traditional building. He looks out and, from his perspective, sums up what the people there think: *You can just see the glow from Princeton University. Everything we do is so wonderful. How can you attack us? How can you say that what we're doing isn't wonderful?* Lapidow is certain that aggressive hubris was going to undergird Princeton's strategy. "They were going to trot out secretaries of state and ambassadors and generals to testify how great Princeton is." That would have been nice, perhaps, but beside the point. "Nobody ever said Princeton isn't a great place; that everything you do isn't wonderful. It's just that you can't use our money to pay for this other stuff. Just because what you do is wonderful doesn't mean you can use our money to pay for all of it!"[116]

In Jessie Washington, who sensed the same attitude about the funds she had investigated, Lapidow found an inside expert's substantiating voice.

Bill Robertson received an email in June 2004 from an attorney at Shartsis Friese. "Ms. Jessie Washington," it said, "would like to speak with you before this"—her story—"hits the press. She is extremely sympathetic to your efforts in this lawsuit. In fact, she has essentially put her reputation on the line (in that she has agreed to be quoted publicly after coming forward with what she has learned, despite any potential threat of breach of confidentiality) because she feels so strongly about your efforts and the injustice you and your family are battling. Ironically, she is also working for the Federal Government at this time; hence, she has a particularly personal understanding of your parents' wishes."[117]

Greg Lebedev, who would later serve as an advisor to the new foundation established as a result of the lawsuit, thinks that Jessie Washington "is courageous." It's almost as if she conscientiously willed herself to defy a core human tendency: "It is difficult to get a man to understand something, when his salary depends upon his not understanding it!"[118] "It takes a lot of guts," Lebedev says, "to work within a particular area and maintain a principle that conflicts with your context—and still act on it. Her action is a wonderful statement about a unique individual."[119]

The Summary Judgments

Along the way of almost any trial, both sides try to clear up some questions so they don't have to be fought over in detail. One way they do this is by asking the judge for what's known as a *summary judgment* on those questions. In the course of litigation, a party might ask the court to issue summary judgments on all or some of the claims involved to either obviate the need for trial or to pare down its scope. Summary judgment is granted only when there is no genuine issue of material fact and the party who files the motion is entitled to judgment as a matter of law.

Altogether, Superior Court Judge Neil Shuster considered seven motions for partial summary judgment. Although the judge rejected efforts to simplify some important legal issues in favor of a trial on the merits, Peter McDonough said the rulings "set up a road map for ultimately ending this case, and doing it rather efficiently, all things considered."[120]

Judge Shuster accepted Princeton's argument that capital gains and appreciation from investments could be considered income, and thus were available to pay expenses for the foundation. The original document spoke only of income, as it was defined in 1961. According to Ron Malone, "The IRS screwed up; instead of using the definition for trust income, it used a definition for corporate income, which unfortunately inadvertently changed the meaning of the provision."[121] It may seem like a technicality, but the Robertsons had agued hard for the stricter definition.

Basically, the judge's ruling meant that the more liberal definition, as the foundation had in fact been relying upon since the mid-1990s, would be sanctioned. To Princeton, this was no small victory; McDonough says this "was one of the University's biggest wins. For us," he says, "it was critically important that the point be made—and be made forcefully—that the inhibition of current and future spending was not going to be one of the outcomes of this very sad and protracted saga."[122]

Ken Logan says it was a "one hundred million dollar-plus issue in the damage calculations that the plaintiff had made." Many times, he says, "a judge will say there are significant contested issues of fact that need to be resolved before he or she can reach a decision. And that's what he did on virtually all the other motions—he deferred a decision on the other matters pending a trial—but on this one, he concluded that there were no material issues of fact that needed to be resolved and that he could decide on the basis of the record he had at that time. It was significant."[123]

The Robertsons wanted a jury to hear the case, but Shuster denied the request, most likely because the case was too intricate and full of legal nuances. In New Jersey a judge has the right to hear the evidence without a jury and he decided to exercise that right.[124] Lapidow explains that jury trials are rare in Chancery Court, which is where this trial would have been conducted, but, he says, "We pressed for the jury trial simply because the idea of having the citizens of Mercer County sit in judgment of the university's action made Princeton crazy."[125]

Still, even with some momentum going Princeton's way, the university's own newspaper acknowledged that the wins were small potatoes. Referring to the income question, it said, "The issue fits a larger pattern of the ruling: a small win . . . that doesn't change the larger claims. Shuster's findings do not reduce the size of the claim the Robertsons would win if the lawsuit were decided wholly in their favor."[126]

One of the wins for the Robertson side—in the sense that a Princeton motion was denied—related to something called the Business Judgment Rule. Regarding the examination of contested business decisions made by the Princeton-dominated board, the judge had to decide whether to apply either the lenient "business decision standard," which assumes that financial decisions were made in good faith, or the more strict "entire fairness standard," which requires every decision to be justified.

Shuster handed the Robertsons a setback when he concluded that they did not make "a sufficient showing that the University-designated Trustees have either been grossly negligent . . . or that they have exercised no business judgment at all." He also did not agree that Princeton's majority vote on the Robertson Foundation board automatically created a conflict of interest, a key consideration in determining whether each decision should be challenged. But the family actually won a bigger point when the judge rejected the idea that the university's spending decisions should be adopted across the board. Instead, Shuster wrote, "the Court finds it more appropriate to determine conflicts of interest, and the existence of self-dealing, on a transaction-by-transaction basis."[127]

The *Daily Princetonian* wrote that if, in the process, a transaction is identified as *ultra vires*—that is, beyond the legal powers of the Foundation—"the money in question would have to be returned to the Foundation. If not, the spending decision would then be examined as a breach of fiduciary duty, the highest legal relationship imposed by law. Princeton has admitted that it has a fiduciary duty to the Foundation. If a breach of fiduciary duty is determined to have occurred, then the appropriate standard — business decision or entire fairness — would be selected."[128]

"Believe me," Frank Cialone said, "we are more than happy to go through all the details of the spending claims and allocations that we've alleged. That is not the silver bullet that Princeton would like it to be."[129] Seth Lapidow says, "It was a huge win for Robertson. The denial of that motion by Princeton meant that they had to individually defend each and every transaction of the $200 million our expert said they diverted. That was a good thing for us."[130]

Nevertheless, Logan asserts, even though the judge "stopped short of agreeing with us and there was a sense of disappointment that he didn't fully adopt the Princeton argument, he did not in fact resolve any factual issues. Princeton had geared up and was prepared to try the case on the basis of explaining each one of its decisions."

That would have been onerous for the university and it's easy to see why the Robertson attorneys declared victory on this point, a point that leads Logan to a broader observation: the way the Robertson legal team was conducting its attack. They "contested virtually every decision made over 40 years as being beyond the authority granted to Princeton under the terms of the certificate of incorporation. Frankly, that's a very extreme, unrealistic position. But they weren't going to give an inch. And they didn't give an inch. That was their strategy." So, according to Logan, Princeton said, "Okay, if that's what you want to do, we'll do it."

As unfair as being required to examine four decades of spending decisions sounds, wouldn't it be logical for the Robertson side to demand a detailed accounting of money that was strongly suspected of being willfully misspent? "Logical, but only if you accept the premise," Logan acknowledges. "It was wasteful and they could have been more selective."[131]

The biggest issue to be decided by summary judgment was whether Princeton would remain the "sole beneficiary." The term, used in the lawsuit, meant that Princeton was the only organization that could receive money from the foundation, and a favorable ruling would provide early assurance that, no matter how other issues were determined, the university would maintain its prized status.

But Judge Shuster provided no such assurance.

While he understood the devastating implications to Princeton of permitting another organization, or other organizations, to receive the Robertson Foundation's revenues, he did not reject the possibility of removing the university's sole-beneficiary status. The court, he said, "should not foreclose an equitable remedy prior to having the full facts. While the court finds that severing the relationship between the foundation and the university . . . may only be appropriate to remedy the most egregious and nefarious of circumstances . . . the court would be remiss if it were to foreclose its ability to grant such remedies at this stage of the litigation." Translation: Yes, severing the foundation from the university would hurt Princeton greatly, but the question was too important and fraught with too many legitimate arguments to be decided prematurely by a judge without all the facts.

Ron Malone was relieved. "Princeton had been hoping to have the possibility of the 'death penalty,'" as the Robertson attorneys called it, "taken off the table." In an interview shortly after the summary judgments were issued, he said, "Not only does our suit allege nefarious and egregious conduct, but we will prove it."[132]

Bill Robertson felt vindicated. "The real beneficiaries of my parents' gift," he says, "were the American people, not Princeton." And he was pleased overall. "Nothing was thrown out in the summary judgments."[133] Princeton's attorneys, according to Logan, didn't see the decisions that didn't go their way as losses; they would just need to be hammered out at trial.[134]

Trouble In the Robertson Camp

Although both sides claimed victory after the decisions were released, as the trial date moved closer, each would have reason to pause. By the summer of 2008, the Robertsons were running out of money, and Princeton was concerned about the uncertainties inherent in a trial and possibly losing a huge portion of its endowment, to say nothing of its continuing battle against the unfavorable perception that the family of one of its most prominent donors had been wronged.

The summer before, in 2007, Lowenstein Sandler, the law firm where Doug Eakeley worked, hired away Judge Shuster's clerk, a move that had delayed the summary judgment decisions by about six months. Robertson saw this as "an extremely dirty trick" on the part of Princeton's attorneys. "The judge went along with it, but I think he regretted it," said Robertson. "So he had no clerk and the State of New Jersey wouldn't provide the funds for a new one until the new fiscal year." Even though parties to a lawsuit don't typically chip in to pay for a judge's law clerk, to keep things going Robertson offered to go fifty-fifty. But "Princeton wouldn't agree to pay for its half. So the judge had to effectively do all this work by himself."

The case was already five years old by the fall of 2007. The delay caused by the absence of a clerk, to say nothing of the anger that it stirred up, exacerbated the financial worries. "If there's a delay in the trial," Robertson said, "it doesn't mean the lawyers stop working. The clock is still spinning and you have to keep paying. At this point we were at about $500,000 a month, maybe a little more, so all of that is going out the door."

Things looked bleak. The money issue unsettled relations between the family and its attorneys.

"The Shartsis Friese firm told me they could guarantee nothing," Robertson says. "After all that we had gone through and all that we had already paid, that seemed to be ethically abhorrent." He remembers the mathematical process they had gone through some years earlier of the probabilities exercise to predict different outcomes. "They said there was a 90 percent chance that we'd get the legal fees back, 60 percent that Princeton would pay X dollars, or whatever, to be reimbursed to the foundation, and I think 50 percent for the money to leave Princeton's control altogether. As we were putting all this together, we were getting good vibrations from the attorneys."

By 2008 his lawyers were telling Robertson that, as a trial seemed inevitable, Princeton was putting together a full staff and the case would be in trouble if they didn't push full-speed ahead. "But that wasn't what I was told earlier on," Robertson says. "I was told that we had an absolute, slam-dunk winner, and that the whole thing was going to cost us between $10 million and $20 million."

In early October 2007, he went to his lawyers to tell them he wasn't willing to pay anything more if things didn't change. At that point, the summary judgments had not yet been decided. "I'm looking at this and saying we can't go on. We can't fund this at $10 million a year for the next five years."

"We wanted to bring Princeton to their knees," Ron Malone says, "but there was a lot of tension." He said he was getting pressure from Robertson not to spend money preparing for a trial. "One line of thinking was that Princeton was going to fold, that they weren't going to let this go to trial," Malone said. "The university's reputation was at stake and, as trials tend to be ugly, no one associated with the university wanted Princeton to be perceived as taking the family of its largest donor to the cleaners."

But there was the other line of thinking: "That Princeton would fight to the death for the foundation and its money, and that the Wilson School's reputation was also very real. We knew," says Malone, "that if we didn't do what we needed to do to prepare for the trial, Princeton would sense in a heartbeat that we didn't have the wherewithal to go through with it—in which case they would crush us." Princeton was outfitting a separate office near the courthouse for a 30-member trial team.

"They would have had a lot of smart people with an unlimited budget," says Malone. "If you're going to trial, you need to be prepared. If you're not prepared, no matter how valid your claims or how much of a smooth talker you are, you'll get trampled."[135] In the summer of 2008 he wrote to Robertson, "The pressure to reduce costs has caused us to decrease the pressure on Princeton at precisely the time when we should be increasing the pressure. This undermines our settlement posture and it emboldens Princeton. It also impairs our ability to be prepared for trial."[136]

"I wasn't accused of bad behavior until I withheld payment from the law firm" in the summer of 2008, Robertson recalls. "But I didn't have any choice. I couldn't accept what the attorneys were telling us. They had to come up with a solution. We'd spent maybe $30 million by this time, which would have gone to naught. Poof! They got crazy and they got my sisters crazy; they threatened to resign. But I made my point, which was: something's got to give here. My sister Katherine called me up and screamed, 'Pay the fee!'"[137]

And then, on the heels of all this, more bad news.

In February 2008 the judge retired.

"We were in shock, absolutely in shock," says Robertson, even though on some level it had to be expected. Shuster's judicial term was up. Although the state could have asked that he stay on, it didn't. "He had been pretty fair," Robertson remembers.[138]

That's an assessment both he and Princeton share. As an example, Ken Logan speaks of the structure that the judge brought to the summary judgment process. "We were comfortable with the analytical framework that he set forth in his summary judgment decisions." Beyond that, Logan thought Shuster was "good. He was a balanced guy and he handled proceedings in the courtroom well. This was probably the most complex and most burdensome case he ever had to try. He did a very fine job and I suspect that the Robertsons had a similar view. We were all disappointed when he stepped off the bench."[139] On perhaps the only sentiment the two sides agreed on, Bill Robertson says, "No one could have replaced him with his institutional knowledge. Shuster was as good a judge as we could have found, and his resignation was a disaster, a blow to the case's continuity."[140]

Shuster's replacement in the lawsuit was Maria Sypek. With 20 years of experience, she was highly regarded and well versed in mediating disputes. One attorney wrote of her, " . . . Be assured that in any mediation with Judge Sypek, counsel and their clients will all receive deeply respectful treatment, careful consideration of their claims, as well as a full opportunity for all sides to be heard."[141] If anyone would do a good job, she appeared to be that person.

Yet Sypek couldn't work miracles. She had to postpone the trial date from October 2008 to January 2009 because the court system and her own schedule were overcrowded. "The best she could come up with was one day a week," says Robertson. "At that pace the attorneys would have tripled the fees."

Aside from the legal costs, however, one day a week simply wasn't going to cut it. So in September 2008, a third judge, John Fratto, recruited out of retirement, was appointed to oversee the proceedings. Fratto said he would be able to devote four days a week to the case.[142]

Although there is no indication that Princeton's hand was in any of this, Robertson felt ambushed. "It turned from our being pretty much assured we would win to almost certain defeat." He wondered if Princeton, as one of the leading and most prestigious organizations in the state, was somehow being protected. The Robertsons were going down because of the delays, and the delays were costing money they didn't have.

In the end, the third judge's appointment was a positive development for the Robertsons. "Princeton fought tooth and nail," Lapidow says, "to prevent the appointment of Judge Fratto. We worked hard to get a judge who could hear the case and they resisted every step of the way. They wanted it to go on forever because they knew they could afford it and that the family could not."[143]

The delays reminded Robertson of a strategic decision recommended by his attorneys made at the outset of the lawsuit, one that he thinks might not have benefited his case. "The idea of litigating cases in New Jersey is not good," Robertson says. "We should have filed the lawsuit in Delaware, where the foundation was incorporated and where the case probably would have gone a lot faster."[144]

Princeton wasn't aware, at least from anything Robertson said publicly, that money was short. "It may have filtered through the grapevine, but I told them point-blank that we had plenty of money," he said. "I made it clear that we were going to try this case." They could have read the Banbury Fund's 990 for 2007 and intuited the Robertsons' financial position, but Princeton could not know for certain how bad things were or the state of angst Robertson was in. "Quite frankly, if they really thought we were running out of money, they would have bargained a lot harder," Robertson says.

After he got caught up financially with his legal team, in the summer of 2008, Robertson asked Robert Ernst, his brother-in-law, as well as an attorney, to talk with Shartsis Friese. He wanted Ernst to kick the tires and find out what could be done to reduce costs. What were the probabilities of various outcomes for the foundation and what would it take to fund those outcomes? "How can we fix it?" Robertson wanted to know. "The lawyers had to figure out a way to turn the case way down."

Ernst recommended that they give up their expectations for a new foundation outside of Princeton. "It seems," he wrote Robertson, "that asking the firm to prepare for the dissolution of the Robertson Foundation and a transfer of the money to a new Robertson Foundation is both very costly and very risky." Ernst then reminded Robertson that earlier that year the lawyers said that such an outcome—the death penalty, from Princeton's perspective—had only a 30 percent chance of succeeding in court.

"On the other hand," Ernst continued, the lawyers "gauge the probability of success on misappropriation with repayment to the Robertson Foundation at 70 percent or better." Ernst said this was a "much more realistic outcome and presumably" would be "a less expensive trial."[145]

The broad choice at this point was between, first, getting the judge to rule that Princeton had misbehaved, but only so much as to warrant that the foundation be reimbursed from the university and, second, getting him to rule that things were so bad that the foundation could rightly be wrested away from the university.

Robertson was disappointed with his brother-in-law's assessment. "He was there"—in the law offices of Shartsis Friese—"for *one day*. I wanted him to study the case in depth. He didn't. I believe that he was persuaded to accept a pyrrhic victory in the case. He backed off from actually analyzing the case, even though that's what I asked him to do." Robertson felt that 30 percent, while it seemed risky to Ernst, represented a strong possibility for success. "I think," Robertson says, "that they told him to back off, so he did."[146]

The going was getting tough and Robertson sensed the growing unease of being alone. While he had led the charge throughout the prior six years, he had the support of his family. Now, he felt, they, and perhaps even his attorneys, were pulling back.

Princeton With Trouble of Its Own

Things weren't going all that well at Princeton either. The nation's financial crisis came into harsh focus in the fall of 2008. On September 14 the *New York Times* reported, "In one of the most dramatic days in Wall Street's history, Merrill Lynch agreed to sell itself on Sunday to Bank of America for roughly $50 billion to avert a deepening financial crisis, while another prominent securities firm, Lehman Brothers, filed for bankruptcy protection and hurtled toward liquidation after it failed to find a buyer."[147] It was the just the beginning of a deluge of bad national and worldwide economic news for the better part of two years. Investment portfolios, especially those with heavy exposure to alternative investments—the kind Robertson was told were "like magic" by the people at PRINCO— were quickly going south. And Princeton's endowment, along with the endowments of many large universities, was caught in the snare.

"With the collapse in the market," Robertson says, "I think Princeton decided that the lawsuit just has to go away." Remember, Robertson, an investment manager, for many years served on the investment committee of the Robertson Foundation. *Money or no money in the Banbury Fund, this has got to go away*, he imagines Princeton thinking as the markets were collapsing. "Princeton had heavy commitments in hedge funds and private equity funds. With the market melting down, the prospect for private equities, because they are less liquid than most stocks and bonds, was not good. It was good money after bad."

But Robertson feels this wasn't the university's most serious problem. "Princeton literally had no cash," Robertson says. "They had 15 percent in marketable equities. And they had five percent in bonds. Maybe." A traditional portfolio, at least before the market run-up of the early 2000s, was more along the line of a 60 percent, 40 percent split between stocks and bonds. Alternative investments comprise a growing component of complex portfolios because they offer a high upside, but they also have a potentially dramatic downside. That potential downside becomes more severe as the portion of the entire investment portfolio in alternatives grows. Contracts in these investments call for layered funding, which means the investor is obligated to provide more money, even if the investment is going south. Their illiquidity means they cannot be sold at the convenience of the investor. As of the end of June 2007, according to a letter delivered to the Senate Finance Committee, Princeton had a full 51 percent of its endowment invested in illiquid hedge funds and private equity.

And Robertson was wrong, but on the right track, regarding Princeton's bond allocation. It wasn't 5 percent; it was only 3.4 percent.[148]

By this time PRINCO had taken over the foundation's account and Robertson was aware of the problems. "Princeton's endowment at the time was about $12 billion and its operating budget was about $1 billion. If you have only a billion dollars in marketable securities—the stuff you can actually sell—you'll run out of money in a year. That doesn't even take into account the potential call for more money in your alternative investments. "Princeton was facing Armageddon. It was a horrible situation," Robertson said. "They borrowed a billion dollars, which they needed for their cash flow. They will probably deny it, but that's what was going on."

Princeton didn't have to deny it. *Barron's* reported in November 2008 that many large endowments are "light on stocks and bonds, and heavy on illiquid assets." Of the woes of Ivy League endowments, the article stated, "Princeton has 70 percent in hedge funds, private equity and real estate assets, while Harvard has 57 percent in those groups." The article also characterized private equity at the time as a "disaster."[149]

Robertson wondered if Princeton was facing insolvency. "With so little of the portfolio liquid, I have no doubt in my mind that was a very real possibility. We as a family had a downside, but Princeton's downside to all this was simply unthinkable."

He then brings up another problem Princeton was facing. "Of course, they didn't want me saying all this at the time because, on top of everything else, their fundraising would have dried up."[150]

Something was happening. In 2004, when the Robertsons filed their amended complaint and when the publicity grew acutely negative, Princeton's total annual voluntary support dropped by an astounding 45 percent, from about $227.5 million to $125 million. According to Ann Kaplan, the author that year of an annual survey conducted by the Council for Aid to Education, "Princeton received its lowest amount in private donations in eight years." Except for Harvard, whose support dropped by a little under three percent, all the other Ivies increased their donations that year. MIT increased its support by more than 50 percent.[151] Nothing catastrophic in the markets was going on that year—the Standard and Poor's Index was up 11 percent—and so, Robertson concludes, "This was a mighty expensive lawsuit in terms of their fundraising."[152]

Princeton denies that the lawsuit was a factor, but Herb Berkowitz, a spokesman for the Robertson family at the time, said that the University "took it on the chin. When people flee an undesirable regime, we say they are voting with their feet. Perhaps there is an equivalent here—people voting with their checkbooks."[153]

That's not just a partisan perspective. Princeton's fundraising not only declined precipitously the year after the lawsuit was filed, it lost its edge in the years following. An analysis of the results compiled in reports of annual support at Ivy League schools shows that Princeton lost comparative ground to its peers. In the nine years preceding the lawsuit, Princeton's average fundraising rank among all colleges and universities was 19th. For the following eight years, the bulk of which was during the lawsuit, the university dropped to 26th. Furthermore, the percentage variance—the increase in fundraising—over the years following the lawsuit's filing dropped continuously through 2010.[154]

Robertson estimates that "Princeton lost somewhere in the neighborhood of $1 billion" in overall voluntary support and characterizes the poor performance as "the biggest smoking gun" of the lawsuit.[155] Of course, many factors contribute to overall fundraising—bequest receipts, for example, are erratic because people don't schedule their deaths—but the evidence that alumni and other supporters were holding back is strong.

In the context of fundraising and Princeton's investment problems, Robertson thought that a settlement, where the lawsuit would simply go away, might be an enticing idea to the university.

The Settlement

Although Robertson is quick to acknowledge that Shartsis Friese did "some very good work on the case," he called David Gelfand at Milbank Tweed, the New York firm that had helped out on the question of whether the Banbury Fund could pay the legal fees, to discuss how a settlement with Princeton might be worked out.

He told Gelfand that he always thought he had a "very strong case for breach of fiduciary duty" and that the "thousands of pages of memos and emails contain powerful evidence against" Princeton. He also told Gelfand that the former judge, Neil Shuster, "largely agrees with us." In addition, Robertson said that he felt that he had "the virtually universal sympathy and support of the media, worldwide. The importance of this case cannot be overestimated. Many people in high office past and present are watching and hoping we can finally strengthen our government as our parents intended and Princeton failed to do." For evidence, Robertson suggested that Gelfand review supportive correspondence from Paul Volcker, George H. W. Bush, and Brent Scowcroft.

"Our family has been assaulted for over 47 years," Robertson passionately stressed. "As a result of this case, higher education as a whole has already been taken to task and forced to improve fundraising methods and reporting to donors to the gratification of donors large and small across the country. And this University," he said, "cannot be exonerated of such self-serving and destructive conduct."[156]

The call to Gelfand wasn't the first time the Robertsons had thought about approaching Princeton to discuss settling the case. In early 2007, over a year and a half earlier, Jonathan Marks, a mediator, was brought in to see what could be done. He reported on January 8 that Princeton "would be willing to consider a settlement that results in a divorce" with "$50 million of the assets of the Robertson Foundation transferred to a new foundation." After Marks conveyed the offer to the Robertsons, on January 19 they came back with a demand of $650 million, that the Robertson Foundation would be dissolved and whatever was left of the assets would be managed by Princeton.

Princeton counter-offered with two possibilities. One was a non-divorce proposal that demanded three new family trustees. Apparently, they felt that getting rid of Robertson, as well as his sister and Bob Halligan, would clear the decks for a new and untainted relationship to begin and grow. The other possibility was the dissolution of the foundation with a cash payment of $80 million. The Robertsons came back, saying they would accept "$620 million in the context of a divorce." Princeton wasn't willing to accept that. Doug Eakeley scoffed at the offer. "Now you know why we don't have much to talk about."[157]

Princeton did not respond after that. Marks wrote, "It appears that the Plaintiffs and the Defendants have reached an impasse." After the judge handed down his summary judgment decisions in October 2007, Marks continued his "inquiries about the possibility of resuming discussions, but concluded that such discussions would not be productive."[158]

A year and a half went by. More summary judgment motions were denied than granted, and the rulings gave neither side a decisive edge. Both sides were spending more and more on attorneys. The economy was tanking. And everyone was getting tired.

Katherine Ernst, Robertson's sister, remembers the lawsuit as "an agonizing process. You'd go into a board meeting," she said, "and you had a big conference room table, and you'd have a Robertson Foundation board member and then you'd have an attorney, then a board member, then an attorney, and then another board member and then another attorney. And on the other side you'd have Princeton, and you'd have a Princeton person and an attorney, a Princeton person and an attorney. It was just like a war zone. And everything was very scripted. And it was very tense.

When we would have a break for lunch, we had separate dining rooms."
Bob Halligan remembers that, before the lawsuit began, everyone would
get together for lunch. "Now," he said, "there was one room for Princeton
and one room for the Robertsons."[159] This tension, says Katherine Ernst,
"consumed the family for more than six years. It was a relief when the
lawsuit ended."[160]

It had to be uncomfortable, with attorneys everywhere. How could
decisions be made? The veneer of civility might have been present, but
the coldness born of resentment and ill will permeated the meetings.

The time had come to take another shot at a settlement. "I thought,"
Robertson remembers telling Gelfand, "that it was time for some grown-
ups to take over and resolve this thing." Gelfand would be the grown-up.
"I offered a settlement of $150 million. Gelfand reported back that
Princeton wanted to talk. He told me that this was a classic case to reach a
settlement. Both sides had pretty much had enough, and both sides were
bleeding."[161]

Gelfand explains that the terms of the settlement were not foremost on
his mind when he first talked with Princeton. "I was not brought in to
size it up and assess a settlement." Instead, he was asked, with an eye on
budget, to think about the right strategy for a trial. The settlement was
the result of Gelfand's review of where things stood and thinking hard
about the prospects of various scenarios. "The result of that assessment
was that it made a lot of sense," after a number of phone calls with family
members and communications with the mediator, "to explore the possibility of a consensual resolution in advance of trial." Gelfand was not
revisiting the merits of the case—the other attorneys had done that well
enough—but was evaluating the different possibilities of how the case
might end up.

The process started out with the hope that Princeton would respond
to the sincerity brought by a new and fresh face. "My purpose," explains
Gelfand, "was to explore whether there would be an appetite on the
part of Princeton to see whether or not a consensual resolution would

be possible." That might seem like a lackluster expectation, but no one could have known whether the rancor that had built up over the prior six years or the failed efforts at a settlement a year and a half earlier ruined any desire Princeton might have had to settle out of court. Neither did, however, and over the following weeks Gelfand engaged in intensive discussions with the family and the university.

"The main question for me," says Gelfand, "was: What were the goals of the family?" Ultimately, it became clear that a major goal was "a separation between Princeton and the family." The end game became a complete dissolution of the Robertson Foundation at Princeton. By this time, he says, "There was no way that a resolution with long-term success could be achieved if the family stayed connected to Princeton. The level of distrust had grown to such a point that they had to go their separate ways."

Gelfand succeeded.

The rationale that both sides agreed to began with this: "Following more than six years of hard-fought litigation, the parties to this derivative action have reached a settlement of all the claims and counterclaims that . . . will achieve three critical goals—furthering the charitable objectives as agreed upon by the Robertson Family and Princeton in 1961, obtaining finality, and avoiding further burdensome litigation and trial."[162]

The essential provisions of the settlement agreement were that Princeton would pay the Robertsons' legal fees, which exceeded $40 million, over the following three years. An additional $50 million, to be paid over a five-year period beginning in 2012, would fund a new foundation. With interest, the total payment was $100 million. In exchange, Princeton rid itself of the biggest thorn ever to prick the most well endowed university, on a per-student basis, in the world. In addition, the founding charter was dissolved and Bill Robertson, his siblings and their heirs would have nothing to do with Princeton on the matter of the generous gift from Charles and Marie Robertson. From the day the settlement went into effect, what would happen to the Robertson Fund—now an endowed fund wholly within the university's ownership and control—was nobody's business except those running the Woodrow Wilson School and Princeton University.

It was the divorce that Robertson wanted all along. After all he had
learned over the years, he did not trust Princeton to carry out his parents'
wishes.

"The remedy of getting the money returned was a very difficult one,"
recalls Ron Malone. "In my heart, in my gut and in my head I was very
confident that we would have gotten a judgment against Princeton for
$300 million or $400 million. Proving that Princeton was guilty of
violating its fiduciary duties and violating the terms of the gift would
have been a big win, but simply reimbursing the foundation would have
been only a pyrrhic victory over time because Princeton is in the game
for the long haul. This generation of the family would die off, the next
generation would come in, and by hook or by crook, the university
would gut that $300 million or $400 million. They'd take it out of one
pocket and put it into the other. Overall," Malone thinks, "it was a very
good result."[163]

Doug Eakeley expressed relief: "This would have been quite a trial.
It would have been an extraordinary opportunity and experience. On
the other hand, the settlement is clearly in the best interests of Princeton
University. And," he points out, "I have my life back." Seth Lapidow feels
much the same. "Charities don't want a Robertson case on their hands,"
he says. "This case underscored that there is a level of adult supervision
that's needed. It's precedential in that respect."[164]

During an evening in early December 2008, Gelfand called Robertson
on his cellphone. He interrupted Robertson, as he was about to take the
first sip of his gin and tonic, to tell him that Princeton's board of trustees
approved the settlement. "I feel," Gelfand says, "the family's cause was
vindicated and that they could come out of this holding their heads high.
They fulfilled their objectives and could claim success."

Gelfand also takes issue with Robert Durkee's comment about how
the Robertsons didn't have any "personal skin in the game," the result of
having the Banbury Fund pay for the family's legal costs. "Even if that
statement were limited to out-of-pocket costs," Gelfand points out, "it
would be overlooking something even more significant than money: the
emotional strains of litigation for non-professional litigants. This is a

family. There is no question that the members of this family had an awful lot of skin in the game. Their family name was the focus of this litigation; they were subject to suffering from adverse publicity. That statement does not stand well with me."[165]

The Public Reacts

The lion's share of public post-settlement commentary supported the Robertsons' perspective. To the outside world the drama may well have seemed to be about an individual going up against corporate arrogance. While Princeton University is a nonprofit, it is also a complex corporate entity, and it must deal with the image of what any large bureaucracy must: criticism from those who feel it mercilessly runs over individuals.

One commentary that embodied the pro-Robertson sentiment was written by Jane Shaw, the president of the John W. Pope Center for Higher Educational Policy. Shaw said the case "sends a message to major donors: watch out when you give your money to a college or university." She added, "It is often easy to think of universities as somehow different from profit-making business, motivated by its lofty goals rather than grubbing for money. But are they? Given Princeton's enormous resources, it could probably outlast any legal challenges, even by heirs to the Atlantic & Pacific Tea Company. The case should remind us that those who run universities are as self-interested as anyone else and that universities are big businesses indeed."[166]

Another supporter of the Robertson cause was Frederic Fransen, the president of Donor Advising, Research & Educational Services, and an author of articles relating to donor intent. His support was evident in a response to an article written by Naomi Levine, the founder of the Philanthropy Center at New York University. In an opinion piece for *Contribute Magazine*, Levine wrote of the lawsuit, "Hogwash," that the Robertson case was not one of donor intent. It was instead, Levine claimed, about money. "The Robertsons simply want more control over the foundation's money."[167] Fransen disagreed. "Her [Levine's] career has been spent working the recipient side of the fundraising game, and her perspective is anything but neutral." He questioned Levine's motivations. "Perhaps her ardent support of Princeton University's position stems more from her belief that colleges and universities, to paraphrase Benjamin Franklin, 'must all hang together, or assuredly, they will all hang separately.'"

Fransen thinks that many universities are intentionally ambiguous when they draft agreements with donors so that "nothing actionable" can ever take place, and so warns donors not to "take fundraisers such as Mrs. Levine at their word." Donors, he says, act out of "legal and moral necessity" when they go to court "not only to provide justice to those such as the Robertsons, but to prevent the contagion from spreading to the entire nonprofit sector."[168]

Fransen didn't like the settlement. "The real shame is that we won't have a chance to hear Princeton officials explain, for example, how the $16,368 rug they purchased for the dean's office with Robertson Foundation dollars contributed to the education of Princeton students for Foreign Service careers." Fransen also said that he hoped "the courts would bring additional clarity to the issue so" donors "won't face similar dilemmas in the future. Instead, the case sputtered to an end with no precedent-setting decision and only partial justice for Charles and Marie Robertson, whose extraordinary 1961 gift began the long saga of bad faith."[169]

Anne Neal, the president of the American Council of Trustees and Alumni, however, finds a measure of satisfaction in the outcome. "We care deeply that colleges and universities adhere to donor intent," she says. "What Bill Robertson was willing to do—and so many others have not done—is essentially draw a line in the sand and say, '*We're not going to accept your failure to abide by donor intent.*' Most donors love their institutions, and, when they are unhappy, too often they are not willing to go public. They just go away. The issue is never pressed. The Robertsons chose to raise the issue rather than hide it. The outcome was very positive and it sent a message."[170]

Note the arc of viewpoints as reflected in the headlines: Jane Shaw's commentary, "An Unsettling Conclusion"; the *Nonprofit Times*,

"Princeton, Foundation Settle Donor Intent Case"; and the *Daily Princetonian*, "University Gains Control Over Robertson Endowment in Settlement."

Perspectives

Ron Malone attended a board meeting of the Robertson Foundation just after the lawsuit was filed and "before we learned about the double dealing and the misappropriations. Several important people were there," he says, "and I made a presentation about the family's concerns." He recalls that he and Anne-Marie Slaughter, the dean of the Wilson School, had a good discussion. "A high-minded conversation," is the way Malone characterizes it.

Shirley Tilghman, who was also at the meeting, said, according to Malone, "Preparing and placing people in nonprofits that do wonderful work in Africa is government service." Malone smiles sadly when he relates what she then said. "You have to understand that things have changed in the world. The government used to do more than it does now and nonprofits do some of the work that government used to do. So when we place people in nonprofits, we're fulfilling the mission. It's really up to us to decide what the mission is and how to fulfill it."

"With all due respect," Malone replied, "I've had some experience with this kind of thing," referring to his work on the Buck Trust and other donor-intent cases. "I've experienced situations where a restricted gift has been made, where some really smart, high-minded people are in a position of administering that restricted gift. When it comes time to spend the money, they ask *themselves* about the best way to spend it. And they answer that question *to themselves*."

He ponders this point, no doubt trying to get into the head of the Princeton president as he recalls his words to her. "They do good things with it, no doubt, and so they're shocked to find out that other people look at it differently. I respectfully suggest," he said to Tilghman, "that instead of asking yourself about the best way to spend the money, you should first ask yourself a few other questions: The first one is, *What did we agree to do?* Then, *What did the donor specify we should do?* Third, *Are we carrying out those instructions correctly?* If people don't ask those questions first, they frequently come up with the wrong answer, and they're shocked to learn that a judge or a jury finds they have violated their fiduciary obligations or the terms of the restricted gift."

Malone stops here, as if his words are reminding him of what he understood as the arrogance to which he was being subjected. "This brilliant woman," he says, referring to Tilghman, "looked at me like I was scum or a moron. 'How dare you suggest we don't know the right questions to ask?' she asked me."[171] It was as if the entire point had been lost on her—and perhaps, he implies, she was inadvertently revealing why Princeton would be forced to argue its case in court.

Peter McDonough looks back and searches for a reason. "There's a sadness here, all throughout this case." Yet he says, "Even though Bill really put a lot of people through a lot of misery, I have always had, and still have, a sense of sadness for him. I think he's led a sad life. It's not something you take any glee from." Doug Eakeley says, "I would substitute the word *pathos* for *sadness.*"

To which McDonough adds, "There's no doubt—and I am certain of this—at the end of this saga, his goal was to hurt Princeton as much as he could, to inflict as much pain as he could upon Princeton."[172]

Robert Durkee feels the same. "Robertson didn't file this lawsuit simply to dissolve the foundation or redirect its spending. He felt that Princeton had done damage to him by diminishing his stature, and now he wanted to do damage to Princeton." And Durkee says Robertson succeeded. "This lawsuit did damage to Princeton, although in the end it produced positive outcomes for Princeton as well."[173]

McDonough asks himself about the *why* of that—the motive for destruction—but, pausing and looking into the middle distance as if trying to retrieve a sliver of logic, he leaves it hanging, trying, but not able, to answer.[174]

Bill Robertson, however, doesn't leave it hanging. "Nothing changed during the lawsuit, except that everything got worse. The negative impressions I had before I brought the lawsuit were exacerbated as it went forward," he says. "But I was most definitely not trying to hurt Princeton as much as possible. I wanted to correct something that was terribly wrong. If, in the process of doing that, I hurt someone . . . well, sometimes it takes a strong stand to tell someone you're serious." Then, after a few moments of further thought, he says, "They have tried to personalize the conflict by blaming me for their misfortune as though I had a scheme, much less the ability, to benefit myself and my family at their expense.

"And 'pathos'? I find that remark to be very condescending. Doug Eakeley does not know me at all. Perhaps that word should be reserved for *him*, as he's the one who led Princeton into this colossal disaster. Or maybe it should be reserved for the university officials who accepted his advice. Remember, he and his firm profited handsomely from this lawsuit. Do those guys realize just how patronizing they are? If they were arrogant before, just look at them today. My life is certainly not one of sadness or pathos."

He remembers, "In the early '70s my father speaks up, saying we're not sending enough people to the United States government, that this has got to change, that we've got to fix it. And Princeton's internal memos were clear. One of them said that even if we—Princeton—wanted to, we couldn't get the faculty to follow this mission. Then John Lewis, the dean, said, 'The university should resist a blind commitment to nation-state parochialism.' So they were saying amongst themselves that we can't do this, and we never can do this."

The comments of McDonough and Eakeley reawaken Robertson's erstwhile mindset for battle. "Then Bill Bowen comes along in 1972 and tells the senior people at the school that *we can't tell the Robertsons we want to allocate funds for other purposes because Charlie and Bill want to hold us very closely to our original promises. But what we can do,* Bowen said, *is support other parts of the university that may contribute to the Woodrow Wilson School.* In other words, *we can spend money over here if it has some relevance to the school.* So," Robertson says, "he was way off base by then. This was a real bait-and-switch operation from the very beginning. They concealed this from my father."

Robertson says his father could have pulled the plug. "Charlie and Marie could have walked in there and said, 'Guys, this isn't working. We want the money back.'" Could they really have done that? "Absolutely," said Robertson. "Here's the donor coming in to say that Princeton University is defrauding my family—for the largest gift in its history? It would have been a catastrophe. He could have blown the whistle. And so they couldn't tell him the truth. They didn't even want to suggest that there was anything amiss." This thought reflects his growing frustration as information became available through the discovery process.

"So, now they downplay my involvement." Robertson interprets what he was hearing from Princeton: "*This next generation is going to have far less importance to this university than your parents had.* Even though this thing was growing like mad. Eventually, it was $900 million. And we're not important enough to be attended to? I'm sure they were certain they had this thing locked up."

As for the assertion that he was trying to hurt the University, he says, "That's not true. And the claim crumbles when you consider that one person—Jessie Lee Washington—came forward and showed that the university was also misusing and diverting the generous gifts of many other donors as well. She had nothing to gain, but perhaps much to lose. The university's conduct was shameful—not just to us, but to others. They were defiant, publicly abusive and dishonest to us. The university's misfortune is of their own doing."[175]

Even though his parents were wealthy, Robertson sees himself as an average person in many ways. He doesn't fill his life with jet-setting glitter and keeps his personal life private. But average people, he says, have the right to fight for their causes. "One of the interesting things about the case is that we—our family, this generation, without any great renown, accomplishment, fame or fortune for that matter—could actually take on an institution of this size and beat them at their own game. That's an interesting aspect: Don't underestimate somewhat humble people, particularly if you've got so many skeletons in the closet. Don't ever forget," he says, "that never in the history of philanthropy has a charity ever returned $100 million to a donor."

Robert Durkee says that neither side won the case.[176] Robertson feels differently. "There's no question," he says, "that we won this case."[177]

Robertson also sees something broader here than his own struggle. "Donors should continue to hope for and expect performance and cooperation from recipients, and we hope that this case has in some way contributed to that notion." [178]

Perhaps it should go without saying: each side vehemently contends that it would have won had the case gone to trial.

In 1878 George Hartford made a deal with George Gilman, the founder of the A&P, to become a partner in the company. The agreement gave Hartford ownership in an establishment that for 60 years in a row, from 1915 to 1975, would be the nation's largest food retailer. The A&P would make Hartford, his children and grandchildren very wealthy. That deal was based on a handshake and, although it provided some estate problems for Gilman some years later, the deal stood. The deal was based on trust, a trust that neither man violated. In contrast, the deal in 1961, hovered over by several attorneys and written with precision, ended up in ashes, the victim of a loss of trust.

It will probably take at least another generation before the bad blood between the Robertson family and Princeton is cleaned up. By then, there may be no blood at all, just an historical footnote in the ledgers and lore of the university's archives and the family's diaries. Right now, however, years after the courtroom battle was settled, it continues in the hearts and minds of those who fought it.

Chapter 6

A Legacy Renewed

Dead at the age of 47, even though its creators intended it to live in perpetuity. The cause of death: broken dreams, broken promises, and severe acrimony. But there was an end-of-life clause: The remains of the Robertson Foundation would be used to create the Robertson Fund, a new fund within Princeton's endowment.[1]

The language in the Settlement Agreement says that the original purpose is always to be pursued "as understood and interpreted solely by Princeton. Plaintiffs shall have no right, expectation or standing to participate in decision-making related to the Robertson Fund." Any decisions made will forevermore be in Princeton's "sole discretion, and not be subject to challenge or inquiry" by the plaintiffs.[2] The family isn't even entitled to any reports the public cannot access. The historic gift at Princeton will never again be the business of any of the heirs.

Then, from death, another birth.

The New Robertson Foundation

The rebirth actually took place before the death. As the lawsuit took its course, Bill Robertson presciently planned for the moment when he would be free of Princeton. Two years before the settlement—in April 2006, when there was no assurance at all that he and his family would recover any money—he set up a new, separate foundation: The Robertson Foundation for Government, or RFG.

Because the lawsuit hadn't yet been settled, the new organization existed only on paper, but it would be what the foundation at Princeton was not. Its purpose closely reflects the original—"Strengthening the United States government and increasing its ability and determination to defend and extend freedom throughout the world by improving the training and education of men and women for government service, with particular emphasis on international relations and foreign affairs"—but the new organization would be more faithful to the words.

In 2010, when Princeton's interest payments began, RFG initiated operations, and in the spring of 2012, four months after Princeton sent its first principal payment of $5 million, the first graduating class of Robertson Fellows delivered a long-awaited satisfaction to the family. Inspired by noble aspirations of making a difference, those young men and women newly personified a mission that was a half-century old.

As if in direct response to the major issues in the lawsuit—whether there was enough interest among students to actually enter government service and whether the government could actually employ people prepared to enter its ranks—the RFG website says this: "Faced with daunting global challenges and the looming retirement of tens of thousands of experienced federal employees, the government's needs couldn't be greater. RFG helps the government meet those needs through a variety of programs and works with colleges and universities throughout the country, with the federal Office of Personnel Management, and with the departments and agencies of the federal government that require international expertise."[3]

"This is not a reinvigorated effort, but a new one," for Robertson. "In my heart," he says, "I truly believe that, from the first day, Princeton did a snow job on my parents." He looks back on the lawsuit years and says he can come to no other conclusion. "So," as he prefers to think of it, "instead of rebuilding it, we are doing what Princeton never did to begin with, something they never even dreamed of doing."[4]

In 2006 Robertson met with Greg Lebedev, the chairman of the Center for International Private Enterprise and a long-term, well regarded and highly accomplished Washington, DC, insider, to get things off the

ground. "Bill's premise," says Lebedev, "was that he needed to find someone who could straddle government and business, with a big dose of
foreign policy as part of the mix."

At the beginning the new foundation was "sequestered," as Lebedev
puts it. "Everyone felt that the original foundation at Princeton was dying
a slow death. There was a growing sense that the patient was ill, and there
was no ability to apply the right medicine because the Robertsons were in
a minority. At the time it was just a shell, but at some juncture we knew
that if we won this thing we wanted to be ready to go." Even in the dark
times, when things were far from certain, Lebedev was confident of victory. "I know Bill to be a tenacious fellow, and I believed in his cause. Bill
said, 'If we win, we're going to launch that foundation, the one my mom
and dad wanted.'" Lebedev was charged with creating a budget and with
planning for the day-to-day operations that would take place once the
new organization was funded. "The Robertson siblings share and carry
forward the passions of their parents," he says. In particular, he notes their
belief in the "importance of public service."[5]

To avoid the Princeton straitjacket, the new foundation chooses worthy university programs where fellows are funded and regularly assesses
how things are going. There are no automatically permanent alliances.
Also, unlike the entrance application at the Woodrow Wilson School for
so many years, prospective fellows are required to express an interest in
a career in international relations before they are accepted. Each student
must commit to working for the federal government for three of the first
five years after graduation. The initial universities the foundation worked
with were: Syracuse, Texas A&M, Tufts, the University of Maryland
and the University of California, San Diego. As private family foundations go,[6] RFG accomplishes much. UC San Diego alone, for example,
announced in late 2012 that the foundation had designated almost $1
million over a period of eight years to fund 24 graduate students.[7]

Lebedev, who continues to oversee many of the new foundation's
activities in Washington, likens the foundation's structure and purpose
to a three-legged stool: the fellowship, the internship and the job. The
internship is an important step to learning the real world of Washington.

"The jobs part," though, "the toughest and most important part," Lebedev says, "was missing at Princeton. It's the work product, if you will, of the foundation's efforts."

An Influential Advisory Board

In addition to a governing board, many charitable organizations compile another group of people, an advisory board, to provide intellectual stimulus and advice related to the mission. RFG began with four advisory board members: two who served in high-level government positions and two academicians.

Chuck Robb and Brent Scowcroft are the two who have served in government. Robb was elected governor and then United States Senator from Virginia. Also, President George W. Bush appointed him co-chair of the Iraq Intelligence Commission, which, among its other mandates, analyzed the information the United States had acquired on weapons of mass destruction in Iraq. In 1967, in a White House ceremony, Robb married the daughter of Lyndon Johnson who, incidentally, was the principal speaker at the dedication in 1966 of Robertson Hall at the Woodrow Wilson School, from which, again incidentally, Robb's daughter and son-in-law both graduated. Scowcroft served as the National Security Advisor to Presidents Gerald Ford and George H. W. Bush. It is no accident that one is a Democrat and the other is a Republican. The members of the governing board are of one mind: all perspectives that promote the cause of competent government service, particularly as they relate to international relations, are welcome, regardless of political affiliation.

Because of his background, Robb sees one of his strengths as an advisor to the new foundation as "having credibility on both sides of the aisle"—he has shown a remarkable ability to collaborate with high-powered people who are prone to be disagreeable—"in helping to define the direction of a program that sponsors young people whose life mission is to serve their government." Robb says his wife Lynda tells him that he "can't be bought" because everyone knows him to be a straight shooter. In explaining the urgency and drama when, in early

2004, President George W. Bush asked him to co-chair the commission that studied the issue of WMD in Iraq, Robb said he was assured that "there would be no politics in the process. Larry Silberman," a politically conservative federal judge and the commission's other co-chair, "and I both agreed and told the President that if there was any hint of politics muddying the investigative process, we could just resign."[8] In addition to his experience, it is that kind of aware, but above-the-fray, mindset that makes Robb's work on the Robertson Foundation for Government so valuable.

Although Scowcroft, like Robb, was not involved in the lawsuit, he thinks about the underlying issues that led to the foundation's creation. "My general sense is that when some universities get bequests, they feel it's their money, and they do whatever they want with the money. They may be using the money for a good cause, but it may not be the cause that the donors wanted pursued." Scowcroft says that the big point is that "what happened at Princeton could have happened anywhere. Princeton," he says, "is just where it happened to be." As far as the outcome of the lawsuit, he admires Robertson's persistence. "Bill should be proud of what he's done. He succeeded. There wouldn't be any foundation if it weren't for his efforts."

"I was immediately enamored with what the family wanted to do with the foundation," Scowcroft says, "because our government is only as good as the people we can get to serve in it." He then echoes Paul Volcker's lamentation. "Everybody now is running against the government, and that's just a deplorable state of affairs for me," which is a large incentive for his service on the advisory board. "I am honored by my affiliation with the Robertson Foundation, especially with the growing mood in the country today that government is evil. The question is," he says, "How do we get the best government possible? By getting young people with idealistic motives to want to go into the government."

Scowcroft and Robb are agreed on the matter of the new foundation's importance and value to society. "It's an extension," Scowcroft says, "of the wishes of Bill Robertson's parents. And, as a matter of fact, it's off to a really fine start." That was in the spring of 2012.

For Scowcroft, idealism is not a cliché. It is an internally directed dictate. "I feel very strongly about this. We need the best people in government" for the sake of the nation, "but it's also important for the individual. There's a reward for working for something that's bigger than you are—like the government." He says that he brings this up all the time when he speaks with young people. "Until you've felt it, you don't even know what it means—because most of us are focused on ourselves. Working for something that is bigger than your own little goals is extremely gratifying."

This is true, he says, even though, "in politics no one is behaving very well right now." Is there anything else we can do for better discourse? "If there is, I don't know. We don't and won't listen. It's almost as if you're poisoning your own ideas if you listen to anybody else. And that's a dreadful statement." Scowcroft, however, as does Robb, considers himself an optimist and thinks the country will figure it out. "I hope the foundation can play a role. It's about serving your country."[9] Robb thinks the RFG can be a major player in husbanding the country's international stature. "Education in government is particularly crucial in international diplomacy, foreign relations and national security. If there's any area where you want to speak with essentially one voice—or, at the very least, where bipartisan cooperation should be paramount—that's it."[10]

Scowcroft's former boss also weighs in on the value of the foundation. George H. W. Bush applauds "any program, particularly a private program, that not only emphasizes the virtue and the value of public service to our country, but also supports those who are willing to maybe set aside other ambitions to try and serve in one form or another. The Robertson Foundation for Government," the former President believes, "is doing the Lord's work in that regard, you might say."

While Bush seems to share the concerns that Scowcroft and Volcker have about the public's confidence in our national government, he is certain people's esteem will rise. "Opinion polls come and go—you're talking to the duty expert on that—but the key thing is our system, our democracy, is resilient. The Founding Fathers who set this grand experiment in self-governance in motion knew what they were doing."

Bush says that most Americans "think about the Foreign Service mostly in times of international crisis. But then, that's why we need organizations like the Robertson Foundation for Government that help strengthen the quality and quantity of our foreign-service personnel—even in times of relative tranquility." Given his extraordinary career, ranging from Congress to the Executive Office, as the highest elected official in the United States as well as the leader of the Central Intelligence Agency and his service as a diplomat, Bush feels that the best way an organization like the Robertson Foundation can make a difference in the country's ability to extend freedom throughout the world and strengthen our democracy is to stay the course. "Keep doing what you are doing," he says, and "keep reaching out, and keep helping others."

Texas A&M named its school of public affairs after Bush and he's pleased with the injection of a number of Robertson Fellows into its program annually. "I am not only happy with the fellowship program at our school—I am overjoyed. At this stage of my very happy and full life, nothing matters to me more than the Bush School and our students. The fact that the Robertson Foundation for Government has decided to partner with us . . . means more to me than mere words can describe."[11]

Renewed Energy for the Original Purpose

Time will need to pass before the new foundation is no longer compared to the old one. Greg Lebedev, for example, points out that almost all of the students have first-year internships and immediately enter government service after they earn their degree. "I would say to Princeton that this *can be done*. I spend my time talking with senior folks in agencies, explaining how wonderful the program is, and how they can bring in talented men and women. This simply wasn't being done at Princeton."[12]

Katherine Ernst, Bill Robertson's sister and the president of the foundation, sees it the same way. "Most of the graduates, from what I understand, did not go into government service and international relations."

Ernst wants the new foundation to attain a level of appreciation that will give it status around the world. "I would hope that it becomes as prestigious as a Fulbright, that when a young person is offered a fellowship, he or she says, 'Wow.'"

Chuck Robb agrees. "Because I have spent most of my adult life in the public policy realm of the governmental arena, I have felt for a long time that we ought to try to attract the best and the brightest to the field of public policy and diplomacy. We see too many instances where people want to go to Wall Street and other places to make a fortune, and too few with a desire to go into government. It's a calling that ought to get a whole lot more credit than it does. Diplomacy is an intricate art, and to the extent that the new foundation can attract more and more people into this field, we'll be that much stronger, both at home and abroad."[13]

Ernst would like to see the foundation grow, and mentions the possibility of adding more universities as fellowship partners. "But having said that," she says, "one of the things that is really special about this foundation is that it has a very personal touch to it, which I give Bo Kemper"—the executive director—"a lot of credit for. He communicates with all the fellows. He writes at Christmas. He congratulates them when they graduate—even when they have a baby—and he encourages them to write thank-you notes. We go out of our way to get together once a year, so they will network with each other and help each other. I would not want to lose that. I hope that the foundation would not get so big that we couldn't maintain that. As president, that's what is so meaningful—the contact with the fellows."[14]

Ernst's sentiments follow her brother's. The *Princeton Alumni Weekly* interviewed Bill Robertson shortly after the lawsuit settlement about his plans for the new foundation. "We are going to have to target our efforts clearly more than we would have with greater funds," he said. "However, we're going to work hard to realize my parents' dream. We want to determine a precise profile for the student applicant for a graduate school of public affairs; I think that's very important to become a leader, to become a devoted federal government professional."

Robertson continued, "Of course, we would like to focus on federal service and encourage whichever schools are recipients of the program to focus in that area. In terms of placement, we would like to implement a real incentive program that will attract graduates into the U.S. government and hopefully keep them there, at least for a significant part of their career. And we would like to actually begin to work on ways to improve the attractiveness of federal government service and to improve the retention of good people in our government. We will be reaching out to other foundations, other institutions to also take an interest in a program like that. So our platter will be full."[15]

Addressing An Ongoing Challenge

The platter is full, not only with possibility but with challenges. The question that haunted Princeton for so many years has become an ongoing concern for RFG, as well: How do you ensure that good and talented students—Paul Light calls them "bright pennies"—will have a job in the government sector when they graduate? Light is a professor at NYU's Wagner Graduate School of Public Service and one of the nation's leading experts on federal government human resource issues. He is also one of the two academicians on the advisory board.

As for the issue of training people to enter government service, he echoes Paul Volcker. "Policy analysis," Light says, "has steadily driven out the study of policy execution. My view is that *how* you're going to do something has to be part of the process from the beginning. It's not just a handoff at the end."

Light refers to the book *Administrative Behavior,* written in 1947 by Herbert Simon, who received the Nobel Prize for Economics in 1978. His work "knocked down, if not out, public administration as a field," says Light. "It was a George Foreman punch to the field. The book was about the field of public administration supposedly being all about *principles*, which suggests empirically derived truths. But Simon comes along and says it's not that at all. Instead, it's all proverbs and homilies. Nothing more. And they aren't supported by any data whatsoever."

"Although any practical activity involves both *deciding* and *doing*," writes Simon, "it has not been commonly recognized that a theory of administration should be concerned with the processes of decision as well as with the processes of action. This neglect stems from the notion that decision-making is confined to the formulation of over-all policy. On the contrary, the process of decision does not come to an end when the general purpose of an organization has been determined. The task of 'deciding' pervades the entire administrative organization quite as much as the task of 'doing'—indeed it is integrally tied up with the latter."[16]

To steer its graduates into government service, Princeton would have needed to pay far more attention than it did to the nuts and bolts of administration.

Not that getting people into the federal government is easy, even though the board and the advisors are of one mind. "The big challenge for the foundation," Light says, "is to stick to its knitting, which is to get these kids in, get them fellowships and get them to honor their agreements" to work in the government. "Unfortunately, the economy is not cooperating with the foundation." He thinks the Robertson Foundation has done an "excellent job of identifying schools to partner with and motivating the fellows, and now they've really got to get them work. In the supply side of the equation, the foundation is doing a great job. The problem is the demand side." The hiring process is arduous; getting a federal job of consequence requires more disclosure and background checks than ever before. In addition, because of budget concerns, federal agencies are holding back. "Despite much more success so far in getting alumni into the federal government than Princeton," Light says, "the times are not cooperating."[17]

Still, according to Bo Kemper, the success rate for the new foundation on this score is about 80 percent.[18]

The question arises: Can a *side-by-sider* qualify as a successful placement? A side-by sider is a person who doesn't work directly for the government but works for a service provider, such as a consulting firm, that in turn has a contractor relationship with the government. Often, two people—one who works for the government and the other who works for a contractor—sit side by side and perform jobs that require the same experience and skills.

The individual hired by the contractor often makes less than the government employee, but that person costs the government more. This is because the contractor's fee is at least as much as the individual's salary. Studies show, Light says, "that a contract employee costs 50 percent to 150 percent more than a government employee."

In a study released in 2011, the Project on Government Oversight (POGO) found that the salary for a federally employed computer engineer would be about $135,000; a contractor might bill the government around $270,000 for similar work. Even taking into account benefits and the process of terminating employees, the cost difference is large. "Our findings were shocking," the report says. "POGO estimates the government pays billions more annually in taxpayer dollars to hire contractors than it would to hire federal employees to perform comparable services.[19] In Washington, actually hiring an employee has become secondary to contracting. Yet anyone with common sense can understand the folly of paying twice as much to hire contractors in the pursuit of trimming government costs.

The mission of the Robertson Foundation is caught in that web. Of course, Robertson Fellows prefer to be government employees as opposed to contractors, as there is more room for advancement and more potential for the professional satisfaction that drove them to the field to begin with. A generation or two into their careers, they hope to be the leaders in government. The question, as Light sees it: "How do you get the fellowship above the tall weeds so that people recognize the recipients as being a real prize?"

Light says that the goal of such an effort, if it is long sustained, is an "improvement in the government's hiring process. We want to help improve the efficiency of government. We want to make government attractive to these students so they don't go to the investment-banking world, or wherever. We want them to *want* to go into government."

But enough unencumbered enthusiasm might be construed, according to Light, "as a lobbying effort," something he describes as "a third rail" in the world of tightly controlled family foundations, at least as far as how restricted they are from becoming politically involved. "It is an absolute violation of federal foundation law for any foundation to lobby," Light says.

That may sound far-fetched—after all, foundations can educate all they want—but Light says, "If you go up to Capitol Hill and say, 'You should give special preference to Robertson Foundation fellows,' now you're really testing the boundary." Light is unimpressed with the process by which government currently recruits—"The federal government is negligent towards it future leaders," he says—and such a concern might make it worse. "The Robertson Foundation has a real opportunity to become a vocal advocate for their fellows, and in doing so make a case for strong leadership in government. That's the case they made in the court," Light points out, referring to the lawsuit. "They were saying that it was not okay to be a side-by-sider."

Light is conflicted about it, however, because the hiring realities today make it almost impossible to expect all Fellows to enter government service soon after they graduate. "The question of what constitutes government service," he says, "is a really important question." That is one of several fundamental questions, according to Light, that need to be addressed. Another is the role of the new foundation as it relates to the original idea of strengthening the United States government. "If the foundation can address these issues, it will be adding greatly to the field." In fact, Light thinks RFG has the potential of commanding a large voice in its niche of public administration. Government needs help, "and the Robertson Fellows are important to providing that help, but government has to get better in handling them."[20] Still, Light is optimistic.

As is John L. Palmer, the other academician on the new foundation's advisory board. Palmer, who contributed his analyses of the Woodrow Wilson School during the lawsuit, says, "The new foundation is doing what Princeton should have been doing and is having considerable success for doing in its early years. I don't think Princeton ever had the goal of placing more than a minority of their MPA graduates into federal service and international affairs. The new foundation aspires to as close to 100 percent as possible." Even if the new effort falls short, he says, "The results will be a lot better than Princeton's ever were.

"We just have to be cognizant of that and understand that more resources have to be brought to bear to help the students. For example," he says, "internships in relevant federal agencies can be a critical way students can get an entrée into a regular job after they graduate. And so we need to put more resources into that effort." The internship component of the Robertson Fellow package is the recognition that the foundation conscientiously moved past merely providing the costs of the fellowships and preparing students academically; it has created a robust infrastructure, including partnerships with strong universities, to help students get connected early on to the various federal departments and agencies that may be their future.

It is this extra dimension—the infrastructure, which is so important yet receives so little attention when philanthropic funding projects take place—that RFG has the ability and mindset to address. And it is this dimension that Princeton overlooked—not because of a lack of money, but because of a lack of will.

"If you go back to the records of the 1970s and 1980s," Palmer says, "Princeton didn't make any attempt to even track their students' subsequent careers. They didn't bring federal recruiters to campus. *The admissions director of the Wilson School was not even aware of the mandate of the Robertson Foundation.* As a result, admissions decisions in no way reflected an emphasis on trying to attract students who had an interest in and intent to go into federal service and international affairs. When the environment got tougher to carry out this mandate," Palmer says, "Princeton broadened its definition of public service rather than doubled down. But, then, it didn't seem to me they originally intended to fulfill the mandate as Charles and Marie Robertson understood it. What you generally got from them was after-the-fact rationalization."

This is important. No one questions Princeton's claim that the highly specific job market the Robertsons envisioned has become increasingly more difficult for students to enter than it was in the 1960s. The difference, which is fundamental as well as philosophical, is that, where Princeton saw the changing environment and threw up its hands—not away from a quality enterprise, but from the specific intentions of the Robertson gift—the new foundation is taking steps to address that difficulty. Another problem was that there was tremendous bureaucratic pressure at Princeton in a time of budget cuts for the money to bleed out elsewhere past what most would describe as its core mission. Perhaps the problem is inherent: not only do budget-cutting senior staff see a well-funded program as a potential feeding ground, the faculty—easier to herd cats than to get them on the same page—was, as we have seen, always at odds with the specificity of the gift's purposes. With that kind of pressure, hindsight being what it is, it was inevitable that sooner or later the program, or at least the funding source of the program, at the Woodrow Wilson School would blow up.

By contrast, Palmer says, "The Robertson Foundation for Government is doing everything it can to carry out that original mission."[21]

The Perils of Family Dynamics

Anyone who has served on or worked closely with a family foundation knows that the mission statement isn't the only challenge in running the place. The dynamics of blood are also part of the picture. The family unity that was so evident during the lawsuit dissolved after the Princeton years. Leo Tolstoy comes to mind: "All happy families are alike, but an unhappy family is unhappy after its own fashion."[22]

Geoff Robertson, Bill Robertson's son and a governing board member of the new foundation, says the lawsuit brought the family together against "the common enemy of Princeton." He feels no particular distinction in being the younger generation's representative on the board with the last name of Robertson, and approaches his responsibilities with a sense of "awe and tremendous responsibility."

He thinks that Bo Kemper has a particularly difficult job. "Not only does he have to make sure the foundation stays on mission, but he also has to deal with family members who don't always see eye to eye."[23] Although it could credibly be characterized as unfair, that is not an uncommon challenge for those in charge of running the operational side of family foundations.

Each of the three surviving children of Charles and Marie—Bill Robertson, Katherine Ernst and Anne Meier—has named two people to the governing board; a seventh position is filled by Robert Halligan, a relative of Charles Robertson but not in the line of his children.

The difficulties inherent in family dynamics, especially when they contend with issues involving money, have not changed over the centuries. The second generation of the Robertson family, the fourth in line after George Huntington Hartford, is not happy. Family members are now grappling with harsh realities and finding their patience limited. Bill Robertson—the family member who led the lawsuit charge—has found himself the subject of his sisters' ire. It began with his request to his sisters and their husbands for additional compensation to lead the legal battle against Princeton. "They turned me down flat," Robertson says. "After much deliberation, they finally agreed to a modest increase."

Relations were further aggravated with the unremarkable results he felt his brother-in-law Robert Ernst, an attorney, had when he visited Shartsis Friese in the summer of 2008 to see about ending the lawsuit on favorable terms to the family. Robertson thinks that it is possible that since "lawyers don't want to discredit one another," Ernst returned with essentially the law firm's line of going forth with modest expectations. "Ernst turned his back on me. He spent only one day there, so he couldn't have learned much, not even to conclude what little he did. How an attorney who could clearly use the business and who has unique reason to protect the family's interests would back away from such an assignment is perplexing."[24]

Keep in mind that this took place at a critical time in the lawsuit—feelings were frayed among Bill Robertson, the attorneys and family members.

Probably no one will ever know the origins of the bad blood, but the bottom line is that Robertson has for all intents and purposes been shut out of the new organization. While he still serves on the board, his position as chair was ignominiously stripped from him. "I understand," he says, "that jealousy among family members is a long-standing practice going back through the ages."[25] It is a sober reminder of how wealth can exacerbate sibling rivalry.

Internal dissent is something many families must address, and the wealthy are hardly exempt. The root issue, whether for philanthropists or for the wealthy who never make a gift to charity, is the same: money. Dr. Lee Hausner, a Los Angeles-based clinical psychologist and the author of the book, *Children of Paradise: Successful Parenting for Prosperous Families,* once explained in an interview, "Money by itself is no longer just a commodity for barter. It has become a substitute for things such as power, control, love, happiness, and self esteem."[26]

When the family is running a foundation, these factors take on a more acute edge. Contemplating this question, Robertson takes a philosophical perspective, and says, "I wanted to hold on to the family dynasty. But then it began to unravel, and I think it began to unravel in earnest after the lawsuit."

Families of wealth interest Bill's daughter Julia, perhaps because they "can act a little crazy. My brother and I were literally ex-communicated" from other family members of her generation, she remembers, "for at least a year. My cousins were told not to talk to either of us because they"— the parents—"were going through this process of change and animosity." And, she says, "Lawyers keep coming into the picture. It's all about money and lawyers at this point."[27] Julia Robertson is not associated with the new Robertson Foundation.

As for Geoff Robertson, even though he is today "not sure how the whole thing is going to work out from a governance perspective"—the outgrowth of all the family difficulties haunting the process—he is optimistic. "This is an interesting and exciting foundation," he says, "and interacting with the fellows is my favorite part."[28]

The dirty little secret at family foundations is that many of them are effectively dysfunctional. If board civility is at times an issue at public charities and large foundations, it is far more severe when family members get together. Although overt personal greed isn't usually a factor, the quest for power and manipulation, much like Hausner says, can rule the day. "Money is like forbidden fruit," according to Bill Robertson. "It can be toxic."[29]

One of the more difficult truths family members of family foundations must realize is that the money is not theirs. *Who's to say you can't hire my girlfriend to do a study? Who's to say my husband isn't qualified to do some marketing for us? Who's to say my charitable priority shouldn't be considered? Why can't we pay ourselves a lot of money?* And more. Desires may be legitimate, but all that can be manipulated to force favor. This is an area the courts and the overseers have not been able to reach.

An example of when overseers reached and were actually able to grab onto something involved the directors of the Gran Marnier Foundation. In August 2001, Eliot Spitzer, then the attorney general of New York, summoned them to respond to complaints that they were overpaid. As Spitzer put it, they violated "their fiduciary duties by paying themselves grossly excessive compensation for their service on the board of directors." They "repeatedly violated their fiduciary duties of care and loyalty, acting in their own interest at the expense of the foundation's well-being." The complaint's focus: "In all, the directors paid themselves more than $3.4 million over a ten-year period." That was about $57,000 per director for a few meetings each year, with no work in between, some of which were all-expenses-paid meetings held in France. This, combined with what Spitzer thought was a far-too-beneficial retirement plan for the board of directors, inspired him to undo the financial transactions and to remove the board members.[30]

Although the Robertson family has had its challenges, they are nothing of the sort that would pique the interest of the IRS or the attorney general's office. And there's nothing to suggest that anyone at the new foundation has anything in mind for the money other than the mission. One casualty of the family's discord, however, was the dissolution of the Banbury Fund. After a remarkable 67-year run, what once was the family's tribute to the idyllic street where Charles Robertson sold a house to Marie Hoffman, was, in 2013, turned into three smaller entities, each controlled by one of the Robertsons' living children.

The New Foundation Looks Forward

Within the understanding that job placement is the number one priority of the foundation, Lebedev and Kemper search for added value the foundation can provide. What can go on top of the three-legged stool?

"The goal for that is to do work that will enhance the standing of public service," says Lebedev. "How can we help that along?" He puts forth the example of when the foundation financially supported the work on a paper commissioned by Paul Volcker and written in 2011 by Paul Light. "That study contributed to the thought process about federal employment," says Lebedev. And it has everything to do with how the new foundation is able to not only enhance its brand but also take steps to improve the federal environment.

In his paper, which addressed the public's understanding of government, Light said, "Confidence in the federal government's ability to respond effectively to national and international, economic and political problems continues to dwindle." He says the big issue is "what can be done to both design and implement a comprehensive reform agenda that would create the high performance government Americans want and so desperately need," and concludes that, "the time for small-scale reform has passed."[31]

"It's a question not only of helping the fellows," says Kemper, "but of getting the best possible work force into the system, as well as improving the system itself. The Volcker study is just one example of adding value to the top of the three fundamental components of the foundation's work."[32]

So the new foundation, perhaps actually buoyed by a second chance, is on its way to doing what Bill Robertson said early on: "Look at what this project could accomplish for the country." In a very real way, the Robertson Foundation for Government, as its predecessor at Princeton was intended to do, has defined and is actively engaged at the heart of the intersection of philanthropy and government.

As he reflects on the work to date, Lebedev connects the weight of the foundation's mission to its beginnings by pointing out that the first A&P store was located at what later would be Ground Zero in New York. "I use that metaphorically to say: Isn't it appropriate that the first Robertsons," by which he means George Huntington Hartford and two of his sons, George and John, "began their enterprise in a place that today has such significance for the country and relevance to the need for strength and vision."[33] Lebedev sees a useful juxtaposition between that and the newly invigorated mission that Charles and Marie Robertson had in mind more than a half-century earlier: "This historic irony perfectly highlights the Robertson family belief that the defense of American liberty begins with the cadre of public servants addressing the increasingly complex global challenges which confront this country on a daily basis."[34]

The words Lyndon Johnson employed so movingly at the 1966 ceremony dedicating the new, but not yet named, Robertson Hall at Princeton could fittingly be applied to today's Robertson Foundation for Government.

"While learning has always been the ally of democracy," he said, "the intellectual has not always been the partner of government. As recently as the early years of this century the scholar stood outside the pale of policy, with government usually indifferent to him." Johnson then suggested that while the feelings of indifference had changed, there were still practical issues to overcome. "More than one scholar has learned how deeply frustrating it is to try to bring purist approaches to a highly impure problem. They have come to recognize how imperfect are the realities which must be wrestled with in a complicated world. They have learned that criticism is one thing, diplomacy another." Johnson, noting the decency and ethical decision-making that must accompany any strong country's diplomacy, quoted the British poet and historian Thomas Babington Macaulay, "The proof of virtue is to possess boundless power without abusing it."[35]

Johnson then took note of the practical challenges, "The responsible intellectual who moves between his campus and Washington knows, above all, that his task is to bring not heat but light to public affairs." There was a time, he said, "when knowledge seemed less essential to the processes of good government," and remembered that President Andrew

Jackson, in that mindset of a different era, "held the opinion that the duties of all public offices were 'so plain and simple' that any man of average intelligence could perform them." But things are very different today, Johnson said. "We are no longer so sanguine about our public service. The public servant today moves along paths of adventure where he is helpless without the tools of advanced learning."

The times were different in 1966, of course, and Johnson spent a few minutes describing the problems in Southeast Asia, as well as the projected growth of government, especially in its foreign relations work. But he made a promise and spoke of timeless truths. He said he would spare "no effort to assist those who select" public service "as their life's work," those who work on the "battlefronts where no guns are heard but where freedom is no less tested." He asked, rhetorically, as Franklin Roosevelt did a generation earlier, if the great dream of democracy can do the job. "It will take," Johnson said, "men whose cause is not the cause of one nation but of all nations—men whose enemies are not other men but the historic foes of mankind." And then, this exhortation: "I hope that many of you will serve in this public service for the world."[36]

It was as if the President were summoning Charles and Marie Robertson's timeless sentiments.

The public service of dreams must be joined with the public service of execution and, even though execution is often dry, it is the ground from which the dream takes flight. Allied with the best public policy programs in academia that are annually monitored for effectiveness and fidelity to mission, along with the assurance from applicants that they have every intention of entering government service, the new foundation has ensured that the original Robertson dream will never go wanting.

Chapter 7

Lessons

Robertson v. Princeton didn't have to happen.

Princeton could have paid more attention, not just to the outcomes the donors wanted for the Woodrow Wilson School, but also to the Robertson family.

Bill Robertson's parents made a gift and, for decades while the purpose was in dispute, his and his father's protestations were ignored. All the while, the evidence strongly suggests, a good deal of money at the foundation was being used for something other than what everyone agreed to. "They took the money and ran," Robertson says today, thinking about how he felt before the dispute went to court. "Those bastards. They destroyed the trust my father counted on. They may have had the money and Princeton may have been king of the hill for 250 years, but they were not going to get away with this."[1]

The broken dreams, broken promises, and severe acrimony resulted in a debilitating loss of trust.

Broken Trust

Trust is one of the most elusive concepts in humankind. "Trust but verify," the expression that President Reagan employed in 1987 to characterize the order of post-cold war relations between the United States and the former Soviet Union, is commonly understood to depict the foundation of a respectful relationship. But the definition of trust—*the acceptance of the truth of a statement without evidence or investigation*—doesn't square with the vow to verify, so the famous phrase is really an oxymoron.

That's the way it is, though. People are always going to try to get the better of you when you're not looking, right? We're forced to set up safeguards, such as contracts, to protect our interests. Civilized society created the legal system for just this reason and, as a result of those safeguards, we can live in some peace. And so we go, anxiously looking over our shoulder for pretty much everything, but with faith in jurisprudence. It isn't ideal, and it certainly doesn't do much to advance the idea of trust, but it works.

Still, although our everyday experiences might suppress our trustworthy nature, and most people seem to have a trustworthy nature, we yearn for at least some pockets of life where we're not always on guard. Down deep, don't we want to be in situations that we can actually depend on people but *not* be forced to verify their intentions?

If there are such situations, isn't one of them in our relationships with charities, where philanthropy is the currency?

While it's true that a big part of the Princeton problem was that the family members of the Robertson Foundation board were not able to verify what was being done with the money, once everybody signed the gift's originating document the need for such verification should have been unnecessary at such a place as Princeton. As a matter of honoring the obligations inherent in the trust that is supposed to follow the signatures of two parties that respect each other, even in our imperfect world, at the very least Princeton should have been able to regularly confirm what had been agreed to.

Yet, as we have seen, Charles Robertson knew better. Despite his life-long love for the university—it had given this middle-class boy many opportunities—he harbored doubts from the beginning about whether Princeton would honor its commitment.

The Scholarship

It should be simple to understand that when a charity accepts a donation for a purpose, it should use the money for that purpose.

A donor once gave $1 million to a boarding school to endow a scholarship. The gift was expected to generate about $50,000 every year. One student would receive a full ride every year he or she was enrolled. After that student graduated, another would receive the same benefit. The gift agreement was clear that the new money was to *establish* a scholarship. After a few years, an accountant in the business office discovered that the money was not being used to provide scholarships. The headmaster had no problem with this. "Donors don't dictate our budget," he said. What was going on? If the accountant was right, how could the headmaster justify himself? Was he saying, despite the gift agreement, that the school had complete discretion, not only over the budget but also in interpreting a donor's wishes?

The headmaster's argument was that there *was* a scholarship that was named after the donor. One million dollars had been put in the endowment for the purpose. Nothing else needed to be known. Everyone should be happy. Case closed.

Alarmingly, leaders at many nonprofits would buy into that logic.

Why alarmingly? The problem is that the school did not *increase* the total amount of scholarship money that was provided to students. Before the gift, the scholarship budget was $3 million. That money came from other revenues the school generated each year, such as tuition payments, the income from prior restricted gifts, the income from unrestricted endowment, and other sources. But, even after the gift, the scholarship budget was still $3 million—it was *not increased* by $50,000. Although the donor's name was slapped on the scholarship so everyone knew the name of the benefactor, the donor's money did not increase the scholarship budget. Instead, the money that had been taken each year from the general fund and put into the scholarship fund could be used for whatever purpose the school wanted.

The donor did little more than subsidize the light bill.

The headmaster was using the concept of fungibility to defend his position.

If this had been explained to the donor—"Your name will be on the scholarship, but our budget for scholarships won't increase"—he might not have made the gift. Is it a stretch to think that the donor, in addition to attaching his name to a scholarship, wanted to increase the money available to deserving kids? No, it's not. This is why charities far too often don't tell donors the whole story when they set up restricted endowment funds. The headmaster was celebrating the naming opportunity and ignoring the donor's real wishes.

And, for what it's worth, as does *trust*, the word *establish* has a definition, and an important part of that definition is that it is *something new*.

Another charity, a large museum, also accepted a restricted gift and for many years never once told the donor how her money was being used. The museum had no idea how to follow the money, or, even that it should have followed the money. When the issue was brought to the attention of the museum's officials, everyone balked, the common refrain being: *This is not something to worry about. It's our money.* They may have been thinking, correctly as it turned out, that the donor's love for the place kept away any of the unpleasantness that would be associated with the demand to be told what was going on.

Flexibility and Variance

If a gift transaction is to be seen as a conduit from place to cause, donors need to be far more diligent in tracking how their money is used. They need to hold the charity accountable.

But the bulk of the burden is on the charity, which has to proactively examine whether it is doing the real work of making sure things are going as donors are led to expect.

As it stands now, nonprofits don't possess sufficient understanding to resolve the issue of donor intent within their current framework of competing but legitimate values: *Do we undertake this obligation, or not? If we do, do we know what we are agreeing to, or, at least, are we and the donor in agreement as to the purpose? And if we are, can we and our successors be reasonably certain to carry forth in both the spirit and the letter of the agreement?*

Are we up to the task?

"Many wise men and women," says Harvey Dale, the NYU law professor, "realize that they are not omniscient and not prescient, and do not impose gift conditions that last forever. But other people, equally wise, say that unless we give donors a say about how their money is going to be used, the money will dry up. And, those people say, donor intent is sacrosanct." Dale then asks the question. "It can't be sacrosanct and it can't be disregarded, so how should the tensions best be addressed?" If the first half of the equation for donors involves understanding the limits their mortality imposes, the second is doing what is possible to make sure future trustees abide by the agreement.

The charity is a crucial player in both parts of the process. Dale says, "I think that what is most important is that institutions should be encouraged to build their own variance power into documents." This would be done on two levels—and here he expands his thoughts on *Donor Intent I* and *Donor Intent II*: "You come to me—I represent a charity—and you're going to give me a large gift. You are going to write out very clearly—we're *not* going to do it orally—what you have in mind. Let's also say that I agree with what you have in mind." Now, Dale says, "Two clauses need to be added to what you've written."

The first clause says something like this: "If there is an argument at some future time, between us or after you are gone, about what this agreement means, here's how it is going to be decided. It may be by arbitration, or it may be decided by going to a judge. Whatever. We don't want our successors to be forced into big litigation. The important thing is that we create a way of solving what we are calling *Donor Intent I*. Both parties get bound by this." Dale makes it clear that this is not a process of discovering any particular truth, but one to create a way to solve a problem that might arise in the future.

Add to that the recommendation from Bill Josephson, the former head of the New York State Charities Bureau, that donors should designate in the gift agreement someone to enforce the gift's provisions, as well as to fund the likely expenses of enforcement.[2]

The second, Dale says, is this: "Suppose we have a problem of, say, impossibility or impracticability." To deal with that potential situation, "let's build in a procedure that permits variance. That's *Donor Intent II*. You're dead now, and you said, for example, that this gift is going to be used only for studying the relief of leukemia. But the problem of leukemia has been solved. This was the March of Dimes problem. Why do you have to go to court for this? Why wouldn't we write into the original agreement that if, in the future, there is a question about whether the money can be practically used for this purpose, then here is the way we will decide how to divert the money to another, similar purpose?"[3]

He puts forth another example, one of a donor who requests that a building be constructed on the corner of Fifth Avenue and 33rd Street in New York City, where the Empire State Building is located. The request for placing a new building there cannot, obviously, be honored. But the donor insists that it can. (Assume that the donor established the bequest before the Empire State Building was constructed, and died, without changing his intentions, afterwards.) How do you solve it? You could go to court. But maybe there's a better way."

He calls this a "double variance power, or double arbitration. I want some way of dealing with *Donor Intent I* if there's a disagreement about what the donor had in mind, and then I want a way of dealing with *Donor Intent II* if circumstances change."

Dale says he would not want a situation in which donor intent is all powerful because he knows that "at some point it will be defeated. We've got hundreds of years of history to prove that. And it's expensive to fix. On the other hand, I don't want to relinquish donor intent because, he says, "it is terribly important."

He would want to keep the tensions. "I don't think there's a simple way of avoiding them," he says. "I'd also want to figure out a way for a mediation process that allows for the appropriate recognition of donor intent, appropriate flexibility for the charitable needs of tomorrow, those that cannot be foreseen today, and a way of avoiding the huge expense and time delay of having to do this through court proceedings. Most important," he advises: "Include *Donor Intent I* and *Donor Intent II* in the instrument somehow."[4]

Victoria Bjorklund, who advised Princeton during the lawsuit and who is on the board of advisors at the Columbia University Training Program for Attorneys General, says one goal for charities is to "explain why charitable enforcement is important. It is very important for them to not allow the public trust in charitable institutions to diminish. On the other hand, they also have to make sure that they do not become tools of donors who have made completed gifts and who may have had changes of heart about various things." Keep in mind, she implores, "Donors who have made completed gifts get their tax benefit and unless they have retained rights of various kinds, they have given that money away. It is no longer their money."[5]

That the money is no longer theirs requires that donors be specific. Bill Josephson describes the process as "making agreements as airtight as possible."[6] And Rae Goldsmith, vice president of advancement resources for the Council for Advancement and Support of Education, says of agreements she likes, "They get into great detail—right down to how the gift will be invested, how the donors will be apprised of changes and what happens if priorities change." She says the goal is to anticipate—and prevent—conflict.[7]

When conflict arises, the potential for confusion and differing interpretations is great. Kenneth Logan, of the Princeton legal team, says, "Where you have multi-generational gifts, the risk of misunderstanding is high." Part of the way to address the issue, he thinks, is with "specificity in the gift instrument. Try to anticipate potential issues." That is impossible to do all the time, however. "Because you have personalities involved," he says, "you'll never reduce the risk to zero."[8] In addition, few restricted gifts produce a paper trail, as the Robertson gift did, of evidence that later can be used to support the heirs' claims.

Respecting the Future

One of the concerns within the donor-intent issue is how long the idea can continue to be relevant. It is not fair to say that just because time passes, the intention will become less important or more difficult to

carry out. The codicil to Ben Franklin's Last Will and Testament established a trust in1790, the corpus of which would benefit Boston and
Philadelphia. "I devote two thousand pounds sterling," he wrote, "of
which I give one thousand thereof to the inhabitants of the town of
Boston, in Massachusetts, and the other thousand to the inhabitants of
the city of Philadelphia, in trust." Five percent each year would be spent
on young apprentices who would repay the money once they were financially stable. By the end of the trust's 200-year term, in 1990, the Boston
endowment was worth a little less than $5 million and the Philadelphia
fund, which was less well managed, was valued at about $2 million.

But here's the thing, and it's closely connected to the duration of a gift's
purposes: Franklin's wisdom was expansive enough to nurture a level of
humility that today's philanthropists would do well to adopt. "Considering
the accidents to which all human affairs and projects are subject in such a
length of time," he wrote, "I have, perhaps, too much flattered myself with a
vain fancy that these dispositions, if carried into execution, will be continued without interruption and have the effects proposed."

As pretty much nothing ever works out as planned, especially when
the planning horizon is two centuries, Franklin's funds did run into obstacles; the idea of apprenticeship, for example, was radically transformed by
the unforeseeable industrial revolution—to say nothing of wars, bad economic times and politics. In the end, however, the basic idea held forth
and both cities received their money. But Franklin was right to be aware
that it might not.

Furthermore, he was not specific about how the money, once the
trust dissolved, would be used. He simply directed that the money
bequeathed to each city be divided up so that one quarter would go to the
two cities and three quarters would go to the states of Pennsylvania and
Massachusetts, "not presuming," he wrote, "to carry my views farther."[9]

Franklin and, as we saw earlier, Andrew Carnegie are reminders that there
are those who know that agreements that go into a long or unmeasur-
able future should not be made capriciously, that decisions about leaving

wealth to a charitable purpose should be made only within an environment of seriousness and humility. The corollary for charities is that, if we accept that the strength of the dead hand should nourish the benefactor's wishes well after death, the manner by which a donor's demands are accepted is the most significant consideration for charities that want to both thrive and stay out of court in the future. Franklin prefaced his gift intentions saying, "if accepted by the inhabitants . . ."[10]

At some point, all of us must come to terms with at least two simple truths: we will not live forever and, over time, the world will change. No matter how wealthy any of us is, we can't control the future. And, no, we can't take our treasure with us. As one Dartmouth College fundraiser once said to a donor, "And even if you could take it with you, in your case anyway, it most assuredly would burn."[11]

With this in mind, is it possible that Albert Barnes's restrictions, for example, were simply too strict to stand the test of time? Or, in his case at least, is there a point past which a donor's wishes become less important than society's needs? Through another prism, donors and charities need to discern the difference between the types of restrictions and intentions put forth by Barnes and Franklin. Not all donor intent is categorically the same. That doesn't necessarily mean that Barnes-like directives are wrong, but it would be clear that over time, as Ken Logan says, with more specificity and more time comes more potential for disagreement.

A Potpourri of Problems

At Princeton, the principal issue was the way the money was being used. That's why, during the discovery phase of the lawsuit, the Robertson legal team closely examined the accounting ledgers. And, that's why Jessie Lee Washington's findings were so relevant. In fact, her conclusions were all the more relevant because she was looking at another part of the university's books and found the same problems the Robertsons did at the foundation.[12]

Fungibility, the interchangability of assets, is not a legitimate defense for not doing what a donor wants after the charity has agreed to do it.

While fungibility wasn't the cause of the Robertsons' original concerns, its murkiness led to other concerns as dire. Money was being used for purposes the family board members did not approve of and, until Princeton's hand was forced, did not know about.

How charities deal with fungibility within restricted accounts is very much related to honoring the donor's intentions. This is not only an accounting issue. It is one that demands the full attention of an informed ethical decision-making process. The solution cannot be to actually follow the physical dollar through the books tracking the value of each fund, but it can involve knowing, and showing, that money is actually getting to its destination without devious legerdemain.

Another issue in the lawsuit, one that Paul Volcker described so persuasively, was the lack of interest in the actual practice of public administration. The Woodrow Wilson School's reliance on the theoretical and not the practical got it into trouble with the Robertsons. Paul Light talks of "Princeton's disinvestment in public administration. The economists and the policy analysts at several schools," he says, "tend to make the argument that success is determined by being published in the right places and that their work is empirically rigorous." Those who criticized Princeton felt that the Wilson School was turning its back not only on the results Charles Robertson wanted but also on the idea that public administration—as distinct from public policy—is a legitimate academic pursuit in its own right. "Paul Volcker," Light says, "was absolutely right to criticize Princeton's approach."[13]

Yet another, the one that never ceded its prominence despite the dramas of misspending and overspending, was why Princeton didn't try to place more people in the federal government. As we've seen, the people there said they tried. But the statistics were disappointing.

And the common thread throughout, sewing all the issues together into one big disaster for Princeton, was the growing lack of trust. The donors and their children never really paused in relief; they never were sure the money was being spent as they wished, as everyone in the beginning had agreed.

If we accept that the gift's purpose wasn't being fulfilled as the donors wanted, then we must wonder why. The Robertson camp pushes the idea that Princeton knowingly and nefariously misused the money. And there is evidence to support that. But it is also true that many charities that don't adhere to a donor's wishes might be guiltier of ignorance than they are of arrogance. For example, when donors give to faith-based organizations, many do so with the feeling they are giving to God, with the understanding that God knows best what to do with the money. Most nonprofit administrators don't believe they are acting with God's wisdom, of course, but donors might think that charities, even when a gift agreement is created, will, without question, do what's best. Therefore, the donor culture of misplaced trust—not because of an organization's bad intentions, necessarily, but because of a lack of accounting aptitude—also needs examination.

That scrutiny might lead to a discovery that nonprofit administrators could learn much from their for-profit counterparts, whose customers are perhaps more likely than donors to require an adherence to sticking to the terms of a deal. It is no secret that many nonprofit administrators have never once set foot in the for-profit arena and have no idea what a customer is or what a customer demands. Or where their salaries really come from. While the for-profit world's ethos should be no blueprint for nonprofits, all too often the dominant component of the charity's ethos is: *Once we get the money, it's ours and we know what's best to do with it. We're the good guys.*

In the for-profit world (where monopolies haven't been formed), a dissatisfied customer can change suppliers. So it's not that much of a stretch to understand Bill Robertson's thinking that, since in his view Princeton wasn't doing the job, he would take the money elsewhere. What was so special about Princeton? While the Wilson School is in many ways world-class, it wasn't world-class—not to either Robertson's satisfaction—in accomplishing the objectives the gift was primarily intended to fund. The essence of the gift wasn't defined by the particular organization where the money resided; it was that the money would be used correctly. Princeton was only Charles Robertson's alma mater; and, as we have seen, he did not respect the way his money was used. That Princeton is an Ivy League school was, of course, significant, but simple stature didn't obviate the need to follow the donor's directions.

From that perspective, it's clear why a deeply dissatisfied Bill Robertson would come up with the solution of taking the fund from Princeton so that he could benefit worthy organizations that would be required to periodically justify themselves.

But, aside from everything else that *Robertson v. Princeton* highlighted, this question persists: While we have seen that donors care very much that their wishes are honored and while we have seen that the states and the courts take those wishes seriously, why is it that we instinctively think that what donors want is so special? What is it about the charitable transaction that gives donors the right to say anything at all?

Why Donor Intent is Important

Money donated to a charity is unquestionably the charity's money. The charity, which includes its future board members, is given the right, the responsibility, actually, to decide what is best for its mission. The IRS is particular about this. Many cases the IRS pursues in its tax-exempt division involve donors who want to retain too much control over how their gifted money is used.[14] The tax dollars that are saved through the deduction are not meant to benefit people close to the donor; that people cannot use charity for their own purposes is evidence of the essential relationship between the nonprofit sector and the rest of society.

So, if it's no longer the donor's money, why is it important that charities keep donors' intentions paramount? Does it really matter, as long as the money is being used for the public good, what Smithers or Buck or Barnes or Robertson wanted into eternity?

Yes, not because charities aren't doing good things, although quibbling about the social importance of the work at various charities will be ongoing. A donor's intentions should be considered sacrosanct because the donor-charity relationship so fundamentally relies on trust.

If we can all agree that nonprofits are not to be fully funded and run by government agencies, or operated as full-fledged profit-making business enterprises, the practical building block of eleemosynary sanctity is that charities need donors.

And donors . . . well, many of them have ideas.

And so it behooves charities to honor their commitments.

Give—in the sense that a person has willingly and without recompense parted with an asset—has a meaning, but so does *agreement*. Any angst the combination of those terms creates in the context of a charitable gift can most easily be alleviated when, after the gift is made and its terms agreed to, the organization does as promised. It's not an issue of a donor demanding something crazy or unanticipated, or even whether the charity owns the money. The rubber meets the road because, while the structured organizations within the nonprofit sector are, from an individual's perspective, the optimum destination for philanthropic treasure, almost no charity or foundation could do its work as well as it does without the support of those with the money.

When the charity agrees to listen, the grip of the donor's dead hand simply needs to be accepted.

Harvey Dale says, "It's perfectly clear that donor intent is really important. I don't think there is anybody who can rationally say that he or she would want to do away with donor intent. Among other things, if donors didn't have the right to specify the uses to which their property is to be put, it would almost certainly chill giving. You certainly want donor intent to be a key and central issue of giving."[15]

Stuart Polkowitz, Bernard and Jeanne Adler's attorney, says, "Donor intent is the most critical aspect of a conditional gift. That was the key legal point in the very first two paragraphs of the Appellate Court's decision in the Adler case. Ultimately, it's *all* about donor intent."[16] Indeed, the ruling said, "A reviewing court's duty is to enforce the donor's original intent by directing the charity to either fulfill the condition or return the gift."[17] The court acknowledged that it is easier to ascertain intentions when donors are alive and disputes arise, but that is no license to act recklessly after the donors have died.

Spending Decisions

It's no secret how money affects people, and as long as humans, and not saints, run nonprofits, the pursuit of economic maximization will not be restricted to corporations. Charities, many of them behemoths of corporations, often feel free to use money the way they want, not only when something comes along that is different from a donor's desires but even when the spending does not strictly support its charitable purposes. Making sure the money is spent correctly—not from the perspective of ideology but of accomplishing a mission—is a tricky area.

The Robertson lawsuit was never intended to do more than get Princeton to do the right thing in the eyes of the family's understanding of the original agreement, in itself a formidable task, but it also brought to light other serious questions about the way colleges and universities, as well as organizations in other charitable sectors, go about spending money.

In a scathing article about the secrecy behind spending decisions at universities, Wick Sloane, a columnist for *Inside Higher Ed* and a former chief financial officer at the University of Hawaii, reported on four studies conducted on behalf of the Massachusetts Service Employees International Union between 2010 and 2011. The studies analyzed important questions involving executive compensation levels, conflicts of interest, the lack of transparency, and the social costs and value of university tax exemptions.[18]

One report quoted Richard Doherty, the president of the Association of Independent Colleges and Universities in Massachusetts, who seemed to endorse an upbeat obfuscation when he told a Boston newspaper, "The benefits of higher education should be so obvious as to render new, number-heavy analyses unnecessary,"[19] a variation of the worn-out response to questions involving value and the nonprofit world: *We're the good guys, so lay off.* The series concluded that more research, as well as far more disclosure, is needed for the public to understand its investment in higher education. As one report said, "A more robust public debate about the costs and benefits of colleges' nonprofit fiscal privileges . . . is badly needed."[20]

In his commentary, Sloane cites the thoughts of a mentor who had once wondered "how so many colleges had become investment-management companies with a few classrooms attached."[21]

Bill Robertson's concerns about PRINCO, as well as the financial crisis that many well-endowed universities endured after the market meltdown in 2007, come to mind. Is it any wonder that much of the public is beginning to think of universities, especially well endowed ones, as little more than palatial playgrounds, where the recess from real life is four years long, where the occasional interruption in the festivities requires an actual assignment? Where the pursuit of a high total return by Wall Street mindsets trumps the job of ensuring that actual money will be available for scholarships and salaries—not only the salaries of star academics but also those of the janitors?

That may sound edgy, but colleges and universities do themselves no favors by investing at risk levels that should be unacceptable for organizations meant to provide ongoing services, all the while doing whatever is needed to tilt the ratings, the most misguidedly popular of which can be found annually in *U.S. News*, toward themselves.

It isn't a chief executive's high salary alone. It's not only an uncomfortable ratio of fundraising or overhead to program expenses. It's when things seem so starkly out of kilter. How can an organization pay so much to its people or experience unnaturally high investment returns and still manage to do so little—say, in the form of scholarships—while keeping the price so high?

What, it must be asked, is the purpose of our nonprofit sector?

Think of this: Charities are tempted to use public money in ways they see fit, and the temptation comes with an inherent conflict: how to dispense that money more for the public good than for the people administering that good.

Nonprofit administrators, including those at Princeton, want to use tax dollars to do big things for their departments. That's natural, and it's easy to justify a department's needs within the greater good. But the concern over how much we benefit private individuals, as well as who decides how that beneficence is bestowed, is a key component to understanding the dangers of capriciously allocating the government's treasury and influence, or using the structure of nonprofits, to spend money poorly. "Poorly" is a subjective term, but the notion that our leading nonprofits—not only in higher education—have somehow left their nonprofit status behind to pursue what for-profit corporations pursue requires them to do more than meagerly offer up: *We're the good guys.*

The impression was critical in the Robertson case. The question of why more people weren't entering government service was legitimate to begin with, but the issue became ensnared in the swirl of money being spent on "the edges of acceptability," as Princeton's counsel Doug Eakeley has said. Eakeley was right to identify the edges as those legitimately gray areas of decision-making, but it behooves administrators to better define and communicate those edges, not only to plan a prudent budget but also to ensure that the public, as well as Congress, is comfortable that a nonprofit really does deserve a special place in our society.

Remember Frederic Fransen's concern about the $16,000 rug in the dean's office at the Wilson School.[22] Remember Harold Shapiro's rationale for the hypothetical football coach.

Public Purpose and Donor Intent

The vitality of the dead hand leads us to another question: Do wealthy people have the right to change or even influence society's priorities?

Isn't that what the large foundations are trying to do today? All the big foundations—Gates, Rockefeller, Pew, Koch and many others—support not only what many believe are good causes, but also specific causes. They are often national causes, and they can understandably be confused with the government's concerns.

Who gave the foundations, and, by extension, individuals who happened to have a lot of money, the right to affect society in major ways? After all, donors are not elected officials and have no agency to change or alter national priorities. That money clearly has been playing a more and more prominent role in our elections and the enactment of legislation is no reason to walk away from the question. Indeed, it focuses the question: Where is the line drawn between helping society and individually altering its objectives?

This is not a new source of anxiety.[23] When George Washington said farewell to public service for good after his second presidential term, he posited an ominous warning:

> The very idea of the power and the right of the people to establish government presupposes the duty of every individual to obey the established government. All obstructions to the execution of the laws, all combinations and associations, under whatever plausible character, with the real design to direct, control, counteract, or awe the regular deliberation and action of the constituted authorities, are destructive of this fundamental principle, and of fatal tendency. They serve to organize faction, to give it an artificial and extraordinary force; to put, in the place of the delegated will of the nation the will of a party, often a small but artful and enterprising minority of the community.
>
> However combinations or associations of the above description may now and then answer popular ends, they are likely . . . to become potent engines, by which cunning, ambitious, and unprincipled men will be enabled to subvert the power of the people and to usurp for themselves the reins of government, destroying afterwards the very engines which have lifted them to unjust dominion.

Washington was not alone. It could be said that an essential pillar of the Constitution itself was born of the idea that there needs to be a construct of supremacy organizing all of government's affairs, as well as the affairs subordinate to public policy. James Madison argued in the Federalist Papers that small groups of people with different interests needed oversight. "The regulation of these various and interfering interests," he wrote, "forms the principal task of modern legislation."[24]

The worry of undue influence was not even born with the Founders, however. We can go back to Niccoló Machiavelli's *Discourses,* in which

he cited a story about a philanthropist who, because his private beneficence was a threat to the state's authority, was put to death for being
charitable.[25]

In 1915, two years before the charitable deduction was added to the
tax code, even though the idea had popular support, some were worried
about its future effect. A concern in the final report of the Commission
on Industrial Relations was how much control the wealthy—as the
deduction mostly benefited, and still does, those in high tax brackets—
would have over national priorities:

> The domination by the men in whose hands the final control
> of a large part of American industry rests is not limited to their
> employees, but is being rapidly extended to control the educa-
> tion and "social service" of the Nation.
>
> This control is being extended largely through the creation of
> enormous privately managed funds for indefinite purposes, here-
> inafter designated "foundations," by the endowment of colleges
> and universities, by the creation of funds for the pensioning of
> teachers, by contributions to private charities, as well as through
> controlling or influencing the public press.

The report cites Rockefeller and Carnegie as examples of foundations
with great wealth.[26]

And so in the 21st Century, Peter Dobkin Hall, a professor of history and theory at the School of Public Affairs at Baruch College, City
University of New York, writes, "The central paradox of American life
is the coexistent ideals of political equality enshrined in our institutions
of law and government and the realities of unequally distributed wealth,
influence and talent." Hall says that foundations—or, "popular interme-
diary bodies"—"not only diminished the sovereignty of the state by representing themselves rather than government as legitimate forums for the
expression of the popular will, they also favored propertied minorities
with the resources to devote to their establishment and perpetuation."[27]

Thus, the purity of altruism is stained. Perhaps it has always been so, and perhaps it must be so. Despite Machiavelli's pragmatism, Jefferson's philosophy, and Washington's warnings, today we accept that society empowers money to address pretty much whatever issues the benefactor wants to address, even though they may not be aligned with public policy.

Washington and those who argued in support of the Constitution's ratification were talking about political factions, or parties, but today we can add *charitable organizations* to *factions* or *associations*. Do that, and you can see how Madison's and Washington's concerns are relevant to today's nonprofit sector, society's orphan, which purports to do its work outside the need for profit and without designs for raw political gain.

The Founders were not necessarily against civil organizations with a public or philanthropic purpose—not as engines to do good, anyway—but they did have a profound understanding of human nature and the tendency of everyone to be an economic maximizer, a propensity shared also by those outside the arena of capitalism. Use enough money on behalf of donors' intentions, in part paid for by foregone taxes, and the idea of economic maximization in the civil sector suddenly seems very real—and with ominous potential. Such groups, as Washington said, were "potent engines, by which cunning, ambitious, and unprincipled men will be enabled to subvert the power of the people and to usurp for themselves the reins of government."

When a nonprofit receives the IRS's tax-exemption blessing, the idea of donor intent gets tested against the concept of public purpose—a step, if it is successful, that legitimizes the donor's wishes. Furthermore, as obtaining tax-exempt status gives no license to the charity to do whatever it wants in the future, feedback mechanisms—which, outside the filing of the 990, pretty much are nonexistent—should demonstrate disclosure, transparency, conflicts of interest, and oversight.[28] And those feedback mechanisms ought to be made publicly available, proactively and willingly, by the charity. The state of affairs at charities today, where secrecy is more the norm than transparency is, defies the very foundation of what societies expect in return for their tax dollars.

The stonewalling in the Robertson lawsuit—think how Princeton refused to provide the information documenting how the Foundation's spending formula was derived—is splayed front and center in the larger arena of charitable spending. Little did the Robertsons and Jessie Washington realize how relevant their questions would become, not only as they related to Princeton's policies but also as they relate to the fundamental question of how society should view nonprofits.

It is within the context of public purpose that charitable activity must be understood. Donor intent is validated by the charity's own public place in society.

This question of using what incontrovertibly is public money to exercise influence must be addressed by charitable organizations individually, as well as by all of them as a group with more or less a single voice. Although there will never be a national consensus on the precise boundaries of such influence, the debate must be ongoing and vibrant. Otherwise, state and local governments, as dysfunctional as they may seem, will be tempted to step in with more regulations than exist on the books today.

While the Robertsons or Princeton cannot be fairly accused of trying to alter the nation's priorities, it is true that the foundation housed and facilitated an intention; a good one, as it turns out, that everyone can agree with, and not in competition with the public's goals. But change the intention, and you can see the root problem.

This is an issue not just because donors can direct public money in the form of diverted tax dollars. It's that the *structure* exists for people to affect national priorities outside the voting booth. The Supreme Court, having dramatically expanded the idea that money can influence elections, has given rise to the number of nonprofit organizations whose donors do *not* benefit from an income tax deduction.[29] The deduction could be eliminated today—indeed, there was no income tax in Washington's day, and so there were no deductions—and the concern would still be valid.

That the Robertsons did not try to usurp anything was, perhaps, the luck of the draw—the uncontroversial goal of promoting the interests of the United States while at the same time not trying to direct those interests involved the rare combination of wisdom and humility—but the fight that followed, in the wake of differences of interpretation of what was to happen after the gift, should cause us all to pause. Donors and charities have a responsibility to address core issues within the question of long-term or perpetual expectations, as well as how those expectations could collide with public policy.

Bill Robertson's Perspective on Princeton

The grocery store heiress and her husband were not interested in upsetting public policy. Princeton was not being asked to do anything that was impossible, impractical or illegal—or, even, outdated. Therefore, it was the university's job to make sure the mandate was executed.

Ron Malone, the Robertsons' attorney, says the problem was "the university's interpretation of the mandate. Princeton was in control of the foundation by virtue of its four to three majority representation on the board, but that control was still subject to the terms of the gift and fiduciary duty." The idea of control, he emphasizes, "does not mean that they could do whatever they wanted."[30]

Greg Lebedev, the consultant to the new Robertson foundation, asks, "How could Princeton have been confused? Even setting aside the charter document, the correspondence was crystal clear about Charles Robertson's wishes."[31] If, for example, as Robert Goheen, Princeton's president at the time the gift was made, acknowledged in his testimony during the lawsuit, the language in the original gift instrument was "unfortunate," referring to what grew to be a large and costly difference of opinion, why didn't Princeton officials *ever* discuss that point with the Robertsons? It appears that Princeton did its work in secret, knowingly violating, or strongly suspecting that it was violating, what Charles and Marie Robertson intended. At the very least, over a period of more than four decades, Princeton was never certain that it was in the good graces of the donors or their children. Princeton could not have been unaware that trouble was brewing.

In the run-up to the trial that never was, considerable evidence was amassed to demonstrate that a first-rate university was trying to pull the

wool over the eyes of the donors and their children. Princeton could have
been more responsive, but they weren't. Even after the lawsuit was filed,
there was plenty of time to work things out. Instead, university administrators, most likely urged by their attorneys, as Paul Volcker surmises,
chose to give no ground. When attorneys get involved, it seems everyone
circles the wagons, and when that happens no one is talking. Regardless
of the legal advice, however, it behooves all nonprofits, behemoths or
not, to pay close attention to their donors—*especially* when the going
gets tough. This should be obvious on a moral level, but, in the pursuit
of enlightened self-interest as well, they should be loath to work out differences with their donors under the harsh and public spotlight of the
courtroom.

Robertson today remains angered by Robert Goheen's deposition
during the lawsuit. "How did Goheen go through 40 years," Robertson
asks, "knowing the whole thing was a lie? How could he have lived with
that? Princeton had just snatched 40 percent of one of America's great
family fortunes of the time." As he wonders about this, Robertson is thinking of the part of Goheen's deposition where he described how "haunted"
he was by what he characterized as a difference between Princeton and
Charles Robertson in executing the gift agreement, an angst that should
never have been necessary as it was always possible to simply pick up the
phone and iron out the differences.

Goheen probably didn't want to do that, however, as he most likely
thought he knew how the conversation would go. Charles Robertson
very well might have said: *You're doing a terrible job, Bob. I've told you
over and over what I expect and, our mutual love of golf be damned, you're
not paying attention. This is not going the way I expected, and not what
I was led to believe when you accepted the responsibilities of managing a
$35 million gift.* For Bill Robertson, it seems to have been far more about
Princeton getting the gift than how to put it to work correctly. He cannot
get out of his mind the moment in the deposition when he heard Goheen
say, "We got the . . .." Robertson knows, had Goheen not caught himself,
the next word would have been *money*.

This—what wasn't said but something everyone knew—is what

should haunt all nonprofits when they are presented with a sizable donation. While some people might think a fundraiser's job is complete when the gift is made, at that moment the nonprofit must begin the process of taking care of it. "The gift was off track from the beginning," says Robertson, "and Princeton was clearly being dishonest."

He further thinks that part of the problem is that each of the presidents during the Robertson Foundation-era at Princeton was an academic, "a tenured professor, and none of them was able to face the reality of the problem of the use of funds." While Ivy League presidents are almost certainly going to arrive at their new desks with a history of impeccable academic credentials, Robertson thinks the saturation in academic bureaucracy prevented each president from seeing the terms of the gift as he knows his parents desired.[32]

Reflecting on this point inspires Robertson to outline a broader blame, one where Robert Goheen is only a lesser culprit. "The real perpetrator," Robertson says, "was Bill Bowen," Goheen's successor. "He got his start in the economics department and as much as admitted that our family's foundation money was using the Woodrow Wilson School as simply a funnel to other departments." Robertson was referring to Bowen's acknowledged yearning that resources should be made available to benefit the "university as well as the school itself." Bowen's goal was to increase resources for other academic departments while at the same time "reduce the charge to the general University funds for those programs."[33] "Goheen was bad," says Robertson, "but Bowen was the guy who actually set the policy. He wanted to siphon off money to the economics department, generously, and he did, and that expanded into the politics and sociology departments, as well as elsewhere. That was a blatant violation of the terms." Robertson adds, "Another culprit in Bowen's flawed policy was Tom Wright, Princeton's general counsel and then secretary of the university for over three decades, who executed many questionable decisions relating to the Robertson Foundation."[34]

By the time Shirley Tilghman became president in 2001, it was becoming clear that the Robertsons and Princeton had not been on the same page for a while. "The Tilghman administration's fatal mistake was in following legal advice, which was to perpetuate and magnify the lie. They were caught red-handed, and," Robertson says as he considers the university's statements in the wake of the lawsuit's settlement, "it appears that they haven't learned from their mistake. They could have avoided the entire disaster had they shown a little honesty and contrition when we questioned them in 2002. But they didn't. They stonewalled us on management of the portfolio, on producing normal corporate records, on spending money on Wallace Hall, and on the mission." Whittled down to a phrase: "Blind arrogance."[35]

If Goheen was bad and Bowen was worse and Tilghman kept it up, then the university itself became the toxic cesspool where trust and respect had long ago been drowned. "There were all kinds of ways this could have been different," Robertson says. They didn't want to give, even a little, because they just thought they couldn't possibly be wrong. Princeton's characteristics were deception, disrespect, and cowardice. They could have discussed all the issues, but they were—What's the word?—they were sneaky. They thought they were so smart they would never have to confront this; they thought they would just outsmart us."[36]

What Can Donors and Charities Do?

Ken Logan, the attorney for Princeton, cautions against searching for sweeping lessons. That the "Robertson Foundation was a unique structure," he says, "precludes a lot of generalizations from the case."[37] But donors have rights even when they don't establish supporting organizations and even when they and their heirs don't have formal voting rights. The very idea of an arrangement in which the charity agrees to spend donated money in a certain way means that someone—the donor, an heir or a regulator—is going to be watching.

Still, there are a few steps that donors can take to ensure their legacies, and a few broad policies that nonprofits can implement to ensure their interests:

For philanthropists:

1. Honestly and humbly consider whether the gift's purpose is enduring and is aligned with the organization's mission.

2. Permit the organization to incorporate an "escape clause" into the gift agreement or default provisions in the event of a dispute or that circumstances change over time.

3. Designate someone you authorize to have standing in court in the event a legal action becomes necessary. As Bill Josephson has written, "Donors who wish to ensure that their restricted gifts can be enforced would be well advised not only to designate in the gift instrument a legal entity to do so, but also to fund the likely expenses of enforcement."

4. Be specific. While Bill Josephson and Ken Logan view the Robertson case from opposing perspectives, each agrees that specificity is key to reducing the potential conflicts that might arise over the years after a gift is made.

5. Hold the charity's feet to the fire by demanding that relevant information is provided in a timely manner.

For nonprofits:

1. Require each board member to review the terms of endowed gifts; in particular, avoid using the phrase "in perpetuity."

2. Actively explore best practices for presenting financials, such as deciding what should be in the board reports and what questions that board members should ask.

3. Develop policies around the allocation of overhead and ask whether it is reasonable for board members to see an annual review of expenses to outcomes.

4. Analyze the effectiveness and fairness of a whistle-blower policy and reiterate the importance of its existence to employees; also encourage them to use it if they see something that management is not addressing.

5. Require that every board member fully review, understand and accept the information reported on the organization's 990.

Within each step for both donor and charity are many other considerations that make the process arduous and complex. But, as we have seen, there really is no shortcut to ensuring a legacy and maintaining the sanctity of the mission. Yes, the two often are at odds, and are inclined to become more so over time, but tensions are healthy. Besides, there is no way to avoid them.

An umbrella over all the suggestions and thoughts for reform is the importance of comprehensive, ongoing, and rigorously honest board training. In this case, it wasn't just the Robertson Foundation board that could have done better; the whole of the Princeton University board, remember, was hurried into accepting the gift. If board members had gone through the process of understanding what is really involved in accepting gifts, it might have been alerted to some of the issues in this particular gift that needed addressing, and a lot of trouble might have been avoided.

This is no criticism of the 1961 Princeton University board of trustees. Since then, there has been much improvement—although not enough—in the awareness of the responsibilities that nonprofit board members undertake when they accept their role. It was once more akin to joining a country club: status with few real risks. Today, in part because of heightened public and regulatory scrutiny, board members have a better idea of what they have signed up for.

But, as important, the message changed over time. What the Princeton board was told was not fully squared with what took place after the gift was accepted.

Finally—and although this may seem obvious, it apparently isn't—the program people at a charity should *never* tell donors that their concerns are exaggerated. Although the dean of the Woodrow Wilson School did not say that directly to Robertson, he wrote it to someone representing his interests. Imagine how that sort of impertinence would affect a donor.

Robertson v. Princeton didn't have to happen, but perhaps it will be a wake-up call for better governance and a healthy respect for the relationship between donor and charity. And trust. Bill Robertson wondered: *Do I trust these people?* And then answered in the negative.

A Judgment and a Legacy

The most consequential finding in a survey taken in 2012 of more than 250 philanthropists from around the world is that emotion drives giving. *Seventy percent said their motivation was from the heart and that they are driven by personal values.*[38] Donors are more than check-off boxes on lists that measure the success of fundraising efforts. The commodity that separates nonprofits from for-profits is honor—the charity can return little else. Thus, the transaction, from the donor's perspective, is far more spiritual than economic.

The spirit transcends death. The checkbook doesn't.

Vartan Gregorian, the president of the Carnegie Corporation, once addressed the spiritual nature of humanity by positing that a major threat to liberty, a value close to the Robertsons' hearts, "is to treat ourselves as only economic units rather than as spiritual beings. America is not an actuality but it's a potentiality. We have to remember that the universe is not going to be seeing somebody like you again in its entire history of creation, so it's up to you to become a dot, a paragraph, a page, a blank page, a chapter in the history of creation."[39]

Nothing better might speak to the importance of the lives beyond. The Robertsons' decision to make their anonymous gift at the height of the Cold War might very well have been driven by a moral hunger to be satisfied only in the lifetimes of future generations.

Seamus Heaney reminded us that the better angels of our nature have the capacity to act well beyond a lifetime:

History says, Don't hope
on this side of the grave.
But then, once in a lifetime
the longed for tidal wave
of justice can rise up,
and hope and history rhyme.[40]

The Robertsons were trailblazers for future philanthropists. They exhibited what every donor wants to be and wants to tell the world. Helping others, including when the others have not yet been born, is a way to act out one of the behaviors most people see as the best of themselves.

We accomplish something big when charity and donor each work together to make the world better by making the other better.

The family's charges weren't vague, but, as they incorporated unclear phrases like *donor intent* and were dependent on the interpretational complexities of accounting, they could be disputed. But the defense was no slam-dunk, as Princeton often indicated it should have been. David Gelfand, the attorney who completed the settlement agreement, says, "If the cause of Bill Robertson and the rest of the family was as frivolous as Princeton was suggesting, this case would not have settled. Princeton would have just pursued it and, ultimately, I think, if they were right the court would have found for Princeton. But I don't think the matter was as straightforward as all of that. If the evidence were so crystal clear that there had been no aberration from the original donors' intent, it's highly unlikely this lawsuit would have gone on for more than six years."[41]

As if to expound on how straightforward the Robertson case wasn't, Ken Logan puts the ordeal in this context. "The adversarial system is a tough way to resolve" the kinds of questions that arose in the lawsuit. While the judge may have admirably juggled many competing values and perspectives, there were far too many issues to be dealt with cleanly in our legal system. "It's inefficient, costly, and time-consuming," says Logan. "I'm not sure what a better system would be, but it's unfortunate.

There are many contexts in which the adversarial system has worked, and historically it's been superb, but there are times when it's cumbersome."

Charles and Marie Robertson did not try to tie down Princeton with short-term conceit; not at all, for example, like Albert Barnes, whose wishes turned out to be more limiting than the passage of time would permit. The Robertsons were the benefactors of a pursuit as benign and timeless as the university's own. Today's federal government is vibrant, and a decent number of its employees are tasked with serving in the arena of international relations and affairs.[42] While there may never be a clear dividing line between honoring and ignoring donor intent—words, no matter how meticulously crafted, will always be subject to interpretation over the ages—the opening sympathy in a dispute, because of the role donors play, must be that the donor has the advantage.

Princeton's defense that:

1. The Woodrow Wilson School is a world-class institution,

2. Its graduates are among society's leaders,

3. A good number of graduates enter public service,

4. Academic freedom is paramount, and

5. The spending outside the direct mission of the Robertson Foundation's mandate was justified

is to be weighed against:

1. Evidence that job results were disappointing,

2. Evidence of the university's scorn toward the foundation's mission,

3. Revelations that important decisions were hidden from the family trustees,

4. The accounting firm's devastating financial revelations, and

5. Jessie Washington's corroborative findings.

Neither a judge nor a jury settled the case. There was no verdict. While many people in the nonprofit world understandably lament the absence of a clear roadmap, especially after such an opportunity so rich with facts and drama arose, in fact any up or down legal decision would have diminished the value of the extralegal and ethical dimensions of each side's rationale. It's not so much the weight of the evidence on each side that interested observers outside the case's participants must take into account, for both sides offered plenty to think about, but the weight of the value system informing our perceptions—the "edges," one might say—of the arguments both sides put forth. That which is actually weighed on the scales of true and messy justice is not easily ascertained; less placing a brick or a feather on a scale than pouring water on it. Still, however, even with the obstacle of complexity, the task of hitting the donor-intent issue head-on is imminent. If nonprofits are to claim a special space in society and in our hearts, they must own a level of responsibility far beyond what any court would require.

In fact, Princeton would have done well to adhere to Lord Thomas Macaulay's words, referenced by President Johnson when Robertson Hall was dedicated: "The highest proof of virtue is to possess boundless power without abusing it."

While we can understand and appreciate the intricacies of spending money in the pursuit of even the simplest ideals—"particular emphasis on the education of such persons for careers in those areas of the Federal Government that are concerned with international relations and affairs"—with a laser eye on the easily understood concepts of *careers*, *federal government*, and *international relations*—an examination of Princeton's fiduciary and stewardship behaviors leads to this layperson's judgment: guilty of misusing the Robertson gift.

Bill Robertson has said, "Look at what this project could accomplish for the country." In a world where the love of humankind reigns—where charity, society's orphan, is paramount to our humanity—Charles and Marie Robertson gave birth to an impressive vision that would one day rhyme with history—and do much for the country.

Epilogue

I'm Proud of You

Dear Bill,

I guess I put us both in quite a pickle, didn't I?

Somebody once said that we are able to write a history only when we hear the people speak. I know how much you've wanted the world to know this story—and so I wanted to speak to you one final time.

First, thank you for saving all those letters. I wrote them to make sure you and the other children would know and never forget what your mother and I were thinking—about Princeton, the gift, her uncles, and you—all of you. We were always grateful that we could provide for you financially. Your mother's fortune was unique in America and I was privileged, beyond anything I deserved, to be her husband. The money, however, wasn't what made my life so filled with promise. Although managing our resources became my life's work, I consider it my highest privilege that I could spend my life with such a remarkable woman. She was remarkable for two things: 1) she never let her wealth turn her into something she wasn't, and 2) she was an extraordinary wife and mother. I am certain that, if it were at all possible, she really would have taken in all those kids from England during the war.

I think you know this, but let me be clear on something very personal. We never played favorites, which is not always the case when a couple has four children. Each of you had—and continues to have—an equally special place in our hearts. People who don't adopt don't know this: every child under a parent's care is the ultimate gift. And I can say this for a fact, because we adopted the three of you and, then, to everyone's surprise, along came Katherine. So we were permitted a special joy.

Still, you were the one whom I thought could do the job for the Robertson Foundation board at Princeton. It's not that you were better than the other children; it's more that I saw in you an interest and a propensity to understand the complexity of investments and budgets that the family side of the foundation would have to understand. You know, I never did trust Princeton to do the job right. For me, the fight was always about getting people into the federal government; that problem was bad enough, but then you discovered things, after I left you, that took my breath away. Not only were job placements disappointing, Princeton was using the money we gave—with what I think were fairly clear instructions—to pay for things we never intended. I don't think anyone else would have been so dogged.

Which is the other reason I wanted you on the board so badly. I sensed in you a uniquely strong devotion to what your mother and I wanted to accomplish. You were right—as you were so many times—when you said that the purpose of the gift wasn't to benefit Princeton but to benefit the American people. During six and a half years, you were called upon to show a great deal of mettle as you kept the interests of your mother and me at the heart of your battle.

Most people with a strong sense of integrity get beaten up a bit. That's just the way it is. When I was on the board, the Princeton board members wouldn't dare overtly show disrespect to your mother or me, of course. Even though they were subtle, however, it was obvious that they were fighting me every step of the way. How many times does one have to point out that not enough graduates are going into the federal government for someone to hear that not enough students are going into the federal government? And, really, we meant it, when we wrote in the founding document, "particular emphasis." The way I see it—and they knew this is how we felt—14 percent doesn't add up to very much emphasis. I would have been happy with 75 percent; actually, anything more than 50 percent would have shown good enough faith. Only from my perspective now can I smile and say how satisfying it is to give an Ivy League university a failing grade.

Please don't misunderstand me, however. My years at Princeton were wonderful, and to this day I have an abiding respect for its history and its place in academia. Not many people know this—I've never seen it pointed out—but, even though we didn't know each other, I admired George Kennan at Princeton. He was one year ahead of me, class of 1925, and even then he knew a lot about world affairs. In fact, I think it was when I listened him speak—we were in a couple of classes together— that I developed my interest in international relations. He was a smart enough fellow, but I'll confide in you that he didn't have many friends on campus. I don't think he felt comfortable with the prep-school elitism permeating Princeton. Maybe it's because he was from the Midwest and everybody else seemed to be from a rich east-coast family. But he was very smart. I knew he was destined for great things but I had no idea he would become such an important and influential diplomat.

Old Kennan! He sensed even then, or seemed to, what was coming in the arena of world affairs. And later on, the United States certainly benefited from his wisdom—from his influence in getting the Truman Doctrine off the ground to his work as the American Ambassador to the Soviet Union. Those Russians were an insecure bunch and he understood that the United States needed to be strong—not only militarily but also diplomatically. He knew the importance of defending and extending freedom. So, yes, I had him and his ideals—which became mine—very much in mind when we drafted the foundation's Certificate of Incorporation. You were right to fight so hard to protect what your mother and I were trying to accomplish.

But back to getting beaten up a bit . . . if I were still physically with you, I would feel sadness, as well as a parental protection, for the challenges you had to undertake in those years during the lawsuit. I realize that was a trying time. The years before, the 1980s and 1990s, might not have been so great for you either. But you endured well. And I'm not at all surprised.

Part of me wants to say, "I'm sorry"; I'm sorry that you had to go through so much. We both know you didn't deserve all the negative comments and I know how much you tried. You really did. But, you see, you were prepared. Although there are times I wish I could have been there with you to protect you, that wasn't possible, and, as things tend to do, everything worked out pretty well.

Let me explain about your mettle.

Your mother and I weren't perfect parents.

Let me amend that: I wasn't a perfect father. I think you were right when you said that I might have been too liberal raising you. I'm reminded (with a smile I can't help form) of that day when you crashed the car through the fence at Teddy Roosevelt's family estate. And of course, I'll never forget when you hid all those people's equipment at the yacht club in the middle of the bay. What were you thinking?

Speaking of Teddy, I'm reminded that he said once, "If you fail to work in public life, as well as in private, for honesty and uprightness and virtue, if you condone vice because the vicious man is smart, or if you in any other way cast your weight into the scales in favor of evil, you are just so far corrupting and making less valuable the birthright of your children.... It is not what we have that will make us a great nation; it is the way in which we use it." That's the kind of thing I had in mind when your mother and I saw, as you have said it so well and so often, what we might accomplish for the people of the United States. And, as you know, I've always wanted that for you, as well.

But somehow, even though parenting is not a perfect

process—you, Anne, and Katherine are, as was Johnny, well aware of that—I knew you'd be okay. Now that the Princeton battle is over—and, again, let me reiterate not only how proud I am of you but also that I think you really beat them—you have other challenges. Your roles at the Banbury Fund and at the new foundation will keep you busy for a long time. One piece of advice: don't let anyone get you down. You're going to have differences of opinion with others on those boards and they with you, but please have the patience and the wisdom to take that in for what it's worth—the cost of living a fulfilling life. Believe me, I had to deal with a lot with those Princeton boys. And I can already see that the fight was worth every minute and every penny spent. Those new students the new foundation sponsors are quite the comers! I'm sure they will do the job for this country as they enter government service.

Whatever the obstacles, the point is to give, to love all of humankind. Your mother was the best example of that. Even though neither she nor I was very religious, she believed what Saint Francis of Assisi once said: "For it is in giving that we receive."

I write from a special place, Bill, a place from which I can watch you every day. I'm asking you not to mind the bumps in the road—and you have to understand that, from where I sit, everything is just a bump in the road—and to forge on with the incredible intensity you showed to Princeton. You did a great job. Thank you for keeping alive the flame of our passion. The world is a better place for your efforts.

Love,
Old Grumble

Timeline of Significant Events

About 1859	George Gilman starts Gilman & Company; a few years later, he and George Huntington Hartford rename it to the Great Atlantic & Pacific Tea Company.
February 13, 1905	Charles Robertson is born.
June 10, 1912	Marie Hartford Hoffman is born.
June 1926	Charles Robertson graduates from Princeton University.
February 1930	The School of Public and International Affairs is founded at Princeton University; the school grants undergraduate degrees only.
December 31, 1931	Marie Hartford Hoffman marries Louis Reed, Jr.
June 18, 1935	Marie and Louis Reed are divorced.
October 1937	Charles Robertson marries Marie Hartford Hoffman.
November 8, 1946	The Banbury Fund is created.
1948	The School of Public and International Affairs adds a graduate-level program and is renamed in honor of Woodrow Wilson; the school begins granting graduate degrees.
September 14, 1949	Bill Robertson is born.
September 21, 1957	The trust established by George Hartford dissolves, an event that gives his grandchildren full access to their portion of the A&P fortune.
March 16, 1961	The Robertson Foundation to benefit Princeton is created.
May 29, 1961	Marie Robertson funds the Robertson Foundation with 700,000 shares of A&P stock, valued at $34,715,625.
September 21, 1962	The IRS grants the Robertson Foundation tax-exempt status.
April 19, 1972	Marie Robertson dies.
June 12, 1973	The Robertsons are publicly identified as the donors of the gift that supports the graduate program at the Woodrow Wilson School.
May 2, 1981	Charles Robertson dies.
July 17, 2002	Bill Robertson and his siblings sue Princeton University.
September 17, 2003	Jessie Lee Washington contacts the Robertsons' legal counsel.
April 3, 2006	The Robertson Foundation for Government is created.
October 25, 2007	Judge Neil Shuster rules on Summary Judgment questions.
December 12, 2008	The Robertsons and Princeton sign the Settlement Agreement; a trial is avoided.
February 29, 2009	The Robertson Foundation at Princeton is dissolved.

Appendix II

People Interviewed for this Book:

1. Victoria B. Bjorklund
    - Legal counsel for Princeton during the lawsuit
    - Partner at Simpson Thacher & Bartlett LLP
    - Leading national expert on nonprofit law
    - Princeton alumna (1973)

2. George H. W. Bush
    - Advocate of the Robertson Foundation for Government, which has a number of scholars at the Bush School of Government and Public Service at Texas A&M
    - Former President of the United States

3. Frank Cialone
    - Legal counsel in the lawsuit for the Robertson family
    - Partner at Shartsis Friese LLP

4. Harvey Dale
    - Expert witness for Princeton on trust issues
    - University Professor of Philanthropy and the Law at New York University
    - Director, National Center on Philanthropy and the Law

5. Robert Durkee
    - Leading public voice of Princeton's perspective during the lawsuit
    - Vice President at Princeton

6. Douglas S. Eakeley
    - Co-lead counsel for Princeton and the individual defendants in the lawsuit
    - Partner at Lowenstein Sandler LLP

7. Katherine Ernst
    - Daughter of Marie and Charles Robertson
    - Plaintiff in lawsuit
    - President of the Robertson Foundation for Government
    - Board member of the Banbury Fund

8. F. Frederic Fouad
    - President of Protect The Hersheys' Children, Inc.

269

- Corporate attorney in private practice
- 2009-2010 Harvard Law School Visiting Scholar
- Adjunct Faculty, Temple School of Law Tokyo Campus

9. Frederic Fransen
   - Wrote articles against Princeton's position in the lawsuit
   - President of Donor Advising, Research & Educational Services

10. David Gelfand
    - The Robertson family's principal negotiator for the settlement of the lawsuit
    - Partner at Milbank, Tweed, Hadley & McCoy LLP

11. Robert Halligan
    - Board member of original Robertson Foundation
    - Board chair of the Robertson Foundation for Government
    - Former employee of the Agency for International Development

12. William Josephson
    - Expert witness for the Robertson family
    - Former Assistant Attorney General in New York and head of the Charities Bureau
    - Leading national expert on nonprofit law

13. Timothy "Bo" Kemper
    - Executive director of the Robertson Foundation for Government

14. Seth Lapidow
    - Legal counsel in lawsuit for the Robertson family
    - Attorney at Blank Rome

15. Greg Lebedev
    - Senior Advisor to the Robertson Foundation for Government
    - Chairman of the Center for International Private Enterprise

16. Paul Light
    - Advisory Board member of the Robertson Foundation for Government
    - Professor of Public Service at New York University's Robert F. Wagner Graduate School of Public Service

17. Kenneth Logan
    - Co-lead counsel for Princeton and the individual defendants in the lawsuit
    - Retired partner at Simpson Thacher
    - Princeton alumnus (1967)

18. Ron Malone
    - Legal counsel in the lawsuit for the Robertson family
    - Partner at Shartsis Friese LLP

19. Peter McDonough
    - General Counsel at Princeton University
    - Oversaw all legal activities for Princeton relating to the lawsuit
    - Negotiated the settlement on behalf of Princeton

20. Dr. Richard Mayeux
    - Recipient of Banbury Fund gifts
    - Chair, Department of Neurology at Columbia University Medical Center where he works to cure Alzheimer's disease

21. Anne Neal
    - President of the American Council of Trustees and Alumni

22. John L. Palmer
    - Advisory Board member of the Robertson Foundation for Government
    - University Professor and Dean Emeritus of the Maxwell School of Citizenship and Public Affairs at Syracuse University

23. Nuala Pell
    - Great granddaughter and oldest living descendant of George Hartford
    - Widow of Claiborne Pell, former United States Senator from Rhode Island

24. Stuart Polkowitz
    - Represented the plaintiffs in the donor-intent case, *Bernard and Jeanne Adler v. SAVE, A Friend to Homeless Animals*
    - Attorney/Member of Brach Eichler LLC

25. Corinne Rieder
    - Executive Director and Treasurer of the John A. Hartford Foundation

26. Chuck Robb
    - Advisory Board member of the Robertson Foundation for Government
    - Former Governor of Virginia
    - Former United States Senator from Virginia

27. Geoff Robertson
    - Grandson of Marie and Charles Robertson
    - Board member of the Robertson Foundation for Government
    - Board member of the Banbury Fund

28. Julia Robertson
   - Granddaughter of Marie and Charles Robertson
   - Board member of the Banbury Fund

29. William Robertson
   - Son of Marie and Charles Robertson
   - Principal plaintiff in the lawsuit
   - Board member of the Robertson Foundation for Government
   - Board member of the Banbury Fund
   - Board member of Cold Spring Harbor Laboratory
   - Princeton alumnus (1972)

30. Brent Scowcroft
   - Advisory board member of the Robertson Foundation for Government
   - National Security Advisor to Presidents Gerald Ford and George H. W. Bush

31. Jessie Lee Washington
   - Reported accounting findings to the plaintiffs
   - Princeton analyst and researcher from 1992 to 1995 and from 1998 to 2003

32. Dr. James Watson
   - Chancellor Emeritus of Cold Spring Harbor Laboratory, which, under the direction of Charles Robertson, was a major recipient of gifts from the Banbury Fund
   - Awarded the 1962 Nobel Prize in Physiology or Medicine for discovering DNA

33. Paul Volcker
   - Former president of the Federal Reserve Bank of New York
   - Former chairman of the Federal Reserve under Presidents Carter and Reagan
   - Chair of the President's Economic Recovery Advisory Board in the Obama Administration
   - Chairman of the Volcker Alliance
   - Princeton alumnus (1949)

34. Dr. Nicholas Yankopoulos
   - Cardiologist
   - First Banbury Fund recipient

( )

July 31 1962

The Robertson Foundation
Room 2500, 63 Wall Street
New York 5, N. Y.

COMPOSITE CERTIFICATE OF INCORPORATION

of

Attachment to Form :

THE ROBERTSON FOUNDATION

As Amended Through July 26, 1961

———◆———

We, the undersigned, in order to form a corporation for the purposes hereinafter set forth, under and pursuant to the provisions of the General Corporation Law of the State of Delaware, do hereby CERTIFY, as follows:

1. The name of the corporation is THE ROBERTSON FOUNDATION.

2. The principal office of the corporation in the State of Delaware is to be located at 229 South State Street in the City of Dover, County of Kent. The name of the resident agent in charge thereof is The Prentice-Hall Corporation System, Inc., 229 South State Street, Dover, Delaware.

3. This corporation is organized and shall be operated exclusively for charitable, scientific, literary, or educational purposes and for no other purpose. In furtherance of such purposes its objective is to strengthen the Government of the United States and increase its ability and determination to defend and extend freedom throughout the world by improving the facilities for the training and education of men and women for government service and to contribute, lend, pay over, or assign the income of the corporation and/or the funds or property of the corporation (any payments of principal being subject to the limitations of article 11(c) hereof) to or for the use of Princeton University for any one or more or all of the following uses:

(a) To establish or maintain and support at Princeton University, and as a part of the Woodrow Wilson School, a Graduate School, where men and women dedicated to public service may prepare themselves for careers in government service, with particular emphasis on the education of such persons for careers in those areas of the Federal Government that are concerned with international relations and affairs;

(b) To establish and maintain scholarships or fellowships, which will provide full, or partial support to students admitted to such Graduate School, whether such students are candidates for degrees, special students, or part-time students;

(c) To provide collateral and auxiliary services, plans and programs in furtherance of the object and purpose above set forth, including but without limitation, internship programs, plans for public service assignments of faculty or administrative personnel, mid-career study help, and programs for foreign students or officials training.

4. In furtherance of the purposes set forth in article 3 and to enable the corporation to carry out such purposes, the corporation shall have the following powers:

(a) To receive by donations, gifts, bequests, devises, contributions or otherwise, any and all kinds of property, real and personal, and to manage, administer, invest and reinvest and dispose of the same.

(b) To acquire by purchase or otherwise, and to own, manage or sell property or any interest therein.

273

(c) To purchase or otherwise acquire or obtain an interest in, hold, sell, assign, transfer, exchange, mortgage, pledge or otherwise dispose of the shares of the capital stock of, or any bonds, notes or other evidences of indebtedness or other securities created by, any other corporation or corporations of the State of Delaware or of any other State, territory or country, or by governments, states, municipalities or other political or governmental subdivisions, and while the owner thereof to exercise all the rights, powers and privileges of ownership, including the right to vote thereon.

(d) Acting through its Board of Trustees and officers, subject to the powers and restrictions of the Certificate of Incorporation, or any amendments thereto and to its By-laws, to do all such acts as are necessary or convenient to the attainment of the object and purpose herein set forth, and to the same extent and as fully as any natural person might or could do.

(e) To have offices and promote and carry on its object and purpose within or outside the State of Delaware.

5. The corporation is not organized for profit and the foregoing object, purpose and powers are each and all subject to the limitation that no part of the net earnings of the corporation shall inure to the benefit of any private member or individual. No substantial part of the corporation's activities shall be carrying on propaganda, or otherwise attempting, to influence legislation; and it shall not participate in, or intervene in (including the publishing or distributing of statements) any political campaign on behalf of any candidate for office. Notwithstanding any provision in this instrument which may be construed to the contrary, the corporation shall not engage in any activities which are not substantially in furtherance of charitable, scientific, literary, or educational purposes within the intendment of Section 501(c)(3) of the Internal Revenue Code, or its then equivalent.

6. The corporation shall not have authority to issue any capital stock.

7. The conditions of membership of the corporation and the rights of the members shall be such as are stated in the By-laws of the corporation.

8. The names and places of residence of the incorporators are as follows:

Names	Residences
Charles S. Robertson	Lloyd Harbor, Huntington Long Island, New York
Marie H. Robertson	Lloyd Harbor, Huntington Long Island, New York
Eugene W. Goodwillie	304 Highland Avenue Montclair, New Jersey

9. The existence of the corporation is to be perpetual.

10. The private property of the members of the corporation shall not be subject to the payment of corporate debts to any extent whatsoever.

11. The following provisions are inserted for the management of the affairs of the corporation:

(a) The number of directors, who shall be known as "trustees" of the corporation, shall be seven, and each member of the corporation shall be a trustee. Any person ceasing to be a member of the corporation shall also cease to be a trustee thereof; and any person ceasing to be a trustee shall cease to be a member.

(b) The Board of Trustees shall have the full power to manage the affairs of the corporation, to invest and reinvest the funds and other property of the corporation, and to determine the use and disposition of the income or corpus of the corporation in accordance with its object and

2

purpose. The Board of Trustees may, by resolution or resolutions passed by five-sevenths of the whole Board, designate an Executive Committee to consist of two or more of the trustees of the corporation which, to the extent provided in the resolution or resolutions, or in the By-laws, shall have and may exercise the powers of the Board of Trustees in the management of the affairs of the corporation and may have the power to authorize the seal of the corporation to be affixed to all papers which may require it. The Board of Trustees may, by resolution or resolutions passed by a majority of the whole Board, provide for such other Committees as it deems advisable from time to time, with such powers and duties as may be assigned thereto by the Board.

(c) Funds or property of the corporation which do not constitute income or accumulated income as defined in Treasury Department Regulations 1.504-1(c), or its then equivalent, shall not be disbursed or paid out unless (1) income of the corporation sufficient to cover the proposed expenditure is not available, and (2) at the time such funds or property is disbursed or paid out, provision is made for repayment out of future income. Payments of principal or capital shall not exceed 5% of the total market value of the corporation's principal or capital assets in any fiscal year computed at the time of such payment.

(d) Unless otherwise restricted by law or the By-laws, any action required or permitted to be taken at any meeting of the Board of Trustees or of any committee thereof may be taken without a meeting, if prior to such action a written consent thereto is signed by all members of the Board or of such committee as the case may be, and such written consent is filed with the minutes of proceedings of the Board or committee.

(e) Any member, trustee or officer performing actual services for and on behalf of the corporation shall be entitled to receive such reasonable compensation therefor as may be approved by the Board of Trustees, and to reimbursement of expenses incurred by him in connection with carrying out the activities of the corporation.

12. In furtherance of purposes set forth in article 3 hereof, the Board of Trustees shall have the power:

(a) To make, alter, amend or repeal any By-laws, subject only to such limitations, if any, as the By-laws may from time to time impose.

(b) To authorize the corporation to borrow money, with or without security, and to authorize and cause to be executed, mortgages, pledges or other liens, without limit as to amount, upon any or all of the real and personal property of the corporation, all on such terms and conditions as the Board of Trustees may determine or authorize in its discretion.

(c) From time to time, to the extent now or hereafter permitted by the laws of the State of Delaware, to sell, lease, exchange or otherwise dispose of any part of the property and assets of the corporation which the Board of Trustees deems expedient and in the best interests of the corporation.

(d) To appoint agents, representatives, consultants, custodians for the corporation's securities and investment advisors to assist the corporation in carrying out its object and purpose, on such terms as the Board of Trustees may determine, including payment of reasonable compensation for services actually rendered and reimbursement for expenses actually incurred in the performance of such services.

13. During the lifetime of Marie H. Robertson and Charles S. Robertson, or the survivor, the corporation may be dissolved only with their prior written consent, or the written consent of the survivor, together with either the unanimous consent given in writing of all of its members without a meeting, or the unanimous vote of all its members given in person or by proxy at a meeting duly called for that purpose. For a period of fourteen years after the death of Marie H. Robertson and Charles S. Robertson, the corporation may only be dissolved with the prior consent in writing of three,

3

or all if there be less than three, persons who are the descendants of both Marie H. Robertson and Charles S. Robertson and who are over the age of twenty-one years, together with either the unanimous consent given in writing of all the members without a meeting, or the unanimous vote of all the members given in person or by proxy at a members meeting duly called for that purpose. Thereafter, the corporation may be dissolved by the unanimous consent given in writing of all of its members without a meeting, or pursuant to the unanimous vote of all of its members given in person or by proxy at a members meeting duly called for that purpose. In the event of dissolution of the corporation, the Board of Trustees shall distribute or transfer the property and funds of the corporation remaining after payment of all proper claims and demands against the corporation to Princeton University which may, for investment purposes, be made a part of the general endowment fund but which otherwise shall be considered and administered as a separate and distinct endowment fund to be known as the "Robertson Fund" and to be used by Princeton University to further the object and purpose above set forth. No part of any such property or funds of the corporation shall pass to any member of the corporation. The term "descendants" as used in this paragraph 13 shall include adopted children.

14. In the event that Princeton University should at any time cease to be an exempt organization, as defined in Section 501(c)(3) of the Internal Revenue Code, or its then equivalent, and not have its status as such "exempt organization" restored within one year from the date it ceased to be an exempt organization, the Board of Trustees shall pay over the income of the corporation and/or transfer its property or funds to any one or more other corporations, trusts, funds or foundations created or organized in the United States which are exempt organizations as defined in Section 501(c)(3) of the Internal Revenue Code, or its then equivalent, for the purpose of carrying out the object and purpose of this corporation.

15. Meetings of the members and trustees may be held outside the State of Delaware, and, subject to the laws of Delaware, and the By-laws, the corporation may keep its books, documents and papers and maintain offices outside the State of Delaware, at such place or places as may be from time to time designated or authorized by the By-laws or by the members or trustees.

16. No amendment of the Certificate of Incorporation shall be effective unless authorized either (a) by the affirmative vote of all of its members given in person or by proxy at a members meeting duly called for that purpose, or (b) by the written consent of all the members without a meeting, provided, however, that paragraph 13 hereof may only be amended in the same manner and with the same consents as is required by the provisions of said paragraph for the dissolution of the corporation.

IN WITNESS WHEREOF, we have hereunto set our hands and seals this 16th day of March, 1961.

MARIE H. ROBERTSON   (L.S.)

CHARLES S. ROBERTSON   (L.S.)

EUGENE W. GOODWILLIE   (L.S.)

STATE OF NEW YORK   }
COUNTY OF NEW YORK } ss.:

BE IT REMEMBERED that on this 16th day of March, 1961, personally appeared before me, a Notary Public in and for the State and County aforesaid, CHARLES S. ROBERTSON, MARIE H. ROBERTSON and EUGENE W. GOODWILLIE, parties to the foregoing Certificate of Incorporation, known to me personally to be such, and they each severally acknowledged the Certificate to be the act and deed of the signers respectively, and that the facts therein stated are truly set forth.

GIVEN under my hand and seal of office the day and year aforesaid.

TOWNSEND J. KNIGHT
Notary Public

TOWNSEND J. KNIGHT
Notary Public, State of New York
No. 31-2156563
Qualified in New York County
Commission Expires March 30, 1961

(NOTARIAL
SEAL)

Notes

Notes for Introduction

1. Author interview with Bill Robertson (01/25/2012).

2. The idea was not unprecedented. Four years after he made a $20 million gift to Yale in 1991, Lee Bass asked for, and received, his money back after the university did not comply with his wishes to promote the study of western civilization.

3. John D. Rockefeller gave $35 million to the University of Chicago over a period of a period of two decades. Carrie Golus, *The University of Chicago Chronicle*, 10/18/2001, Vol. 21, No. 3, http://chronicle.uchicago. edu/011018/donors.shtml (accessed on 11/13/2012).

4. Robert Durkee, "Princeton Has Done the Right Thing," *Wall Street Journal* (10/18/2007), http://online.wsj.com/article/SB119266801424862832. html (accessed on 04/02/2012).

5. The book was inspired by a lawsuit in Texas in the mid-1990s that claimed charities had violated state and federal laws in the pursuit of gifts. Charities won the battle. See "The Texas Lawsuit," a chapter in *Charity on Trial*, by Doug White (Barricade Books, 2007).

6. Author interview on Channel 9, Washington, DC (12/18/2006), http:// www.youtube.com/watch?v=FhCtP4hT1dQ (accessed on 02/10/2013).

7. Doug White, *The Nonprofit Challenge: Integrating Ethics into the Purpose and Promise of our Nation's Charities* (Palgrave Macmillan, 2010), p.122.

8. In late 2012 the Robertson Foundation for Government moved its office from Juno Beach, FL to Washington, DC.

9. "Colleges with the Biggest Endowment Per Student," cnbc.com (03/01/2011), http://www.cnbc.com/id/41834274/Colleges_with_the_ Biggest_Endowment_Per_Student, (accessed on 08/05/2012); in 2011 Princeton's endowment per student was more than $1.85 million; Yale came in second with just under $1.5 million per student.

10. Kelly Gifford, "The Tax Man Cometh: Residents Go After Princeton's Nonprofit Status," *New York Observer*, (07/02/2013), http://observer. com/2013/07/the-tax-man-cometh-residents-go-after-princetons-nonprof- it-status/ (accessed on 08/22/2013). In 2013 a group of Princeton, New Jersey, residents filed a lawsuit against Princeton University, claiming that the

school's income from royalties and commercial ventures makes it ineligible for its tax-exempt status. According to the newspaper, "The suit argues that the Ivy League school's commercial activities . . . make it a business like any other. The school also made $127 million in patent licensing profits last year and has distributed $118.5 million in royalty profits to faculty since 2005".

11. The author did not have access to certain documents that were ordered destroyed pursuant to the Settlement Agreement.

12. http://www.princeton.edu/robertson/about/ (accessed on 08/15/2013).

Notes for Chapter 1

1. John F. Kennedy, speech at the University of Michigan, Ann Arbor (10/14/1960) http://www.peacecorps.gov/index.cfm?shell=about.history.speech.

2. Ibid.

3. Lawrence Leamer, *The Kennedy Men: 1901–1963*, HarperCollins (2001); pp. 337-338.

4. John Coyne, "Josephson and His Executive Order" (01/06/2011) http://peacecorpsworldwide.org/babbles/2011/01/06/josephson-and-his-executive-order/.

5. Author interview with Bill Josephson (03/03/2012).

6. Author interview with Robert Halligan (02/17/2012).

7. John F. Kennedy, Inaugural Address (01/20/1961).

8. The History Channel, http://www.history.com/topics/house-un-american-activities-committee (accessed on 03/25/2012).

9. Eugene McCarthy was not directly involved with HUAC, the House Committee on Un-American Activities; he was a Senator, not a member of the House of Representatives. He chaired the Senate Government Operations Committee and its Permanent Subcommittee on Investigations.

10. United Press International, *New York Times*, (04/12/1961), p. 1 http://query.nytimes.com/mem/archive/pdf?res=F60913FB385912738DDDAB-0994DC405B818AF1D3 (accessed 03/25/2012).

11. Memo from John Kennedy to Lyndon Johnson; (04/20/1961) http://history.nasa.gov/Apollomon/apollo1.pdf (accessed on 04/01/2012).

12. Kennedy Library Archives; http://www.jfklibrary.org/Research/Ready-Reference/JFK-Speeches/Special-Message-to-the-Congress-on-Urgent-National-Needs-May-25-1961.aspx (accessed on 04/01/2012).

13. John Kennedy (09/12/1962) (http://er.jsc.nasa.gov/seh/ricetalk.htm); (accessed 03/25/2012).

14. United Press International; http://www.upi.com/Audio/Year_in_Review/Events-of-1961/Death-of-Dag-Hammarskj/12295509433760-4/ (accessed on 03/24/2012).

15. Certificate of Incorporation of the Robertson Foundation (03/16/1961).

16. "History of the Woodrow Wilson School," as part of the press release for the dedication of the school (05/11/1966).

17. http://wws.princeton.edu/about_wws/history/.

18. "Special Convocation for the Dedication of the New Building of the Woodrow Wilson School of Public and International Affairs" (05/11/1966).

19. Ibid..

20. Certificate of Incorporation of the Robertson Foundation (03/16/1961).

21. Letter from Charles Robertson to John Gardner (01/08/1977).

22. Charles Robertson, note to himself on the gift (03/08/1960).

23. Charles Robertson, note to himself on the gift (03/19/1960).

24. Letter from Charles Robertson to Bill Robertson (02/09/1978).

25. Robert Goheen, at the unveiling of the Robertson Foundation (06/12/1973).

26. *Princeton Alumni Weekly* (12/14/2005), http://paw.princeton.edu/memorials/12/28/index.xml (accessed on 12/14/2012).

27. Letter from Robert Goheen to Charles Robertson (12/05/1960).

28. Letter from A. J. Goodpaster to Charles Robertson (12/20/1960).

29. Letter from A. J. Goodpaster to Charles Robertson (02/21/1961).

30. Ibid. (author's italics).

31. Letter from Robert Goheen to Charles Robertson (12/05/1960).

32. Gardner Patterson obituary, *New York Times* (07/04/1998), http://www.nytimes.com/1998/07/04/business/gardner-patterson-82-ex-world-trade-official.html (accessed on 04/01/2012).

33. Charles Robertson memo (12/15/1960).

34. Robert Goheen, Deposition on *Robertson v. Princeton* (06/21/2004), p.103.

35. Author interview with Victoria Bjorklund (03/28/2012).

36. Author interview with Seth Lapidow (07/02/2013).

37. Weather Underground http://www.wunderground.com/history/airport/KISP/1961/3/16/DailyHistory.html (accessed 03/29/2012).

38. Letter from the IRS to the Robertson Foundation (09/21/1962).

39. "Wilson School Endowers Identified as L.I. Couple," *New York Times* (06/14/1973), http://query.nytimes.com/mem/archive/pdf?res=FA0A-16F93959137A93C6A8178DD85F478785F9 (accessed 07/07/2012); beginning in 1890 with his initial gift of $600,000, over a period of two decades John D. Rockefeller gave more than $35 million to establish the University of Chicago http://chronicle.uchicago.edu/011018/donors.shtml (accessed 03/30/2012).

40. Michael Barbaro, "$1.1 Billion in Thanks from Bloomberg to Johns Hopkins," *New York Times* (01/27/2013), http://www.nytimes.com/2013/01/27/nyregion/at-1-1-billion-bloomberg-is-top-university-donor-in-us.html?hp&_r=0 (accessed on 01/27/2013) .

41. Executive Summary, *Giving USA* 2012, p. 10.

42. Letter from Charles Robertson to Bill Robertson (07/03/1962).

Notes for Chapter 2

1. Marc Levinson, *The Great A&P and the Struggle for Small Business in America* (New York: Hill and Wang, 2011), pp. 3-12.

2. Avis Anderson, *A&P: The Story of the Great Atlantic & Pacific Tea Company,* (Charleston, SC: Arcadia Publishing, 2002), p. 9.

3. William Walsh, *The Rise and Decline of the Great Atlantic & Pacific Tea Company* (Barricade Books, 1986), p. 18. One of the three last ceremonial golden spikes of the transcontinental railroad was driven in by Leland Stanford, the president of the Central Pacific Railroad and later the founder, with his wife Jane, of Stanford University.

4. Levinson, *The Great A&P,* p. 33.

5. Ibid., pp. 33-34.

6. Ibid., pp. 44-48.

7. Ibid., pp. 44-49.

8. Ibid., p. 249.

9. *New York Journal American* (09/07/1948), p. 1.

10. Even though Marie Robertson established temporary residency in Nevada, she actually lived in New York..

11. *The American Weekly* (11/07/1948), p. 4.

12. Ibid., p. 4.

13. Ibid., p. 4.

14. Notice of Motion; Supreme Court: New York County; Reed against

Robertson (09/01/1948).

15. *The American Weekly* (11/07/1948), p. 4.

16. *The Troy Record* (02/02/1950).

17. *Daily Mirror* (11/25/1948), p. 3.

18. Letter from Charles Robertson to Bill Robertson (02/09/1978).

19. Levinson, *The Great A&P,* pp. 60-61.

20. Author interview with anonymous source (01/20/2012).

21. Author interview with Nuala Pell (03/23/2012).

22. Obituary, *The New York Times* (05/06/1981), http://www.nytimes.com/1981/05/06/obituaries/charles-s-robertson-ex-investment-banker-and-a-philanthropist.html (accessed on 08/12/2013); the information on Charles Robertson's war service was written on an undated hand-written note from the father of one of Robertson's crew.

23. Author interview with Nuala Pell (03/23/2012).

24. Author interview with Bill Robertson (01/25/2012).

25. Author interview with Bill Robertson (05/23/2012).

26. Ibid.

27. Author interview with Nuala Pell (03/23/2012).

28. Levinson, *The Great A&P,* pp. 247-248.

29. Avis Anderson, "The Story of the Great Atlantic & Pacific Tea Company" (2002) Arcadia; p. 48 .

30. 2011 IRS Form 990, John A. Hartford Foundation.

31. Author interview with Corinne Rieder (05/03/2013).

32. Levinson, *The Great A&P,* p. 253 .

33. Letter from Charles Robertson to Bill Robertson (02/09/1978).

34. Author interview with Bill Robertson (01/24/2012).

35. Letter from Charles Robertson to Bill Robertson (02/09/1978).

36. Ibid., 02/09/1978.

37. Levinson, *The Great A&P,* p. 254.

38. Levinson, *The Great A&P,* p. 11.

39. Levinson, *The Great A&P,* pp. 254-259.

40. Author interview with Bill Robertson (01/25/2012).

41. Richard Kirkland, Jr., "Should You Leave It All to the Children?" *Fortune* (09/29/1986), http://money.cnn.com/magazines/fortune/fortune_archive/1986/09/29/68098/index.htm (accessed on 08/15/2013); the

sentence from the article that contains the quote is: "To him the perfect amount to leave children is 'enough money so that they would feel they could do anything, but not so much that they could do nothing.'"

42. Letter from Charles Robertson to Bill Robertson (02/09/1978).

43. Ibid.

44. Author interview with Bill Robertson (01/24/2012).

45. Author interview with Katherine Ernst (06/27/2012).

46. Author interview with Nicholas Yankopoulos (06/30/12).

47. Columbia Psychiatry website, http://asp.cumc.columbia.edu/facdb/profile_list.asp?uni=rpm2&DepAffil=Psychiatry (accessed on 06/29/2012).

48. Author interview with Dr. Richard Mayeux (06/04/2012).

49. Author interview with Dr. James Watson (06/25/2012); the two people who "couldn't work together" were Drs. Maurice Wilkins and Rosalind Franklin..

50. James Watson, *Avoid Boring People,* (Vintage Books, 2010), p. 289.

51. Author interview with Dr. James Watson (06/25/2012).

52. Cold Spring Harbor Laboratory 2011 Annual Report, p.32 .

53. Letter from Charles Robertson to Bill Robertson (02/09/1978).

Notes for Chapter 3

1. Cleveland Foundation, www.clevelandfoundation.org/about/history (accessed 12/28/2012).

2. Sir Arthur Hobhouse, *The Dead Hand: Address on the Subject of Endowments and Settlements of Property,* Chatto & Windus, 1880, Google Books, p. viii, https://play.google.com/books/reader?id=lI0BAAAAQAAJ&printsec=-frontcover&output=reader&authuser=0&hl=en&pg=GBS.PR3 (accessed 005/16/2013).

3. Alan Howson, "Community Foundations—An Idea Whose Time Has Come," The Winnipeg Foundation, p. 7.

4. Hobhouse, p. 6.

5. Hobhouse, p.123.

6. Ibid. p. 4.

7. *Trustees of Dartmouth College v. Woodward,* 1819; http://www.law.cornell.edu/supct/search/display.html?terms=religion%20and%20free%20or%20establishment&url=/supct/html/historics/USSC_CR_0017_0518_ZO.html (accessed 06/22/2012); Marshall actually said, "A corporation is an artificial being, invisible, intangible, and existing only in contemplation of law."

8. Cleveland Foundation; op. cit.

9. Thomas Jefferson to Samuel Kercheval, July 12, 1816. ME 15:42.

10. William Allen, *Modern Philanthropy: A Study of Efficient Appealing and Giving* (New York, Dodd, Mead, 1912) p. 189, http://archive.org/stream/ modernphilanthr01allegoog#page/n227/mode/2up (accessed 06/06/12).

11. Allen, p. 190.

12. A comprehensive work on this topic is "The Problem with Donor Intent: Interpretation, Enforcement, and Doing the Right Thing," by Susan N. Gary (05/14/2010); another is "Standing to Sue in the Charitable Sector," New York University School of Law (1993).

13. Mary Grace Blasko, et. al., "Standing to Sue in the Charitable Sector" (1993) http://www1.law.nyu.edu/ncpl/pdfs/Monograph/ Monograph1993StandingtoSue.pdf (accessed 06/12/2012) This comprehensive article collects almost all cases from 1800 to the present on who has standing to sue.

14. Author interview with Harvey Dale (02/22/2102).

15. Supreme Court, Appellate Division, First Department, New York, *Smithers v. St. Luke Roosevelt Hospital Center* (05/05/2001).

16. Ibid.

17. Ibid.

18. Ibid.

19. In re: The Estate of R. Brinkley Smithers, Surrogate's Court, Nassau County, New York (04/01/2003).

20. New York Charities Bureau, http://www.nycharities.org/about_us/index. asp (accessed on 03/24/1012).

21. Author interview with William Josephson (06/20/2012).

22. The center was eventually sold and, after the medical community's opinion that such a center would actually benefit patients more if it relocated inside a clinical environment, moved into a hospital wing of St. Luke's.

23. Supreme Court, Appellate Division, First Department, New York, *Smithers v. St. Luke Roosevelt Hospital Center* (05/05/2001).

24. William Josephson, "New Prudent Management of Institutional Funds Act," *New York Law Journal* (12/03/2010).

25. Author interview with William Josephson (06/20/2012).

26. Author interview with Harvey Dale (02/22/2012).

27. Pamela G. Hollie, "Belridge Rides Oil Price Boom," *New York Times* (09/04/1978), http://query.nytimes.com/mem/archive/

pdf?res=F10B11FE3D5C12728DDDAC0894D1405B898BF1D3 (accessed on 08/13/2013).

28. The will did "not restrict the beneficiary class to Marin residents: as long as the funds are spent within Marin, the benefits can flow outside of the County"; see Harvey Dale, "The Buck Trust," article, pp. 1-4; 03/18/87. http://www.nyu.edu/projects/hdale/buck%20Trust%20Article%20by%20HPD%20_1987_.pdf (accessed 06/16/2012).

29. Harvey Dale, "The Buck Trust," article, pp. 1-4; 03/18/87; the trust's value by 1987 was $450 million, making it at the time one of the 20 largest foundations in the United States and probably larger than any other community trust. As of June 2012, it was worth over $1 billion.

30. In 1979 the population of Marin County was just under 223,000; by 2011 it had grown to just over 255,000; see http://quickfacts.census.gov/qfd/states/06/06041.html (accessed on 08/11/2013).

31. Harvey Dale, "The Buck Trust," article, pp. 1-4; 03/18/87; p. 4; Trial Brief of Co-Trustee John Elliott Cook, January 23, 1986 (hereinafter Cook Trial Brief), at 9.

32. Ibid., p. 10.

33. Author interview with Ron Malone (04/11/2012).

34. Harvey Dale, "The Buck Trust," article, pp. 1-4 (03/18/87), p. 7.

35. Author interview with Ron Malone (04/11/2012).

36. Author interview with Harvey Dale (02/22/2012); also see Dale's article "The Buck Trust," 1987, http://www.nyu.edu/projects/hdale/buck%20Trust%20Article%20by%20HPD%20_1987_.pdf (accessed on 02/27/2013).

37. An article with the title "de Medici in Merion," written by A. H. Shaw, appeared in *The New Yorker* magazine on 09/22/1928.

38. Ibid. p. 87.

39. Martin Morse Wooster, "The Great Philanthropists and the Problem of Donor Intent," (*Capital Research Center* 2007), p. 86.

40. *Barnes Foundation. v. Keely*, 171 A. 267 (Pa. 1934).

41. Ilana Eisenstein, "Keeping Charity In Charitable Trust Law: The Barnes Foundation And The Case For Consideration Of Public Interest In Administration Of Charitable Trusts," *University Of Pennsylvania Law Review*, Vol.151: 1747, 2003, p. 1755; Eisenstein quotes Lewis Simes's "The Dead Hand Achieves Immortality: Gifts to Charity."

42. Opinion By Mr. Justice Musmanno, *Commonwealth v. Barnes Foundation*, The Supreme Court of Pennsylvania (03/22/1960).

43. Martin Morse Wooster, "The Great Philanthropists and the Problem of Donor Intent," (Capital Research Center 2007), p. 89.

44. "Albert C. Barnes—The Controversy" *The Philadelphia Enquirer* http://www.philly.com/philly/entertainment/museums/144401855.html#Controversy, narrated by Stephan Salisbury (2012) (accessed 06/23/2012).

45. "Art Held Hostage: The Battle over the Barnes Collection," a book by John Anderson, and the film, "The Art of the Steal," provide comprehensive background on the Barnes Foundation story.

46. Richard Blow, "Picture Perfect Party; Gallery Opens Show of French Masterworks" *Washington Post*, (04/19/1993).

47. Chris Mondics, "Opponents of the Barnes move soldier on," *Philadelphia Inquirer* (05/20/2012), http://www.philly.com/philly/business/20120520_Opponents_of_the_Barnes_move_soldier_on.html (accessed on 06/24/2012).

48. "Albert C. Barnes—The Controversy" *The Philadelphia Enquirer* http://www.philly.com/philly/entertainment/museums/144401855.html#Controversy, narrated by Stephan Salisbury, 2012 (accessed on 06/23/2012).

49. "Hearings Before the Committee on Ways and Means, House of Representatives" (02/18-20/1969), p. 94, https://ftp.resource.org/gao.gov/91-172/000064D6.pdf, (accessed on 12/15/2012).

50. Author interview with Harvey Dale (02/26/2013).

51. Ibid.

52. Susan Gary, "The Problems with Donor Intent: Interpretation, Enforcement, and Doing the Right Thing," *Chicago-Kent Law Review* (05/14/2010).

53. Katherine Mangan, "Tulane U. Wins Donor-Intent Lawsuit Over Closing of women's College," *Chronicle of Higher Education* (02/21/2011), http://chronicle.com/article/Tulane-U-Wins-Donor-Intent/126465/ (accessed on 07/01/2012).

54. Katherine Mangan, "Tulane Had the Right to Close Its College for Women, a State Judge Rules," The Chronicle of Higher Education, 08/31/2009; http://chronicle.com/article/Tulane-Had-the-Right-to-Close/48246/ (accessed 07/01/2012).

55. Associated Press, 01/25/2012; http://music-mix.ew.com/2012/01/25/garth-brooks-hospital-case/ (accessed on 07/01/2012).

56. "Milton Hershey School—Second Restated Deed of Trust (As of November 15, 1976)", pp. 3, 8; http://www.mhs-pa.org/assets/files/page-341/file-55.pdf (accessed on 09/01/2013).

57. F. Frederic Fouad, "Hershey's Charity for Children Became GOP Slush

Fund," *The Nation* (10/17/2012), http://www.thenation.com/article/170640/hersheys-broken-trust# (accessed on 12/01/2012).

58. Bob Fernandez, "Settlement ends Hershey Trust probe," *Philadelphia Inquirer* (05/10/2013), http://articles.philly.com/2013-05-10/news/39144622_1_hershey-charity-board-members-golf-course (accessed on 05/13/2013).

59. Bill Keisling, "AG Kane's Agreement with Hershey Trust Disappoints Reformers," *realreporting.org* (05/09/2013), http://newslanc.com/2013/05/09/ag-kanes-agreement-with-hershey-trust-disappoints-reformers/ (accessed on 05/13/2013).

60. Author interview with F. Frederic Fouad (12/28/2012).

61. Samuel P. King and Randall W. Roth, "Broken Trust: Greed, Mismanagement, and Political Manipulation at America's Largest Charitable Trust," University of Hawaii Press, 2006. p. 1 .

62. King and Roth, ibid., p. 301.

63. King and Roth, ibid., p. 195.

64. The merger took place in 2006.

65. Author interview with Stuart Polkowitz (08/08/2013).

66. New Jersey Appellate Court Decision, *Bernard and Jeanne Adler v. SAVE, A Friend to Homeless Animals* (08/05/2013), pp. 22-23.

67. Author interview with Stuart Polkowitz (08/08/2013).

68. *McKenzie v. Trustees of the Presbytery of Jersey City,* 67 N.J. Eq. 652, 672-73 (N.J. 1905).

69. New Jersey Appellate Court Decision, *Bernard and Jeanne Adler v. SAVE, A Friend to Homeless Animals* (08/05/2013), p. 37.

70. New Jersey Appellate Court Decision, *Bernard and Jeanne Adler v. SAVE, A Friend to Homeless Animals* (08/05/2013), pp. 27, 34-35.

71. Author interview with Stuart Polkowitz (08/08/2013).

72. Author interview with Bill Robertson (08/08/2013).

73. Bill and Melinda Gates website, http://www.gatesfoundation.org/about/Pages/gates-foundation-asset-trust.aspx (accessed on 07/01/2012) .

74. Jim Dwyer, "Philanthropist Wants to Be Rid of His Last $1.5 Billion," *New York Times* (08/07/2012), http://www.nytimes.com/2012/08/08/nyregion/a-billionaire-philanthropist-struggles-to-go-broke.html?emc=tnt&tntemail0=y&_r=0 (accessed on 01/11/2013).

75. According to the Foundation Center, the Ford and Getty Foundations each had approximately $10.5 billion under management in 2011, while the Gates

Foundation had more than $37 billion under management http://foundationcenter.org/findfunders/topfunders/top100assets.html (accessed on 12/30/2012).

76. Adam Meyerson, "When Philanthropy Goes Wrong," *Wall Street Journal,* 03/09/2012, http://online.wsj.com/article/SB10001424052970203370604577263820686621862.html (accessed on 12/20/2012).

77. Marta Tellado, letter to the editor, *Wall Street Journal* (03/26/2012).

78. Ibid.

79. Martin Morse Wooster, "The Great Philanthropists and the Problem of Donor Intent," (Capital Research Center, 2007), p. 27.

80. Website, Carnegie Corporation of New York, http://carnegie.org/about-us/mission-and-vision/ (accessed on 02/25/2013).

81. Peter Ascoli, "Julius Rosenwald's Crusade: One Donor's plea to Give While You Live," *Philanthropy Magazine*, Philanthropy Roundtable, June 2006, http://www.philanthropyroundtable.org/site/print/julius_rosenwalds_crusade (accessed on 01/09/2013).

82. John J. Miller, "Giving and Taking Away," *National Review* (03/14/2006), http://old.nationalreview.com/miller/miller200603141618.asp (accessed on 01/05/2012).

83. Martin Morse Wooster, "The Great Philanthropists and the Problem of Donor Intent" (Capital Research Center 2007), p. xi.

84. Author interview with Ron Malone (04/11/2012).

85. Author interview with Anne Neal (06/26/2013).

86. Author interview with Bill Robertson (05/31/2012).

Notes for Chapter 4

1. Letter from John Myers to Robert Goheen (05/05/1961).

2. Memo from John Myers to Robert Goheen (04/28/1961); one half is less than the income tax rate of 91 percent, and $32 million is not equal to $35 million. We don't know why there is a discrepancy between what he wrote about the tax effect and the tax rate at the time; the gift tax rate in 1961 was just under 60 percent. Also, although the Robertsons had decided to establish the foundation, the actual gift amount had not yet been determined when Myers was meeting with the IRS.

3. Memo from John Myers to Robert Goheen (04/28/1961).

4. Author interview with Victoria Bjorklund (03/28/2012).

5. Memo from John Myers to Robert Goheen (05/04/1961) .

6. Memo from John Myers to Robert Goheen (04/28/1961).

7. Letter from Robert Goheen to the Commissioner of Internal Revenue (05/01/1961).

8. Memo from John Myers to Robert Goheen (05/04/1961).

9. Robert Goheen, Deposition on *Robertson v. Princeton* (06/21/2004), pp. 68-69.

10. Letter from J. Worley, Chief, Exempt Organization Branch of the IRS, to the Robertson Foundation (09/21/1962).

11. Gary, Susan The Problems with Donor Intent: Interpretation, Enforcement, and Doing the Right Thing (05/2010); Chicago-Kent Law Review (Volume 85:3).

12. Letter from Charles Robertson to John Myers (08/07/1970).

13. "Hearings Before the Committee on Ways and Means, House of Representatives" (02/18-20/1969), p. 12-13, https://ftp.resource.org/gao.gov/91-172/000064D6.pdf, (accessed on 01/14/2012).

14. Think of a public charity as the kind of organization people give money to, such as a university, museum, faith center, and other organizations that need donations to do their work, and a private foundation as an organization that essentially has enough money and makes grants to public charities.

15. Form 4653, "Notification Concerning Foundation Status," signed by Charles Robertson on 08/20/1970.

16. Form 4653, "Notification Concerning Foundation Status," signed by Charles Robertson on 08/20/1970, attachment.

17. Charles Robertson memo, "Summary of the Results of Our Talks in Washington" (12/15/1960) .

18. The top post at the Woodrow Wilson School was elevated from Director to Dean in 1964; Bernstein served in that position from 1964 to 1969.

19. Memo from R. A. Lester to Marver Bernstein (11/07/1966).

20. Ibid.

21. Master of Public Administration.

22. Memo from Charles Robertson to John Lewis (11/10/1970).

23. Memo from Charles Robertson to John Lewis (07/04/1971).

24. Letter from G. A. Lincoln to William Marvel (12/14/1971).

25. Memo from Roger Jones to John Lewis (10/21/1971).

26. Report, "Placement Activities (12/30/1971).

27. Letter from John Lewis to Roger Jones (01/20/1972).

28. Author interview with Bill Robertson (05/31/2012).

29. Letter from John Leslie to Charles Robertson (04/26/1972).

30. Letter from John Leslie to Charles Robertson (04/26/1972).

31. Letter from William Marvel to Charles Robertson (05/24/1972).

32. Letter from John Gardner to Charles Robertson (06/14/1972).

33. Press information, "History of the Woodrow Wilson School," "Special Convocation for the Dedication of the New Building of the Woodrow Wilson School of Public and International Affairs" (05/11/1966).

34. "The Road to Xanadu," *Time Magazine* (01/18/1963), pp. 54-64.

35. Letter from Charles Robertson to his children Anne, John, Bill, and Kate (05/04/1979).

36. Robert Goheen, "The Unveiling of the Robertson Foundation" (06/12/1973).

37. "Wilson School Endowers Identified as a Long Island Couple," *New York Times* (06/14/1973), http://query.nytimes.com/mem/archive/pdf?res=FA0A16F93959137A93C6A8178DD85F478785F9 (accessed on 07/07/2012); although the newspaper attributed the quote to one of Charles Robertson's two sons, Bill Robertson said in an interview with the author on 10/18/2012 that it was actually his father who was quoted, but did not want the comments to be attributed to him.

38. Letter from Charles Robertson to Bill Robertson (11/27/1972).

39. Letter from John Gardner to Charles Robertson (06/14/1972).

40. Letter from Charles Robertson to his children (11/27/1972).

41. Ibid.

42. Robert Goheen, Statement about the Robertson gift (09/22/1961).

43. Pew Research Center for the People & the Press, "Public Trust in Government: 1958-2010 (04/18/2010), http://www.people-press.org/2010/04/18/public-trust-in-government-1958-2010/ (accessed on 07/18/2012).

44. Letter from A. J. Goodpaster to Charles Robertson (04/14/1972).

45. Letter from Livingston Merchant to Charles Robertson (04/14/1972).

46. Letter from Charles Robertson to William Bowen (11/18/1972).

47. "Report of the Review Committee Concerning the Woodrow Wilson School MPA Program" (04/05/1996), pp. 2, 7.

48. Paul Volcker, "A Challenge Worthy of Princeton (Even Larger Than the Future of Wrestling)," undated essay.

49. Letter from Paul Volcker to Shirley Tilghman (10/24/2001).

50. Author interview with Paul Volcker (03/06/2012).

51. Letter from Paul Volcker to Shirley Tilghman (10/24/2001).

52. Paul Volcker, "A Challenge Worthy of Princeton (Even Larger Than the Future of Wrestling)," undated essay.

53. Letter from Paul Volcker to Shirley Tilghman (10/24/2001).

54. Bill Robertson, "*Robertson v. Princeton*," (advertisement) *Princeton Alumni Weekly* (12/13/2006).

55. Memo from Charles Robertson to Eugene Goodwillie (01/27/1972).

56. Author interview with Bill Robertson (05/23/2013).

57. Letter from Charles Robertson to John Gardner (01/08/1977).

58. Letter from Charles Robertson to Bill Robertson (02/09/1978).

59. Letter from Roger Jones to Bill Robertson (02/05/1979).

60. Composite Certificate of Incorporation of the Robertson Foundation (07/26/1961), p. 4.

61. Letter from Roger Jones to Charles Robertson (02/05/1979).

62. Harold Shapiro, "The President's Page: The Robertson Endowment," *Princeton Alumni Weekly* (11/02/1998).

63. Author interview with Bill Robertson (04/12/2012).

64. Author interview with William Josephson (03/13/2012).

65. PRINCO was not the only group to buy into the mantra of alternative investments; many other large university endowments, including those of Harvard, Yale, and the University of Virginia, dramatically increased their investments in this asset class.

66. Author interview with Bill Robertson (04/12/2012).

67. Author Interview with William Josephson (03/13/2012).

68. James Stewart, "University Endowments Face a Hard Landing," the *New York Times* (10/12/2012).

69. Author interview with Bill Robertson (08/17/2012).

70. Michael Lewis, "How the Eggheads Cracked," *New York Times Magazine* (01/24/1999), http://www.nytimes.com/1999/01/24/magazine/how-the-eggheads-cracked.html?pagewanted=all&src=pm (accessed on 12/02/2012).

71. Author interview with Ron Malone (04/11/2012).

72. Author interview with Paul Volcker (03/06/2012).

73. Author interview with Bill Robertson (08/17/2102).

74. Susan Warner, "Thriving on a World in Crisis; Life at the Woodrow Wilson

School, a Training Ground for Policy Wonks, After Sept. 11," *New York Times*, (12/23/2001), http://www.nytimes.com/2001/12/23/nyregion/thriving-world-crisis-life-woodrow-wilson-school-training-ground-for-policy.html?pagewanted=all&pagewanted=print (accessed on 03/14/2013).

75. Author interview with Robert Halligan (02/17/2012).

76. Author interview with Bill Robertson (05/31/2012).

77. Author interview with Peter McDonough and Douglas Eakeley (07/24/2012).

78. Ibid.

79. Author interview with Bill Robertson (02/01/2013).

80. Author interview with Bill Robertson (08/17/2012).

81. Doug White, *The Nonprofit Challenge: Integrating Ethics into the Purpose and Promise of Our Nation's Charities* (Palgrave Macmillan 2010) p.130.

Notes for Chapter 5

1. Maria Newman, "Princeton University Is Sued Over Control of Foundation," *New York Times* (07/18/2002), http://www.nytimes.com/2002/07/18/nyregion/princeton-university-is-sued-over-control-of-foundation.html?pagewanted=print (accessed on 08/27/2012).

2. Author interview with Robert Durkee (08/21/2012).

3. Kelly Heyboer, "Big Stakes as Donor's Heirs Fight Princeton," *Star Ledger* (11/28/2004) http://www.freerepublic.com/focus/f-news/991707/posts (accessed on 10/29/2012).

4. Author interview with William Josephson (03/13/2012).

5. Author interview with Ron Malone (04/11/2012).

6. An *ultra vires* act is one that is beyond the scope or power allowed by a charter or bylaw.

7. *Promissory estoppel* is the doctrine that provides that if a party changes his or her position substantially, either by acting or forbearing from acting in reliance upon a gratuitous promise, then that party can enforce the promise although the essential elements of a contract are not present.

8. "Defendants' Motion to Strike Plaintiffs' Jury Demand" (10/25/2007), p. 2 (quoting the original verified complaint, 07/17/2002).

9. "Verified First Amended Complaint" (11/12/2004), pp. 59-68.

10. "Summary Judgment: Defendants' Motion to Strike Plaintiffs' Jury Demand" (10/25/2007), p. 7.

11. "Verified First Amended Complaint" (11/12/2004); pp. 2-5.

12. John Hechinger and Daniel Golden, "Fight at Princeton Escalates Over Use of a Family's Gift," *Wall Street Journal* (02/07/2006) http://online.wsj.com/article/SB113927779413766787-search.html#printMode (accessed on 09/21/21012).

13. Peter McDonough, "Endowments and Donor Restrictions," paper submitted at the Georgetown University Law Center conference on tax-exempt organizations (04/24-25/2008).

14. Author interview with Peter McDonough and Douglas Eakeley (07/24/2012).

15. Victoria Bjorklund, "*Robertson v. Princeton*—Perspective and Context," (01/2008), p. 3.

16. Author interview with Victoria Bjorklund (03/28/2012).

17. Author interview with Peter McDonough and Douglas Eakeley (07/24/2012).

18. Author interview with Bill Robertson (11/12/2012).

19. Victoria Bjorklund, "*Robertson v. Princeton*—Perspective and Context" (01/2008), p. 8.

20. Author interview with Ron Malone (04/11/2012).

21. Author interview with William Josephson (03/13/2012).

22. Robert Durkee, Letter to the Editor of the *Chronicle of Philanthropy* (01/29/2009).

23. Author interview with Bill Robertson (08/17/2012).

24. Robert Goheen, Deposition on *Robertson v. Princeton* (06/21/2004), p. 96.

25. Ibid., pp. 62-63.

26. Author interview with Bill Robertson (05/31/2012).

27. Ibid.

28. Robert Goheen, Deposition on *Robertson v. Princeton* (06/24/2004), pp. 372-374.

29. As recounted in an email from Ron Malone to others on the Robertson legal team (12/20/2004).

30. Author interview with Seth Lapidow (07/02/2013).

31. Summary Judgment Decision on "Plaintiffs' Motion for Partial Summary Judgment Regarding 'Fiduciary Duties' and 'Business Judgment Rule'" (10/25/2007), p. 6.

32. Ibid, p. 7-8.

33. Victoria Bjorklund, "*Robertson v. Princeton*—Perspective and Context" (01/2008), pp. 2-3.

34. Victoria Bjorklund, "*Robertson v. Princeton*—Perspective and Context" (01/2008), p. 10.

35. Peter McDonough, "Endowments and Donor Restrictions," paper submitted at the Georgetown University Law Center conference on tax-exempt organizations, 04/24-25/2008, p. 8; McDonough's cite: Sweezy v. New Hampshire, 354 U.S. 234, 261 (1957) (Frankfurter, J., concurring).

36. Author interview with Bill Robertson (11/12/2012).

37. Author interview with Seth Lapidow (07/02/2013).

38. "Highlights of the Graduate Program 2001-2006," Woodrow Wilson School (03/13/2006), p. 3.

39. Ibid., p. 31.

40. Colin Powell, Address at Princeton University (02/20/2004), *The Woodrow Wilson School of Public and International Affairs Princeton University, Highlights of the Graduate Program 2001-2006.*

41. In November 2012 David Petraeus abruptly resigned from his post as the Director of Central Intelligence after it became known that he was conducting an extramarital relationship.

42. Author interview with Peter McDonough (07/24/2012).

43. Amanda Loerch, "Oboist Joseph Robinson Joins George Mason Faculty," *Examiner.com*, 06/21/2012, http://www.examiner.com/article/joseph-robinson-joins-george-mason-faculty (accessed on 11/13/2012).

44. Despite the plaintiffs' criticism of the overall numbers of Woodrow Wilson School graduates who did not enter government service, no one, to the author's knowledge, has criticized Mr. Robinson for his career choice. Bill Josephson, one of the expert witnesses for the plaintiffs, calls the oboist "a very good friend of mine and one of the supreme oboe players in the world."

45. Charles Robertson memo on contemplating an expanded Woodrow Wilson School (12/15/1960).

46. Author interview with Seth Lapidow (07/02/2013).

47. Statistics compiled by Princeton University (2008).

48. http://grad-schools.usnews.rankingsandreviews.com/best-graduate-schools/top-public-affairs-schools/public-affairs-rankings (accessed on 11/06/2012).

49. Summary Judgment Decision on "Plaintiffs' Motion for Partial Summary Judgment Regarding 'Fiduciary Duties' and 'Business Judgment Rule'" (10/25/2007), p. 10.

50. "Best Grad Schools," *U.S. News*, 2012, http://grad-schools.usnews.

rankingsandreviews.com/best-graduate-schools/top-public-affairs-schools/
public-affairs-rankings (accessed on 04/14/2013).

51. Author interview with John Palmer (12/31/2012).

52. Author interview with Bill Robertson (08/17/2012).

53. Shirley Tilghman, "Settlement Retains Princeton's Control, Use of
    Robertson Funds - Endowment Will Continue to Support Wilson School
    Graduate Program" (12/10/2008), http://www.princeton.edu/main/
    news/archive/S22/81/66C43/index.xml?section=topstories (accessed on
    09/24/2012).

54. Each year nonprofits must file Form 990 with the IRS; the form summarizes
    the organization's fiscal activities as well as other information.

55. Peter McDonough, "Endowments and Donor Restrictions," paper submit-
    ted at the Georgetown University Law Center Conference on Tax-Exempt
    Organizations (04/24-25/2008), pp. 1-2.

56. Author interview with Bill Robertson (08/17/2012); also Banbury Fund
    financial reports and 990s from the years 2000 through 2006.

57. McDonough, "Endowments and Donor Restriction," p. 22.

58. Author interview with Victoria Bjorklund (03/18/2012).

59. Ben Gose, "Family Uses Nonprofit Funds to Pay Legal Expenses in Princeton
    U. Case," *Chronicle of Philanthropy* (10/24/2007), http://philanthropy.com/
    article/Family-Uses-Nonprofit-Funds-to/62726/ (accessed on 09/24/2012);
    By invoking "another egregious example," Dorfman was presumably referring
    to the many number of problems charity executives and board members have
    created by using their organizations' money improperly.

60. Author interview with Peter McDonough and Douglas Eakeley
    (08/21/2012).

61. Letter from Charles Robertson to the directors of the Banbury Fund
    (08/23/1962).

62. James Sligar memorandum to Bill Robertson, Anne Meier and Katherine
    Ernst (10/09/2003).

63. A private letter ruling is an opinion that the IRS issues publicly on fact-
    specific cases but it does not provide authority for any other situation; a
    revenue ruling has more weight than a private letter ruling and therefore can
    be applied more broadly.

64. IRS Private Letter Ruling 200649031 (12/08/2006).

65. IRS Private Letter Ruling 8615076 (01/14/1986).

66. IRS Revenue Ruling 73-613, 1973-2 CB 385, IRC Sec(s). 4941.

67. Marcus Owens Deposition (08/25/2005), p. 154.

68. William Josephson Deposition (08/09/2005), pp. 195-196.

69. Author interview with Ron Malone (04/11/2012).

70. Ibid.

71. Author interview with Seth Lapidow (07/02/2013).

72. Author interview with Bill Robertson (02/01/2013).

73. Author interview with Robert Durkee (08/21/2012).

74. Author interview with Bill Robertson (08/18/21012).

75. Author interview with Ron Malone (04/11/2012).

76. Author interview with Frank Cialone (04/11/2012).

77. Summary Judgment Decision on "Plaintiffs' Motion for Partial Summary Judgment Regarding 'Fiduciary Duties' and 'Business Judgment Rule'" (10/25/2007), p. 19.

78. Author interview with Frank Cialone (04/11/2012).

79. Summary Judgment Decision on "Plaintiffs' Motion for Partial Summary Judgment Regarding 'Fiduciary Duties' and 'Business Judgment Rule'" (10/25/2007), p. 19.

80. Author interview with Peter McDonough and Douglas Eakeley (07/24/2012).

81. Matthew Hersh, "Heirs to A&P Fortune Say University Misused Foundation's Assets," *Town Topics*, 06/23/2004, http://www.towntopics.com/jun2304/story2.html (accessed on 10/05/2012).

82. Author interview with Peter McDonough (07/24/2012).

83. Verified First Amended Complaint (11/12/2004). pp. 31-33.

84. PricewaterhouseCoopers and Deloitte vie for the number 1 position each year; while each generates roughly equal revenues, Deloitte employs more people. The other two firms of the big four are Ernst & Young and KPMG.

85. "Expert Witness Report of Michael G. McGuire," undated; although the findings in McGuire's report were subject to change at the time it was presented, the relevant information reported here did not change.

86. Author interview with Seth Lapidow (07/02/2013).

87. "Expert Witness Report of Michael G. McGuire," undated.

88. Marcus Owens deposition (08/21/2008), pp. 56-57.

89. Named after William Bowen, the economist and former Princeton president, it allocated costs related to the Wilson School's undergraduate and graduate programs based on activity at the time of the Robertson gift, while allocating expenses relating to the expanded graduate program to the Foundation. The Foundation Board approved the Bowen Formula in 1965.

90. Author interview with Peter McDonough and Douglas Eakeley (08/21/2012).

91. Linda Stein, "University Funds Diverted," *Trenton Times* (02/10/2006), http://www.freerepublic.com/focus/f-news/1576359/posts (accessed on 11/06/2012).

92. John Hechinger, "Princeton Reimburses Donors' Foundation," *Wall Street Journal* (03/13/2007).

93. Author interview with Ron Malone (04/11/2012).

94. Author interview with Seth Lapidow (08/21/2012).

95. Author interview with Seth Lapidow (07/02/2013).

96. Author interview with Peter McDonough and Douglas Eakeley (08/21/2012).

97. Author interview with Seth Lapidow (08/21/2012).

98. Raj Hathiramani, "Robertson Family Seeks to Amend Complaint," *Daily Princetonian* (09/13/2004), http://www.dailyprincetonian.com/2004/09/13/10684/ (accessed on 01/17/2013).

99. Summary Judgment Decision on "Plaintiffs' Motion for Partial Summary Judgment Regarding 'Fiduciary Duties' and 'Business Judgment Rule,'" 10/25/2007, pp. 16-17.

100. "Memorandum of Law in Support of the Plaintiffs' Motion in Limine," p. 12.

101. Author interview with Seth Lapidow (07/02/2013).

102. Author interview with Kenneth Logan (07/25/2013).

103. Author interview with Seth Lapidow (07/02/2013).

104. Summary Judgment Decision on "Plaintiffs' Motion for Partial Summary Judgment Regarding 'Fiduciary Duties' and 'Business Judgment Rule'" (10/25/2007), pp. 17-18.

105. Author interview with Peter McDonough (07/24/2012).

106. Author interview with Jessie Lee Washington (04/03/2012).

107. Jessie Lee Washington, "Religious Life Endowment Review: Summary of Findings" (02/2003).

108. Deposition of Jessie Lee Washington, *Robertson v. Princeton* (06/15/2005), pp. 44-45.

109. Author interview with Jessie Lee Washington (04/03/2012).

110. Raj Hathiramani, "Robertson Family Seeks to Amend Complaint," *Daily Princetonian* (09/13/2004), http://www.dailyprincetonian.com/2004/09/13/10684/ (accessed on 01/17/2013).

111. Letter from Janet Smith Dickerson to Jessie Lee Washington (05/27/2002).

112. Author interview with Jessie Lee Washington (04/03/2013).

113. Ibid.

114. Ibid.

115. Ibid.

116. Author interview with Seth Lapidow (08/21/2012).

117. Email from Cecily Freyermuth to Bill Robertson (06/03/2004).

118. Sinclair Lewis, I, *Candidate for Governor: And How I Got Licked,* (1935), reprinted by the University of California Press, 1994, p. 109.

119. Author interview with Greg Lebedev (04/04/2012).

120. Michael Juel-Larsen, "Princeton Scores Small Wins with Summary Judgments," *Daily Princetonian* (10/26/2007), http://www.dailyprincetonian.com/2007/10/26/19165 (accessed on 11/01/2012).

121. Author interview with Ron Malone (04/11/2012).

122. Michael Juel-Larsen, "Princeton Scores Small Wins with Summary Judgments," *Daily Princetonian*, 10/26/2007; http://www.dailyprincetonian.com/2007/10/26/19165 (accessed on 11/01/2012).

123. Author interview with Kenneth Logan (07/25/2013).

124. Summary Judgment on Defendant's Motion to Strike Plaintiffs' Jury Demand, 10/25/2007, Superior Court of New Jersey Chancery Division General Equity Part Mercer County, Docket No. C-99-02, p. 14.

125. Author interview with Seth Lapidow (07/02/2013).

126. Michael Juel-Larsen, "Princeton Scores Small Wins with Summary Judgments," *Daily Princetonian*, 10/26/2007; http://www.dailyprincetonian.com/2007/10/26/19165 (accessed on 11/01/2012).

127. "Summary Judgment Decision on "Plaintiffs' Motion for Partial Summary Judgment Regarding 'Fiduciary Duties' and 'Business Judgment Rule'" (10/25/2007), p. 80.

128. Michael Juel-Larsen, "Princeton Scores Small Wins with Summary Judgments," *Daily Princetonian*, 10/26/2007; http://www.dailyprincetonian.com/2007/10/26/19165 (accessed on 11/01/2012).

129. Ibid.

130. Author interview with Seth Lapidow (07/02/2013).

131. Author interview with Kenneth Logan (07/25/2013).

132. Ben Gose, "Judge Rules That High-Stakes Case Against Princeton U. Can Proceed," *Chronicle of Philanthropy* (10/25/2007), http://philanthropy.com/article/Judge-Rules-That-High-Stakes/62729 (accessed on 11/15/2012).

133. Author interview with Bill Robertson (10/18/2012).

134. Author interview with Kenneth Logan (07/25/2013).

135. Author interview with Ron Malone (04/11/2012).

136. Memo from Ron Malone to The Banbury Fund, Bill Robertson, Kate Ernst, Anne Meier and Bob Halligan (08/08/2008).

137. Author interview with Bill Robertson (10/18/2012).

138. Ibid.

139. Author interview with Kenneth Logan (07/25/2013).

140. Author interview with Bill Robertson (10/18/2012).

141. From Maria Sypek's press biography on the website of JAMS; http://www.jamsadr.com/sypek/ (accessed 11/03/2012).

142. Matt Westmoreland, "Retired Judge to Decide Robertson Lawsuit," *Daily Princetonian* (11/03/2008), http://www.dailyprincetonian.com/2008/11/03/21930/ (accessed on 11/06/2012).

143. Author interview with Seth Lapidow (07/02/2013).

144. Author interview with Bill Robertson (03/26/2013).

145. Letter from Robert Ernst to Bill Robertson (07/17/2008).

146. Author interview with Bill Robertson (04/09/2013).

147. Andrew Ross Sorkin, "Lehman Files for Bankruptcy; Merrill Is Sold," *New York Times* (09/14/2008), http://www.nytimes.com/2008/09/15/business/15lehman.html (accessed on 11/05/2012).

148. Letter from Shirley Tilghman to Senators Max Baucus and Charles Grassley, the chair and ranking Republican member, respectively, of the Senate Finance Committee (02/22/2008).

149. Andrew Bary, "Crash Course," *Barron's* (11/10/2012) http://online.barrons.com/article/SB122610188023510005.html#articleTabs_article%3D1 (accessed on 11/16/2012).

150. Author interview with Bill Robertson (08/17/2012).

151. Internal Report, "Ivy league Annual Voluntary Support: 2000 through 2010."

152. Author interview with Bill Robertson (08/17/2012).

153. Joyce Howard Prince, "Gifts to Princeton Drop Sharply," *Washington Times* (03/29/2005), http://www.washingtontimes.com/news/2005/mar/29/20050329-122720-6243r/?page=all (accessed on 12/08/2012).

154. These conclusions are the result of the author's analysis of raw numbers provided in reports, including "Ivy League Schools Annual Voluntary Support of Education," from the years 1995 through 2010.

155. Author interview with Bill Robertson (02/10/2013).

156. Memo from Bill Robertson to David Gelfand (08/26/2008).

157. Ben Gose, "Judge Rules That High-Stakes Case Against Princeton U. Can Proceed," *Chronicle of Philanthropy* (10/25/2007), http://philanthropy.com/article/Judge-Rules-That-High-Stakes/62729 (accessed on 04/17/2013).

158. Jonathan Marks, "Confidential Mediation Document" (09/25/2008), pp. 1-6.

159. Author interview with Robert Halligan (02/17/2012).

160. Author interview with Katherine Ernst (06/27/2012).

161. Author interview with Bill Robertson (08/18/2012).

162. Memorandum of Law in Support of the Parties' Joint Motion on Consent Seeking the Court's Approval of Settlement Agreement and Dismissal of Action (12/09/2008).

163. Author interview with Ron Malone (04/11/2012).

164. Linda Stein, "*Robertson v. Princeton:* Colossal Costs Finally," *ESQ* (03/16/2008), pp. 16-26.

165. Author interview with David Gelfand (12/12/2012).

166. Jane Shaw, "An Unsettling Conclusion," The John William Pope Center (12/15/2008), http://www.popecenter.org/commentaries/article.html?id=2106 (accessed on 11/06/2012) .

167. Naomi Levine, "Courtroom Clash," *Contribute Magazine* (09/22/2008), http://www.contributemedia.com/opinions_details.php?id=205 (accessed on 11/06/2012).

168. Author interview with Frederic J. Fransen (11/06/2012).

169. Frederic J. Fransen, "*Robertson v. Princeton*—A Post-Mortem," *Pittsburgh Tribune-Review* (01/04/2009), http://home.ease.lsoft.com/scripts/wa-HOME.exe?A3=ind0901&L=NAS-NET&E=quoted-printable&P=1280700&B=------%3D_NextPart_000_0218_01C9780F.10681930&T=text%2Fplain;%20charset=iso-8859-1&header=1 (accessed on 01/08/2013).

170. Author interview with Anne Neal (06/26/2013).

171. Author interview with Ron Malone (04/11/2012).

172. Author interview with Peter McDonough and Douglas Eakeley (07/24/2012).

173. Author interview with Robert Durkee (08/21/2012).

174. Author interview with Peter McDonough and Douglas Eakeley

(07/24/2012).

175. Author interview with Bill Robertson (03/19/2013).

176. Author interview with Robert Durkee (08/21/2012).

177. Author interview with Bill Robertson (05/31/2012).

178. *Princeton Alumni Weekly* interview with Bill Robertson (01/28/2009), http://paw.princeton.edu/issues/2009/01/28/pages/5507/ (accessed on 11/13/2012).

Notes for Chapter 6

1.   Composite Certificate of Incorporation of the Robertson Foundation, as amended through July 26, 1961, pp. 3-4.

2.   Agreement of Settlement (12/08/2008), p. 5.

3.   "About" Section, Robertson Foundation for Government website, http://www.RFG.org/about.html (accessed on 11/15/2012) .

4.   Author interview with Bill Robertson (11/12/2012).

5.   Greg Lebedev, Paper on The Robertson Foundation for Government, 09/2010 ("Lebedev Paper").

6.   As of 2010, the National Center for Charitable Statistics reports, there were 120,810 private foundations in the United States, with a combined total asset base of over $582 billion, http://nccsdataweb.urban.org/PubApps/profileDrillDown.php?state=US&rpt=PF (accessed on 01/18/2013).

7.   Karen Kucher, "Foundation Gives Nearly $1 Million for UC San Diego Grad Students," *U-T San Diego News* (11/01/2012), http://www.utsandiego.com/news/2012/nov/01/private-foundation-gives-nearly-1-million-support-/ (accessed on 11/17/2012).

8.   Author interview with Chuck Robb (05/25/2012).

9.   Author interview with Brent Scowcroft (05/14/2012).

10. Author interview with Chuck Robb (05/25/2012).

11. Author interview via email with George H. W. Bush (08/09/2012).

12. Author interview with Greg Lebedev (04/04/2012).

13. Author interview with Chuck Robb (05/25/2012).

14. Author interview with Kathryn Ernst (06/27/2012).

15. Interview with Bill Robertson, *Princeton Alumni Weekly* (01/28/2009), http://paw.princeton.edu/issues/2009/01/28/pages/5507/ (accessed on 11/13/2012).

16. Herbert Simon, Administrative Behavior, Free Press, p.1 (fourth edition).

17. Author interview with Paul Light (12/05/2012).

18. Author interview with Bo Kemper and Greg Lebedev (01/24, 2013).

19. Project on Government Oversight, http://www.pogo.org/our-work/reports/2011/co-gp-20110913.html#Executive%20Summary (accessed on 01/11/2012).

20. Author interview with Paul Light (12/05/2012).

21. Author interview with John L. Palmer (12/31/2012).

22. Leo Tolstoy, "Anna Karenin" (Penguin Books, Ltd., 1954), p. 13.

23. Author interview with Geoff Robertson (03/26/2013).

24. Author interview with Bill Robertson (04/26/2012).

25. Author interview with Bill Robertson (02/10/2013).

26. Charles W. Collier, *Wealth in Families,* second edition, (President and Fellows of Harvard College, 2006), p. 44.

27. Author interview with Julia Robertson (04/11/2012).

28. Author interview with Geoff Robertson (03/26/2013).

29. Author interview with Bill Robertson (09/01/2013).

30. Complaint from Eliot Spitzer to Michel Roux, Jerry Ciraulo, Joel Buchman, Maxime Coury, Jacques Marnier-LaPostolle, and Francois de Gasperis (08/30/2001), p. 1-10 .

31. Paul Light, "The Campaign for High Performance Government" (06/15/2011), p. 1.

32. Author interview with Bo Kemper and Greg Lebedev (01/25/2013).

33. Author interview with Greg Lebedev (04/04/2012).

34. Lebedev Paper.

35. The actual words were, "The highest proof of virtue is to possess boundless power without abusing it," which were spoken by Lord Thomas Babington Macaulay, British poet, historian, politician (1800-1859).

36. Lyndon Johnson, "Remarks of the President at the Dedication of the New Building at the Woodrow Wilson School of Public and International Affairs" (05/11/1966); the name of the building was not made public then out of deference to Marie Robertson's wishes that the gift remain anonymous.

Notes for Chapter 7

1. Author interview with Bill Robertson (05/31/2012).

2. Josephson, William "New Prudent Management of Institutional Funds Act,"

New York Law Journal (12/03/2010).

3. Author interview with Harvey Dale (02/22/2012).

4. Author interview with Harvey Dale (02/22/2012).

5. Author interview with Victoria Bjorklund (03/28/2012).

6. Author interview with Bill Josephson (03/13/2012).

7. Lori Aratani, "Johns Hopkins Lawsuit Highlights Questions About Schools' Obligations to Donors," *Washington Post* (02/20/2012) http://www.washingtonpost.com/local/trafficandcommuting/johns-hopkins-lawsuit-highlights-questions-about-schools-obligations-to-donors/2012/02/17/gIQAVMH0PR_story.html (accessed on 09/01/2013).

8. Author interview with Kenneth Logan (07/25/2013).

9. Ben Franklin, Last Will and Testament, The Franklin Institute, http://www.fi.edu/franklin/family/lastwill.html (accessed on 07/18/2013) .

10. Ibid.

11. Anecdote anonymously told to the author.

12. That her findings weren't enthusiastically received internally at Princeton suggests an additional and entirely different problem.

13. Author interview with Paul Light (12/05/2012).

14. Among the biggest challenges for the IRS is verifying the amount donors deduct for donated assets that are not easily valued.

15. Author interview with Harvey Dale (02/22/2012).

16. Author interview with Stuart Polkowitz (08/08/2013).

17. New Jersey Appellate Court Decision, *Bernard and Jeanne Adler v. SAVE, A Friend to Homeless Animals* (08/05/2013), p. 2.

18. The reports, conducted by the Tellus Institute and funded by the Massachusetts Service Employees International Union, are "Academic Excess: Executive Compensation at Leading Private Colleges and Universities in Massachusetts" (09/2011); "Errors of Omission: Transparency and Disclosure of Trustee Conflicts of Interest at Leading Private Colleges and Universities in Massachusetts" (04/2012); "Public Investment in Private Higher Education: Estimating the Value of Nonprofit College and University Tax Exemptions" (09/2012); and "Education Endowments and the Financial Crisis: Social Costs and Systemic Risks in the Shadow of the Banking System, A Study of Six New England Schools" (05/27/2010).

19. "Public Investment in Private Higher Education: Estimating the Value of Nonprofit College and University Tax Exemptions" (09/2012), p. 3.

20. "Academic Excess: Executive Compensation at Leading Private Colleges and Universities in Massachusetts" (09/2011), p. 15.

21. Wick Sloane, "Clear-Eyed Reports on Foibles of Higher Education Finance," *Inside Higher Ed* (03/28/2013), http://www.insidehighered.com/users/wick-sloane (accessed on 07/19/2103).

22. The IRS acknowledges a rug used in the office of a nonprofit administrator as a legitimate purchase or related-use gift; the issue for the public, however, is one of degree.

23. Many people cite the Supreme Court case *Citizens United v. Federal Election Commission* as a key to understanding the influence money has in today's political process.

24. The Federalist Papers, #10, New American Library, 1961, p. 74.

25. Niccoló Machiavelli, *Discourses on Livy,* 1531; the chapter with the story is "That The Actions Of Citizens Ought To Be Observed, For Many Times A Beginning Of Tyranny Is Hidden Under A Pious Act".

26. "Final Report of the Commission on Industrial Relations," (Barnard and Miller Print 1915) p. 118 http://ia600308.us.archive.org/0/items/finalreportofcom00unitiala/finalreportofcom00unitiala.pdf (accessed on 08/20/2013).

27. Peter Dobkin Hall, *Philanthropic Foundations,* edited by Ellen Condliffe Lagemann, (Indiana University Press, 1999), p. 3.

28. These are the four pillars of ethical decision-making at nonprofits, as described in "The Nonprofit Challenge," written by the author.

29. The Supreme Court expanded the role money plays in the political process in *Citizens United v. Federal Election Commission* (2010); donors have since flocked to 501(c)(4) organizations, or social welfare organizations, donations to which are not eligible for an income tax deduction.

30. Author interview with Ron Malone (04/11/2012).

31. Author interview with Greg Lebedev (01/25/2013).

32. Author interview with Bill Robertson (02/10/2013).

33. Summary Judgment Decision on "Plaintiffs' Motion for Partial Summary Judgment Regarding 'Fiduciary Duties' and 'Business Judgment Rule'" (10/25/2007), pp. 16-17.

34. Author interview with Bill Robertson (03/16/2013).

35. Author interview with Bill Robertson (03/19/2013).

36. Author interview with Bill Robertson (08/17/2012).

37. Author interview with Kenneth Logan (07/25/2013).

38. "Next Generation Philanthropy: Changing the World," Forbes Insights in Partnership with Credit Suisse, 09/2012, p. 8; 264 philanthropists were surveyed.

39. Vartan Gregorian; documentary "The Statue of Liberty" (1985); aired on PBS (09/30/85); Ken Burns.

40. Seamus Heaney, "The Cure at Troy" (1961).

41. Author interview with David Gelfand (12/12/2012).

42. The Department of State alone employs over 23,000 people in its foreign and civil service divisions, http://careers.state.gov/learn/what-we-do/mission (accessed on 05/15/2013).

Index

T

Taub Institute for Research on
    Alzheimer's Disease and the Aging
    Brain 44
Taylor, George 33
Tellado, Marta 87, 289
Texas A&M 215, 219
The Great Atlantic & Pacific Tea
    Company
    A&P 22
Tilghman, Shirley 115, 116, 123, 128,
    161, 176, 180, 207, 208, 255, 256,
    291, 292, 296, 300
Tolstoy, Leo 226
Trussell, James 151
Tuck School of Business (Dartmouth)
    181
Tufts University 215
Tulane University 78

U

Ultra vires 140, 154, 189, 293
United Nations 5-7
United States Constitution 249, 251
United States Supreme Court 153
University of California, San Diego 215
University of Hawaii 246
University of Maryland 215
University of Michigan 1, 129, 280
Upper Canada College 35
U.S. Department of the Treasury 155
U.S. Government Accountability Office
    155
U.S. Office of Management and Budget
    155

V

Variance power 69, 70, 236, 237, 238
Vietnam War 3, 100, 106, 112
Volcker, Paul 114-117, 126, 131, 200,
    217, 218, 221, 230, 242, 254, 272,
    291, 292

W

Wallace Hall 118, 122, 123, 130, 140,
    256
Washington 3, 6, 9, 11, 279, 287, 290,
    300, 304
Washington, DC 74, 90, 214
Washington, George
    1st President 249, 251, 252
Washington, Jessie Lee 181-187, 210,
    241, 252, 261, 268, 272, 298, 299
Watergate 107, 108, 112
Watson, James, Dr. 46-48, 272, 284
Wilkins, Maurice 46, 284
Wilson, Woodrow 6, 7, *135*
WMD (Weapons of Mass Destruction)
    217
Woodrow Wilson School xi, xii, 6-11,
    13, 14, 18, 19, 29, 34, 43, 92, 96-
    100, 102-110, 113-120, 122, 123,
    126, 127, *136*, 141, 142, 146, 148,
    149, 151, 154-160, 164, 169-173,
    175-181, 193, 203, 207, 209, 215,
    216, 221, 224-226, 233, 242, 243,
    248, 255, 259, 261, 268, 281, 282,
    285, 290, 291, 293, 295-297, 303
Wooster, Martin Morse 87, 89, 286, 287,
    289
World Bank 155
World Trade Center 22, 106
World War II 2, 3, 5, 10, 30, 43, 157

X

Y